Inflation Targeting, Debt,
and the Brazilian
Experience, 1999 to 2003

Inflation Targeting, Debt, and the Brazilian Experience, 1999 to 2003

edited by Francesco Giavazzi,
Ilan Goldfajn, and Santiago
Herrera

The MIT Press
Cambridge, Massachusetts
London, England

MIT Press books may be purchased at special quantity discounts for business or sales
promotional use. For information, please email special_sales@mitpress.mit.edu or write
to Special Sales Department, The MIT Press, 5 Cambridge Center, Cambridge, MA 02142.

This book was set in Palatino on 3B2 by Asco Typesetters, Hong Kong, and was printed
and bound in the United States of America.

Library of Congress Cataloging-in-Publication Data

Inflation targeting, debt, and the Brazilian experience, 1999 to 2003 / edited by Francesco
Giavazzi, Ilan Goldfajn, and Santiago Herrera.
    p.   cm.
Includes bibliographical references and index.
ISBN 0-262-07259-9 (alk. paper)
1. Monetary policy—Brazil. 2. Inflation (Finance)—Brazil. 3. Debts, External—Brazil.
I. Giavazzi, Francesco. II. Goldfajn, Ilan. III. Herrera, Santiago.
HG835.I529   2005
339.5′0981′090511—dc22   2004056776

10 9 8 7 6 5 4 3 2 1

Contents

Contributors

Persio Arida
Núcleo de Estudos de Politica
Econômica,
Casa das Garças
Rio de Janeiro

Edmar Lisboa Bacha
Núcleo de Estudos de Politica
Econômica,
Casa das Garças
Rio de Janeiro

Olivier Blanchard
Massachusetts Institute of
Technology
Cambridge

Eliana Cardoso
Universidade de São Paulo
São Paulo

Dionísio Carneiro
Pontifícia Universidade Católica
do Rio de Janeiro (PUC-Rio)
Núcleo de Estudos de Politica
Econômica,
Casa das Garças
Rio de Janeiro

Carlo A. Favero
IGIER-Bocconi University and
CEPR
Milan

Arminio Fraga
Gávea Investimentos
Rio de Janeiro

Márcio Garcia
Pontifícia Universidade Católica
do Rio de Janeiro (PUC-Rio)
Rio de Janeiro

Francesco Giavazzi
CEPR, NBER, and IGIER-Bocconi
University
Milan

Ilan Goldfajn
Pontifícia Universidade Católica
do Rio de Janeiro (PUC-Rio)
Partner, Gávea Investimentos
Rio de Janeiro

Santiago Herrera
World Bank
Washington, DC

André Lara-Resende
Núcleo de Estudos de Politica
Econômica,
Casa das Garças
Rio de Janeiro

Joaquim Levy
Secretary of the National
Treasury of Brazil
Rio de Janeiro

Eduardo Loyo
Pontifícia Universidade Católica
do Rio de Janeiro (PUC-Rio)
Banco Central do Brasil

Pedro S. Malan
Chairman of the Board,
Unibanco
Pontifícia Universidade Católica
do Rio de Janeiro (PUC-Rio)
Rio de Janeiro

Marcus Miller
University of Warwick
Warwick, England

Alessandro Missale
Universitá di Milano
Milan

Affonso Celso Pastore
A.C. Pastore & Associados
São Paulo

Maria Cristina Pinotti
A.C. Pastore & Associados
São Paulo

Roberto Rigobon
Massachusetts Institute of
Technology
Cambridge

Kannika Thampanishvong
University of Warwick
Warwick, England

Rogério L. F. Werneck
Pontifícia Universidade Católica
do Rio de Janeiro (PUC-Rio)
Rio de Janeiro

Charles Wyplosz
Graduate Institute of
International Studies,
CEPR
Geneva

Lei Zhang
University of Warwick,
Warwick, England

Overview: Lessons from Brazil

Francesco Giavazzi, Ilan Goldfajn, and Santiago Herrera

Why Brazil?

Brazil adopted inflation targeting in early 1999, after floating its currency and a 50 percent depreciation. This development ended a period during which the exchange rate had been the main anchor for monetary policy. Inflation targeting was one element of a wider policy regime that entailed, in particular, the announcement, a year earlier, of a sequence of higher primary budget surpluses. The new monetary regime worked well: the initial inflation targets were set at 8 percent for 1999 and 6 percent for 2000—with a 2 percent tolerance range. In December 1999 the 12-month inflation rate was 8.9 percent, and the following December 6 percent, exactly on target.

The successful start was followed by two difficult years: contagion from Argentina, a domestic energy crisis, a widening of bond spreads worldwide, a sudden reversal in capital flows amounting to 6 percent of GDP, and finally the political uncertainty surrounding by the 2002 presidential campaign. During this period the *real* depreciated again —20 percent in 2001 and 50 percent in 2002; inflation temporarily increased to as much as 16 percent, but by March 2004 it was back to 6 percent.

Overall the new policy regime survived such a severe stress test. This book is about how this happened and what lessons other countries that either adopt or consider adopting inflation targeting can learn from the experience of Brazil.

In his overview of inflation targeting in emerging market economies, Mishkin (2004, p. 29) concludes that "to ensure that inflation targeting produces superior macroeconomic outcomes, emerging market countries would benefit by focusing on institutional development, while international financial institutions like the IMF can help by providing these countries with better incentives to engage in this development." The importance of domestic institutions, fiscal institutions, in particular, and of the incentives offered by international institutions is highlighted by the experience of Brazil: hadn't inflation targeting been accompanied by institutional development, as the adoption of the Law of Fiscal Responsibility and the agreements with states and local governments, it is unlikely that Brazil would have managed the crisis. Further, at a critical moment during the 2002 presidential campaign, an IMF agreement provided the necessary framework to coordinate the candidates' public support for maintaining sound policies in the future.

The first chapter in the volume, by Affonso Pastore and Maria Cristina Pinotti, reviews macroeconomic events in Brazil since 1999: we will refer to that chapter for understanding Brazil's macroeconomic landscape in the period we study. In this overview we focus, instead, on the factors that, in our opinion, made it possible for Brazil to manage the crisis and on the lessons that can be drawn.

Inflation Targeting under Stress

During 2002 Brazil underwent a severe "stress test." Due mainly to the uncertainties related to the presidential campaign, but also to the widening of spreads worldwide, especially on US corporate bonds, there was a sudden stop in capital flows[1] amounting to 6 percent of GDP, an exchange rate depreciation of almost 50 percent, and a substantial increase in the spread over Treasuries of Brazilian bonds. The real depreciation and the sudden stop in capital inflows required a sharp adjustment in the current account (5 percent of GDP, from 2001 to 2003) and a corresponding reduction in domestic absorption, mostly private consumption and investment.

The sudden stop and the resulting depreciation also led, because of the composition of Brazilian public debt, to an increase in the amount of debt as a fraction of GDP. Both domestic and external public debt were linked to the exchange rate: 30 percent of domestic debt was indexed to the nominal exchange rate and, as in most emerging markets, all public external debt is denominated in strong currencies. As a result the ratio of net public debt to GDP jumped, in a few months, from 0.54 to 0.63.

The composition of public debt in Brazil has been an important issue for a while. The unwillingness of the private sector to bear currency risk limits the ability of the government to reduce the dollar-linked component of the debt. After two years (1999–2000) of continuous reduction, the proportion of dollar-linked debt increased again in 2001. Only after the crisis, since mid-2003, the government has been able to reduce once again this component of the debt. As we will discuss at the end of this overview, it remains an open question by how much and at what speed the Brazilian government should continue reducing its exposure to currency risk.

As public debt increased, and investors became suspicious regarding the economic policies that would be adopted after the election, doubts regarding the sustainability of the debt mounted. At one point, in mid-2002, the market began to price into Brazilian bonds a risk of default within the coming 12 months. The EMBI spread (the difference between the yield on dollar-denominated bonds issued by Brazil and that on equivalent US Treasury bonds) moved from 700 basis points in the spring to 2,400 at the end of July.

The uncertainty regarding the sustainability of public debt induced market participants to reduce their exposure to public debt or seek shorter government securities. As a result the discount on long-term domestic government securities widened substantially and the debt maturity was shortened. The average maturity of Selic-indexed debt held by the market fell from 36 months in March 2002 to 20 months in January 2003 and the percentage of debt coming due in the following 12 months rose from 6 percent to about 50 percent.[2]

The inflation-targeting regime also underwent a direct stress test: the exchange rate depreciation had led to higher expected inflation: one-year-ahead inflation expectations increased from 4.5 percent in the spring to 5.3 percent in early August and 10 percent in October.

How Brazil Managed the Crisis

The sudden stop confronted the government with a number of challenges. First, the government had to restore confidence on future policies to avert the net capital outflows and reduce doubts regarding debt dynamics. Second, the central bank had to evaluate whether the impact of the exchange rate depreciation would be limited to a once and for all change in the level of prices, or inflation would remain higher even after the exchange rate had stabilized. In this regard, how fast and by how much should interest rates be raised? Third, the government had to manage the sharp fall in the demand for longer term government securities and avoid a rollover crisis.

Inflation Targeting and Debt

As was noted above, the depreciation had rapidly increased the ratio of public debt to GDP. This called for an increase in the primary surplus if the level of the debt was to remain stable at the new level; alternatively, the debt level could fall as the result of a reversal of the exchange rate depreciation. Confidence in future fiscal policies was necessary, but there was widespread uncertainty as to the policy that the future government would adopt.

In a situation of uncertainty about future fiscal policy, monetary policy alone may not be sufficient to stabilize the economy. In chapters 2 and 3 Blanchard, and Favero and Giavazzi, argue that in 2002 raising interest rates to offset the inflationary effects of the exchange rate would have added doubts regarding debt dynamics. This could have led to more capital outflows and further currency depreciation.[3]

Given the need for a coordinated approach and while evaluating the consequences of the shock to inflation, the central bank refrained from raising nominal interest rates. In mid July 2002 the target Selic rate was in fact cut from 18.5 to 18 percent. Real rates, measured using the one-year-ahead inflation forecast, fell, though it remained at a still relatively high level of 11 percent.

The situation called for a change in expectations regarding future fiscal and monetary policy. But, how to achieve a commitment on future fiscal policy by the leading candidates in the midst of the campaign? And how should monetary policy act in the process?

A first response came in August 2002, when the IMF granted Brazil a US$30 billion loan—the largest ever in IMF history—conditional on Brazil maintaining "responsible policies" in the next few years: fiscal primary surpluses, inflation targeting, a floating exchange regime and respect of contracts, including the public debt. The purpose of the loan was not only to provide the central bank with foreign exchange reserves but also, and importantly, to provide a mechanism that would help the main candidates coordinate their public support for sound policies—precisely as suggested in Mishkin (2004). The statements from the candidates came, though some were more vague than had been hoped, but they certainly helped avoiding a further deterioration of market conditions ahead of the October elections. More important, the leading candidate started sending stronger signals that he was pre-pared to adopt the fiscal stance required to stabilize debt dynamics.

At the same time, it became progressively clearer that the exchange rate depreciation would have persistent effects on inflation (we explain in detail below how the central bank confronted the rise in inflation). At this point monetary policy acted aggressively: on October 15 the Selic was raised from 18 to 21 percent, followed by a further rise to 25 percent in mid-December; the real rate jumped from 11 to 18 percent, consistent with a monetary policy rule that responds more than pro-portionately to an increase in inflation expectations. Eventually Presi-dent Lula delivered on his promises: the new government maintained the floating exchange regime and inflation targeting, made clear that public debt would be honored, and increased the primary surplus by a half percent of GDP.

Far from falling into a vicious circle, the economy rapidly stabilized. By the end of December the EMBI spread had fallen to 1,500 basis points: a year later, when Brazil's rating was raised from a B to B+, the spread fell to 450 bp, 100 less than in February 2002, before the crisis had started. As it had happened on the way up, part of this reduc-tion can be explained by a simultaneous reduction in the US corporate bond spread, which fell 200 bp between October 2002 and December 2003, nevertheless, there is little doubt that market perceptions of Brazil had shifted. The exchange rate stabilized and inflation expecta-tions, which had been rising for six months, by December 2003 were back to 5.8 percent. Eventually the central bank could lower rates: by late 2003 the Selic was reduced to 16.5, two points below its level before the crisis had started.

Why was such a small shift in fiscal policy—half a percent of GDP—sufficient to produce a large change in expectations and put the econ-omy in equilibrium? As we explain in the following paragraphs, much hard work on the budget had already been done and the perceived change in fiscal policy stance was—notwithstanding the small shift in the actual primary surplus—quite large. In mid-1998, before the exchange rate peg was abandoned and Brazil shifted to inflation tar-geting, the primary surplus was close to −1 percent of GDP. In early 2002, before the crisis, the primary surplus had reached 3.5 percent. The composition of the change in the surplus is also important. Two-thirds came from improvements in the federal budget, and one-third from improvements in the fiscal positions of the states. The sharing of the burden of fiscal adjustment between the federal government and the states is at the core of Brazil's success—another theme of the book: it is also, in our view, the main underlying reason why Brazil eventually survived while Argentina collapsed. We explain how Brazil managed to get the states to contribute to the fiscal consolidation of the federal government in the next section.

Inflation Targeting and the Exchange Rate

Understanding the response of price setters to changes in the exchange rate was crucial to determine the optimal monetary policy response. In theory, the larger and the more persistent the effect is on prices, the longer is the horizon needed for inflation to return to the target path. Brazil's most recent experience prior to the crisis was that of 1999: after a 60 percent depreciation, inflation increased temporarily to 9 percent, but at the end of 2000 it was back to 6.0 percent, the midpoint of the central bank's target range.

There was, however, a big difference between 1999 and 2002: the level of the real exchange rate before the depreciation. In 1999, before the devaluation, Brazil's effective real exchange rate (measured relative to 13 currencies and normalized to 100 in 1994) was 95.7—a fall in the index indicating a real appreciation. In 2002, it was 150. As shown by Goldfajn and Werlang (2000) the level of the real exchange rate before a devaluation is an important factor in determining the pass-through from the exchange rate to prices. When the real exchange rate is weak, foreign exporters enjoy large margins and can afford to cut them to preserve their market shares, thus dampening the pass-through. This was the case in 1999, but not quite the situation in 2002.

In January 2003, as soon as the new administration came into office, the central bank recognized that inflation would overshoot the initial target: adjusting the target was thus necessary to retain credibility. By discussing alternative paths for inflation and why a new path using the adjusted target was chosen, the central bank was able to demonstrate that it was not an "inflation nutter" who only cares about controlling inflation and gives no weight to output fluctuations. In an open letter sent to the Minister of Finance in January 2003,[4] the bank first explained why the exchange rate had overshot, and made explicit estimates of the size of the shocks and their persistence. It estimated the shock from administered prices to be 1.7 percent and the inertia from past shocks to be 4.2 percent of which two thirds was to be accepted, resulting in a further adjustment of 2.8 percent. The central bank added these two numbers to the previously announced target of 4 percent to get an adjusted inflation target for 2003 of 8.5 percent ($= 4 + 1.7 + 2.8$ percent). Specifically, the bank indicated that an attempt to achieve an inflation rate of 6.5 percent in 2003 would entail a fall of 1.6 percent in GDP, while trying to achieve the nonadjusted target of 4 percent would lead to an even larger decline of GDP of 7.3 percent. As a result inflation in 2003 ended up at 9.3 percent, very close to the adjusted target, and the GDP declined by 0.2 percent. As noted by Mishkin (2004), the role of the central bank in this accomplishment provides a good example for other emerging markets considering adopting inflation targeting: the way the central bank articulated the reasons why the initial inflation target was missed, how it responded to the shock, and how it planned to return to its longer-run inflation goal.

Fiscal Achievements and Fiscal Failures in the Late 1990s

As noted by Mervin King (2004, p. 11), "the key to macroeconomic success in emerging market economies is not primarily their choice of exchange rate regime, but rather the health of the countries' fundamental macroeconomic institution." Starting in mid-1998 Brazil increased substantially its overall primary fiscal surplus: a shift of 5 percentage points of GDP, when comparing 1997 to 2003. Figure 1 through 3 show why Argentina eventually collapsed, while Brazil was able to withstand the consequences of the crisis: the reason is the sharp difference in fiscal policy.

Strong fiscal adjustments require developing rules and institutions over time. In Brazil there were two main developments: (1) the agreements between the federal government and the states and local governments since 1997, and (2) the Fiscal Responsibility Law, an important piece of legislation on fiscal rules and limits, approved in May 2000.

The Consolidation of State Debts

Starting in 1997 (with discussions as early as 1996), 25 of Brazil's 27 states signed debt-restructuring agreements with the federal government. According to such agreements the federal government accepted to consolidate the states' debts transforming them into 30-year bonds with a fixed real interest rate of 6 percent. In turn, the states agreed to commit a minimum of 13 percent of their income to servicing the debt,

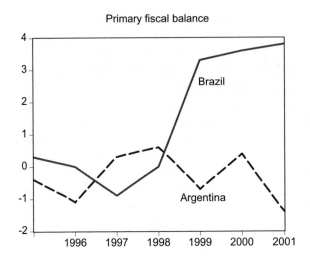

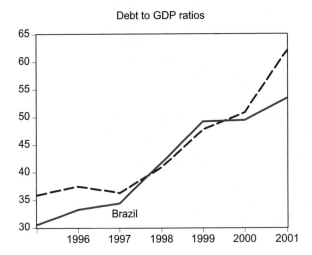

Figure 1
Brazil and Argentina: Primary budget surplus and percentage of GDP compared

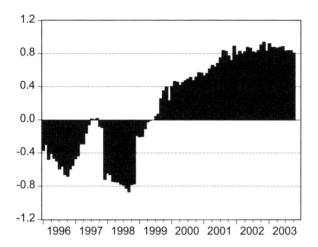

Figure 2
Primary fiscal balance of states and municipalities in Brazil, 1996 to 2003, as percentage of GDP

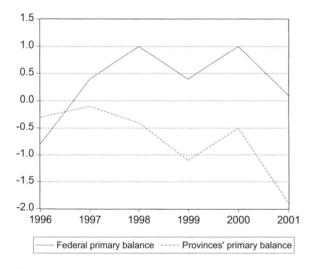

Figure 3
Primary fiscal balance of the federal government and the provinces in Argentina, 1996 to 2003, as percentage of GDP

and to earmark privatization proceeds to redeem it. These commitments were accompanied by a guarantee that gives the federal government direct access to the states' income and to the transfers they
receive from the federal government itself. In the case of a default, the
contracts give the federal government the authority to seize the transfers or, if this is not enough, to withdraw the amount due directly
from the state's bank accounts.[5]

The agreements produced a rapid shift in the fiscal position of the
states; they also survived, which is rare for fiscal rules of this kind. As
shown in figure 2, the aggregate annual primary surplus of states and
municipalities improved by 1.1 percent of GDP over the period 1999 to
2003. The fiscal adjustment mostly came from a reduction of payroll
expenditures: in 1997 personnel expenditure represented more than 70
percent of the net revenue of the states; in 2001 it was reduced to less
than 60 percent. As a result state and municipal debt has stabilized, despite low growth and the exchange rate devaluation.

The Fiscal Responsibility Law

In 2000 Congress passed the Fiscal Responsibility Law which sets a
general framework for budgetary planning, execution, and reporting
for the three levels of government.[6] The law consists of three fiscal
rules: general targets and limits for selected fiscal indicators, corrective
institutional mechanisms in case of noncompliance, and institutional
sanctions for noncompliance.

The law introduced several important changes in fiscal procedures:
limits for expenditure on personnel, annual fiscal targets and ceilings
on the public debt, rules requiring the compensation of any new permanent expenditures and any reduction in tax revenues, and rules to
control public finances in electoral years. But the most important innovation was the prohibition of the federal government from financing
state and local governments beyond the yearly legal transfers. This
guaranteed that the debt rescheduling agreements would be respected.

The Rise in the Debt Ratio

Before 1999 the underlying reason for the increase in the debt ratio was
low primary surpluses. Only in 1999 did Brazil start producing significant and consistent primary surpluses. Notwithstanding the improvements in fiscal policy and the new fiscal rules, Brazil's debt–GDP ratio
kept rising, from 35 percent in 1998 to 57 percent in 2002. Two factors
pushed the debt ratio up. First, as already mentioned, the depreciation
of the exchange rate (figure 1.1 in chapter 1 by Pastore and Pinotti

documents the correlation between the debt ratio and the real exchange rate). Second, the recognition, over time, of previously hidden liabilities, "skeletons" in Brazilian jargon.

Lessons from Brazil

The experience of Brazil during 2002 to 2003 points to four main lessons that may be of more general interest:

• Fluctuations in the exchange rate and/or in risk premia cause corresponding fluctuations in the debt ratio—the wider, the larger is the share of dollar denominated debt. If the debt is perceived as unsustainable, the economy may fall into a circle of further depreciation and further increases in the debt ratio. In such a situation monetary policy cannot work alone; fiscal policy has to be adjusted to the change in the real exchange rate or risk premia.

• The share of dollar-linked debt is partly the result of history, partly it is a choice by the government. When the private sector wishes to reduce its exposure to exchange rate risk, as was the case in Brazil during 2001, the government can limit the depreciation of the exchange rate by issuing dollar debt or currency swaps. If the shock is deemed to be permanent, this is essentially an intertemporal choice between depreciation today or tomorrow (a decision to smooth the shock). In contrast, in the case of overshooting, there might instead be an argument for intervention. In both cases intervention could take place using foreign exchange reserves. We are not aware of analyses of such trade-offs in the literature.

• Economic policy in an emerging market economy is often portrayed as an impossible task: it is not necessarily so. Provided that the authorities have the willingness to act and the correct framework to build upon, much can be done in a relatively short period, in fact at a speed not very different from that of financial markets. But this depends on previous institutional development.

• In Brazil, inflation targeting (coupled with a floating exchange rate regime) helped absorb the severe shocks that hit the economy, while at the same time maintaining inflation under control. The latter was an essential ingredient for producing the real exchange rate depreciation (as opposed to only nominal depreciation) and therefore the external adjustment. Following the depreciation the central bank assessed the nature and persistence of the shock; then it built different inflation and output trajectories associated with different interest rate paths. Based on its aversion to inflation variability, it chose the optimal path for output and inflation. If the shock is abnormally large and/or persistent, its inflationary effect may last more than a year. In such a case the optimal inflation path may imply a 12-month-ahead inflation above the previous annual target. In such a case it is not possible, nor optimal, to pursue blindly the central point of the old target. The target should be adjusted in order to take into account the effects of the change in relative prices. Eventually, although at longer horizons, inflation must converge to its target path.

Looking Forward

Looking forward, it is clear that a successful path in the case of Brazil requires a continuation in the institutional development that allows the country to reduce uncertainty arising from economic policy, in particular, from fiscal policy. Charles Wyplosz in chapter 3 discusses how the Fiscal Responsibility Law can be improved.

The next issue is the level of real interest rates. Brazil has emerged from the crisis with a level of real rates that remains unusually high. There are two common explanations for the level of real rates: (1) Brazil is caught in a bad equilibrium of high real interest rates and bad debt dynamics, and simply lowering real rates would be sufficient to shift the economy to a good equilibrium; (2) real rates are high because fiscal fundamentals are still perceived to be weak. (Chapter 5 by Garcia and Rigobon shows how an increase in macroeconomic volatility raises the level of the primary surplus that is required to stabilize the debt. In the presence of macroeconomic risk there are paths along which the debt will be unsustainable). We share the view expressed by Arminio Fraga, in his comments in the book: real rates are temporarily high and will come down over time, provided that fiscal policy keeps being consistent. Arida, Bacha, and Resende pursue, however, in chapter 8, an alternative and potentially interesting explanation, based on "jurisdictional uncertainty." They argue that interest rates are high because investors do not want to extend long-term credit in the domestic jurisdiction.

Vulnerability will not be reduced until the duration and maturity of the debt are lengthened and its link to the dollar is reduced. Missale and Giavazzi in chapter 4 discuss the optimal structure of the Brazilian public debt: they conclude that the portion of the debt that is linked to foreign currencies should be as small as possible, and argue in favor of price-indexed and fixed-rate nominal bonds. They find that issuing fixed-rate bonds in exchange for Selic-indexed bonds increases the probability of debt stabilization even if the 12-month term premium is as high as 4 percent.

As mentioned above, one of the reasons such a large share of the domestic debt is indexed to the dollar is the demand for hedge by the private sector. In Brazil most of the exchange rate risk is borne by the government and the central bank: the private sector hedges its dollar exposure by entering into swap contracts with the central bank. Such a large amount of outstanding hedge may not be rapidly reduced: the currency tends to fall whenever the central bank announces that it will not fully roll over the outstanding stock of hedge. The current account surplus that Brazil is now running offers an opportunity to reduce the demand for hedge by the private sector. In fact in March 2004 the stock of dollar-linked debt had fallen to 17 percent of total domestic, almost one-half of its level during the crisis.

Since vulnerability to exchange rate risk is valued by investors, an even lower share of dollar-denominated debt could reduce the risk premium on the Brazilian debt. A more aggressive retiring of dollar-linked debt would leave, however, less room for the accumulation of reserves, and vice versa. A higher stock of foreign exchange reserves reduces the likelihood of liquidity or self-fulfilling crises. Additionally a number of "vulnerability indicators" depend on the stock of reserves, such as the ratios of exports to reserves or M2 over reserves. So what is the optimal strategy? How much is a dollar of debt retired worth, compared with one more dollar of reserves?

The experience of Brazil does not offer an unambiguous answer to this question: it points however to a missing link in the literature on financial crises in emerging markets, one that we would hope is soon addressed. The ingredients are all there: a model of self-fulfilling crises (e.g., à la Obstfeld 1996) where vulnerability depends on two parameters, the reserve ratio and the composition of the debt.

The volume starts with a survey by Affonso Pastore and Maria Cristina Pinotti who carefully describe Brazil's macroeconomic landscape in the period we study. This is then followed by three chapters: the first analyzes the interaction between monetary and fiscal policy; the second looks at fiscal institutions and debt management; finally, chapter 4 analyses the Brazilian experience with the spectacles of the "political economist."

Notes

1. The expression "sudden stop" reflects a rapid collapse in net capital inflows into the country and is defined and analyzed in Dornbusch et al. (1995).

2. Mutual funds, which held 30 percent of the domestic public debt, were particularly vulnerable to the widening of the discount on longer term securities. Since these institutions were issuing de facto very liquid liabilities against long-term government bonds, the losses on their assets induced heavy withdrawals from depositors. Moreover some funds were delaying the recognition of the losses on their balance sheets, increasing the risks of runs on their liabilities. In order to avoid this, the central bank forcefully enforced the mark-to-market regulations, leading in the short run to more recognized losses and withdrawals. Eventually, and partially as a result of central bank intervention, the discounts stop widening, further losses were prevented, cutting short the withdrawals.

3. The evidence analyzed in these chapters could also be of interest for a growing literature that has extended the "fiscal theory of the price level" to open economies and to debts bearing risk premia (see Daniel 1999; Uribe 2003).

4. Under the presidential decree that introduced inflation targeting, the Central Bank of Brazil is required to submit an open letter to the Ministry of Finance explaining the causes of any breach of the inflation target and what steps will be taken to get the inflation rate back down.

5. When tested, the guarantees proved to be effective: the governors of Minas Gerais, Itamar Franco, and of Rio de Janeiro, Rosinha Garotinho, (among others), all had their revenues and transfers seized by the federal government when they stopped paying. Furthermore states failing to comply are denied federal guarantees on new state borrowing (even if within the limits agreed upon by the federal government), and violations can trigger interest penalties on the debt rescheduled with the federal government.

6. This law has the status of a complementary law. Thus any modifications require a qualified majority of Congress.

References

Daniel, B. C. 1999. A fiscal theory of currency crises. Mimeo. University at Albany.

Dornbusch, R., I. Goldfajn, and R. O. Valdés. 1995. Currency crises and collapses. *Brookings Papers on Economic Activity* 2: 219–315.

Fraga, A., I. Goldfajn, and A. Minella. 2003. Inflation targeting in emerging market economies. *NBER Macro Annual 2003*. Cambridge, MA. http://www.bcb.gov.br/pec/wps/ingl/wps76.pdf.

Goldfajn, I., and S. Werlang. 2000. The pass-through from depreciation to inflation: A panel study. Working paper 423. PUC, Rio de Janeiro. www.econ.puc.rio.pdf/td423.pdf.

King, M. 2004. The institutions of monetary policy. NBER working paper 10400.

Mishkin, F. 2004. Can inflation targeting work in emerging market countries? Presented at the Conference in Honor of Guillermo Calvo, April 15–16, 2004. Washington: IMF.

Obstfeld, M. 1996. Models of currency crises with self-fulfilling features. *European Economic Review* 40: 1037–47.

Uribe, M. 2003. A fiscal theory of sovereign risk. Mimeo. Duke University.

I

Economic Policy in Brazil, 1999 to 2003

1

Fiscal Policy, Inflation, and the Balance of Payments in Brazil

Affonso Celso Pastore and
Maria Cristina Pinotti

1.1 Introduction

In this chapter we review Brazilian macroeconomic policy in recent years. Brazil's public debt is large, and the sizable proportion tied to the dollar makes it sensitive to the real exchange rate. Brazil's exchange rate behavior is highly dependent on capital flows, and fears of a weakening of the government's commitment to generating large primary fiscal surpluses reduces the demand for public sector bonds, raising risk premiums and reducing net capital inflows, depreciating the exchange rate, and increasing the public debt in relation to GDP. As we show in section 1.2, fears of the public debt sustainability were the main reason for the sharp rise in risk premiums, and for exchange rate depreciation in 2002. The maintenance of high fiscal surpluses is important to decreasing the size of the debt, and the reduction of the exchange rate corrected proportion of the public debt is fundamental to cutting dependence of its dynamic on abrupt swings in capital flows. In section 1.3, we evaluate monetary policy. The inflation-targeting regime in Brazil has functioned well, but the sudden stops in capital flows have forced the central bank to be more flexible, and to respond with temporary increases in the inflation targets in order to accommodate the primary inflationary effects of shocks, reducing the output decline. The central bank has also intervened in the foreign exchange market to reduce exchange rate volatilities. In section 1.4, we investigate the effects on GDP growth of the central bank's reaction raising the interest rate to avoid the inflationary consequences of internal and external shocks. The sequence of external and internal shocks since 1995 and the high real interest rate produced a decline in gross investments, decelerating the growth of the capital stock. In recent years the high interest rate also induced a decline in the output–capital ratio, further decelerating the growth rate. In section 1.5, we analyze the effects of the floating exchange rate on the current account. Real exchange rate depreciation has been the main factor in this result, working through expenditure-switching and expenditure-reduction effects. The floating exchange regime has been responsible, together with the more flexible inflation targets, for mitigating the recession of 2003, without hindering control of inflation.

1.2 Fiscal Policy and the Public Debt

Since the adoption of a floating exchange rate in early 1999, the net public debt–GDP ratio in Brazil has practically doubled from its average of the five previous years. It had already been rising since the monetary reform of 1994: increasing from 30 percent of GDP that year to 40 percent at the end of 1998, stabilizing at around 50 percent between 1999 and 2000, and growing again in 2001 and 2002, accompanying real exchange rate depreciation (figure 1.1). At the end of 2003 the debt–GDP ratio came close to 58 percent.

Although debt levels are as high as this, or even higher, in some industrialized countries, it is very high for the Brazilian economy.

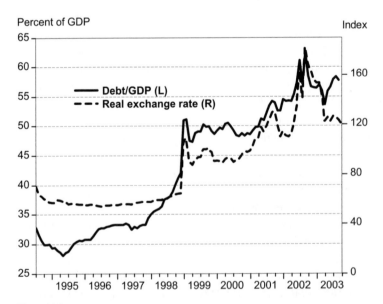

Figure 1.1
Consolidated net public sector debt as a ratio to GDP and the real exchange rate

Brazil has a history of resorting to artificial mechanisms to reduce the public debt. Its real interest rates are much higher than those of industrialized countries, and its vulnerability to external shocks increased after the 1994 monetary reform. Even though interest rate volatility has diminished since the adoption of a floating exchange rate, real interest rates are still high.

It was only at the end of 1998 that Brazil started generating primary fiscal surpluses, trying to control its public debt dynamic. More recently the government has made explicit its objective of keeping primary surpluses high enough for several consecutive years in order to cut the debt–GDP ratio. This is a correct strategy. Like many other emerging markets, Brazil suffers from debt intolerance, which is the "inability to manage levels of debt that are manageable for advanced industrial countries" (Eichengreen, Hausmann, and Panizza 2003). This is also the diagnosis of Fischer (2003), who argues that "although economic theory has not provided a great deal of guidance about an optimal debt–GDP ratio, it should be smaller for an emerging market than for an industrialized country," and concludes that "a 60 percent ratio for an emerging market country is too high, and rates nearer 30–40 percent are much safer."

Primary surpluses had occurred in some isolated years before 1999, but never were persistent and never had been calibrated in such a way to at least stabilize the debt–GDP ratio. After the exchange rate crisis of 1999, clearer fiscal rules were defined, along with a set of measures to attack the high debt–GDP level. The states and municipalities signed agreements to restructure their debts with the federal government, and were subjected to the new Law on Fiscal Responsibility. State-owned banks were liquidated or privatized, stricter controls were established over government-owned companies and many were privatized, and the federal tax revenue was increased (Goldfajn 2003). From this point forward regional governments and state-owned enterprises began showing primary fiscal surpluses of just under 1 percent of GDP, and the federal government heightened its efforts in this respect, at first maintaining primary surpluses of around 2 percent of GDP, then raising this to nearly 3 percent of GDP in 2003, as can be seen in figure 1.2.

Even with these primary surpluses, the risk premiums on Brazilian sovereign debt rose with the contagion from the Argentine crisis in 2001, and even more so due to the political uncertainties surrounding the 2002 presidential election. Although primary surpluses are high,

Percent of GDP

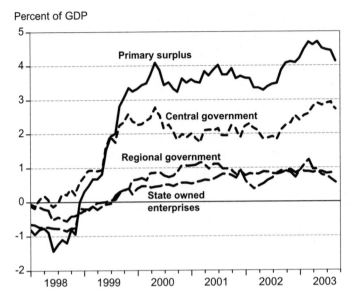

Figure 1.2
Primary fiscal surpluses

there has been criticism of the quality of the fiscal adjustment, realized mainly through higher revenues from new taxes with the potential to create greater distortion than traditional ones. We will now discuss each of these points in more depth.

1.2.1   The Public Debt Dynamic and the Real Exchange Rate

A significant part of Brazil's consolidated net public debt is corrected by the exchange rate, whether because it is external or because, despite the fact that it is domestic, it is represented by bonds tied to the exchange rate or to the value in *reais* of the exchange rate swaps contracts sold by the central bank. So public debt has a positive correlation with the real exchange rate, as shown in figure 1.1.

The exchange rate is dependent on capital flows, which explains its correlation with the risk premiums on Brazilian sovereign debt (figure 1.3). There is no suggestion of causality in this correlation. Contagion from the Argentine crisis in 2001 and concerns over the sustainability of the public debt in 2002 simultaneously generated two phenomena: (1) lower demand for Brazilian government bonds in the secondary market reduced their prices and raised risk premiums, and (2) since these bonds are substitutes for newly issued bonds (public and pri-

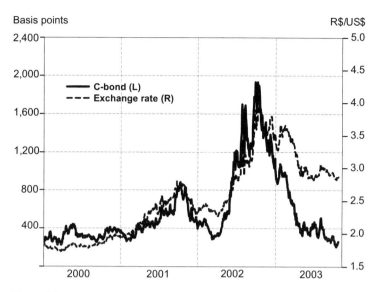

Figure 1.3
Spreads on sovereign Brazilian debt and the exchange rate based on daily data

vate) in the international financial market, there was also a decline in demand for new bonds, reducing capital inflows and driving down the exchange rate.

Exchange rate depreciation was particularly strong in 2002, not only due to uncertainties over the fiscal policy of the new government, but also due to the higher degree of risk aversion in the international financial market. Even with the extremely low interest rates on fed funds since 2001, capital inflows suffered in 2002 because of risk aversion, which raised the risk spreads for the majority of emerging markets sovereign debt bonds. This effect is illustrated by the co-movements of the spreads on Brazilian C-bonds and those in many other emerging markets,[1] as well as by the spreads on high-yield bonds, taken as a proxy for the degree of general risk aversion (figure 1.4).[2] In other words, not all of the rise in risk premiums on Brazilian debt occurring during those years can be attributed to fears over the sustainability of Brazil's public sector debt—the behavior of the international financial market certainly played a role.

The exchange rate pass-through to consumer prices remained low even with the precipitous fall in the exchange rate in 2002, and because of this, there is a high positive correlation between the nominal and real exchange rates.[3] The co-movements between risk premiums and

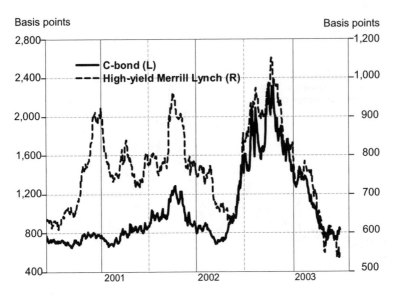

Figure 1.4
Spreads of high yield and sovereign bonds

the nominal exchange rate, and the positive correlation between the nominal and real exchange rates, establish the connection between the perception of the government's solvency and growth of the debt–GDP ratio. Without guarantees of continuing primary surpluses, the dynamic of the public debt becomes dependent on political cycles, and subject to self-fulfilling prophesies: doubts about the government's commitment to primary surpluses high enough to stabilize the public debt cause risk premiums to rise and the real exchange rate to fall, validating the expectation of higher debt. This was largely the cause of the crisis experienced in 2002. The ship was only righted when the outgoing government took the initiative to ease things for the incoming one by reaching a transition agreement with the IMF,[4] establishing explicit targets for primary surpluses, and when the new Lula government hewed to this agreement, expressing its intention to generate high enough primary surpluses to reduce the size of the public debt over a reasonable horizon.

Co-movements between the risk premiums on sovereign debt and the exchange rate did not exist under the crawling-peg regime in place between 1994 and 1998. Unlike what happened after the exchange rate was allowed to float, when external shocks were predominantly

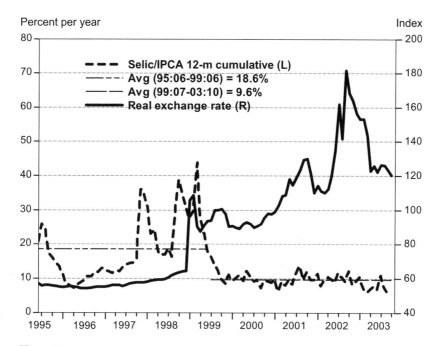

Figure 1.5
Real interest rate and real exchange rate

absorbed by the real exchange rate, under the crawling-peg regime these shocks were absorbed by the basic interest rate, a behavior consistent with the empirical evidences for industrialized as well as developing countries (Frankel, Schmukler, and Servén 2000). The differences in the behavior of the real interest rate and real exchange rate are shown in figure 1.5.

As expected, after the adherence to the floating exchange rate regime, the volatility of real interest rates dropped significantly, with the interest rate fluctuating around an approximately constant level. The average real interest rate declined from 18.6 percent a year between June 1995 and June 1999, with a standard deviation of 7.8 percent a year, to 9.6 percent a year from July 1999 to the present, with a standard deviation of just 1.9 percent a year (table 1.1).[5] Under the crawling-peg regime, the central bank responded to external shocks by raising the interest rate to defend the exchange rate. Now, under a floating rate regime, external shocks increase risk premiums and depreciate the real exchange rate, with very small alterations in the real

Table 1.1
Real interest rates and GDP growth under two exchange rate regimes (% per year)

	Period I	Period II
	1994:02 to 1998:04	1999:01 to 2003:02
Average quarterly GDP growth	2.13	1.90
	1995:06 to 1999:06	1999:07 to 2003:10
Real Selic	18.6	9.6
Standard deviation	7.8	1.9

interest rate. But despite this important change, the real interest rates have remained high, and since the exchange rate is sensitive to risk premiums and absorbs shocks, it becomes fundamental to have high primary fiscal surpluses, and strong credibility in their remaining high.

This point is important because in principle a falling real exchange rate alone would not be capable of triggering a crisis of credibility over the sustainability of the public debt. The argument lies in the empirical evidence on the behavior of the real exchange rate, showing that even though purchasing power parity is not valid in the short run, in the great majority of cases in the long run the real exchange rate tends to revert to its mean, although with a high half life (Froot and Rogoff 1995). In other words, depreciation of the real exchange rate would only generate temporary rises in the debt–GDP ratio, and could not cause an explosive debt dynamic. The question would boil down to tolerating the persistence of these shocks to the public debt, which is just as high as the persistence of shocks to the real exchange rate, and calibrating the primary surpluses according to the desired objective for future behavior of the public debt, given the real interest rate, the real rate of economic growth and size of that debt. Based on this argument, the crisis experienced in 2002 had no justification, only existing due to market hysteria.

The equation of the public debt dynamic tells us that the primary surplus that stabilizes the debt–GDP ratio b is given by $-s_t = [(r-g)/(1+g)]b$, where r and g are respectively the real interest rate and rate of growth. With the values of r and g shown in table 1.1, primary surpluses of 5.76 percent of GDP would be necessary to stabilize a debt–GDP ratio of 35 percent, which existed before 1999, and the absence of primary surpluses in that period largely explains the growth of the public debt.[6] In the second period, with a higher debt–GDP ratio of nearly 50 percent at the start of 2002, with an average real interest rate of 9.6 percent per year and GDP growth of 1.9 percent a year, a primary surplus of 3.85 percent of GDP would be necessary to stabilize the debt–GDP ratio. This is near the average of surpluses effectively occurring from 1999 onward. We do not want to minimize the importance of exercises such as this. As Goldfajn (2003) showed in his counterfactual exercise, if the government had paid attention to this simple equation, and had maintained a primary surplus of 3.5 percent of GDP since 1995, with the same real exchange rate path that effectively occurred until 2002, and with the same acknowledgment of "hidden debts," the debt–GDP ratio would have fallen to 30.7 percent in 2002, and probably we would not even be discussing the problem of debt intolerance in Brazil. Nevertheless, even with primary surpluses near those required to stabilize the debt–GDP ratio, in 2002 Brazil faced a crisis in which the markets raised the country's risk premiums to over 2,400 basis points above T-bills, indicating a high probability of a default.

This exercise with the equation of the public debt dynamic tells only part of the tale. If we combine several ingredients, such as a large public debt sensitive to the real exchange rate, and nominal and real exchange rates positively correlated with risk premiums, given that these are very sensitive to the degree of government commitment to primary surpluses, the real exchange rate begins to decisively influence the public debt dynamic. In the presence of indications that the government may relax its commitment to primary surpluses, even before this occurs, the risk premiums rise and both the nominal and real exchange rates go down, creating the conditions for a self-fulfilling prophecy. From that point onward, everything depends on the reaction of the government. It is possible that if the risk premiums and real exchange rate remain stable, the government will maintain the same primary surpluses that stabilize the debt–GDP ratio. But, faced with the depreciation of the exchange rate, it would not be willing to also cut spending and raise taxes. In this case there would be a continuously rising debt.

It is evident that an important reason for the possibility of this double equilibrium would disappear if some binding rule of economic policy could oblige the government always to maintain primary surpluses adjusted so as to reduce the debt–GDP ratio, or if the portion of the debt currently in dollars were substituted by debt in *reais*. Despite passage of the Fiscal Responsibility Law, there is nothing that ties the hands of the government, requiring it to hew to sufficiently high primary surpluses, and for different reasons the portion of the debt in

Percent of total debt

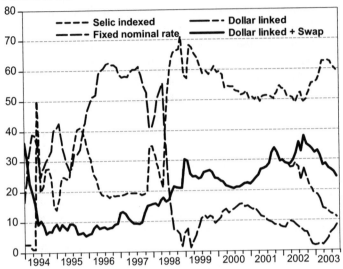

Figure 1.6
Composition of the federal public debt

dollars grew both under the crawling-peg regime and more recently under the floating one.

Figure 1.6 shows the composition of the internal federal government debt. Between 1994 and 1998, the debt in dollars grew in order to defend the exchange rate regime—rising from 10 percent of the total to over 20 percent by the end of 1998—but this total ignores the value of the exchange rate swap contracts sold by the central bank in the months before the balance of payments crisis of January 1999.[7] The wager during that exchange regime was that if the government accepted more dollar debt, it would be signaling to the private sector its commitment to the crawling peg, offsetting the most important source of speculative attack on reserves. The size of the overvaluation, however, made the current account deficits unsustainable, and as in nearly all cases where current account rises to unsustainable levels even in industrialized countries, (Freund 2000), as well as cases of exchange rate appreciations in emerging economies (Goldfajn and Valdés 1996), it was inevitable that sooner or later the *real* would have to fall. In this case the sale of hedge instruments to the private sector only made the public debt more vulnerable to exchange rate depreciation, increasing instead of reducing the probability of an exchange rate crisis.

The growth in the proportion of bonds corrected by the dollar has nevertheless continued even after adoption of the floating exchange regime. But at the end of 2002 the central bank changed its strategy: the strong elevation in 2002 came from the sale of exchange rate swap contracts, lowering the proportion of bonds corrected by the exchange rate. The growth in this phase is closely related to the central bank's interventions in the foreign exchange market, in an effort to reduce exchange rate volatility, as we will see shortly.

The other important change shown in the graph, one that occurred after adoption of a floating exchange rate, is represented by the large-scale substitution of debt issued at prefixed nominal rates (even with short maturities) with bonds indexed to the Selic rate. The volatility of the Selic rate under the crawling-peg regime produced swings in fixed interest rate bond prices, and to reduce the risk premiums and the cost of the debt, the average maturity of these bonds was shortened. With adhesion to the floating exchange regime, the volatility of the Selic rate decreased, but even so it was great enough to lead to high-risk premiums. This is the chief reason authorities opted mainly to issue bonds indexed to the short-term interest rate of the central bank. Certainly risk premiums were lower than previously, but from that moment on, increases in the Selic rate started to directly influence the cost of the public debt.

1.2.2 The Primary Fiscal Surplus

The largest contribution to higher primary surpluses has come from the federal government. Between 1999 and 2002 the primary surpluses of the federal government rose due to rising revenues, while spending remained stable as a proportion of GDP in 1999 and 2000, grew in 2001 and 2002, and declined in 2003. The vertical distance between the two curves in figure 1.7 is exactly the federal government's primary surplus.

The growth of revenues did not come from higher rates of existing federal taxes, which grew only slowly between 1997 and 2003 but rather from new taxes—the so-called contributions—that unlike other taxes are not subject to revenue-sharing with the states. These grew from 4 to nearly 8 percent of GDP between 1998 and 2002 (figure 1.8a). These contributions are basically cascading taxes, which are more distorting than traditional taxes, with a stronger anti-trade bias.[8] Considering the states and municipalities as well, we find that total tax receipts rose from 26 to 36 percent of GDP between 1998 and 2003.

Percent of GDP

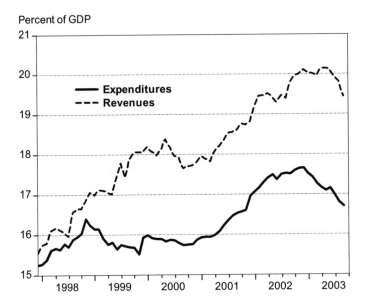

Figure 1.7
Net nonfinancial expenditures and revenues of the federal government

This rising tax burden has accentuated the crowding-out of consumption, and accelerated the fall in investments, also provoked by high real interest rates and growth of risks, derived from the succession of external shocks and uncertainties over macroeconomic policy.

After rising significantly in 2001 and 2002, expenditures contracted in 2003. The drop in special revenues in 2003, and the economic slowdown in the first half of the year, caused total revenues to fall (figure 1.7). This situation provided an important test of the government's commitment to its primary surplus target, and it reacted correctly. It could not cut social security expenses, which in any case grew more slowly due to readjustment of the minimum salary[9] below inflation levels, and cuts had to be made in other spending areas. The greatest savings occurred in the public payroll, where salaries were falling in real terms, achieved mainly by cutting discretionary spending, of which the other cost and capital expenditures (OCC) are the dominant component (figure 1.8b).

The behavior of the government in cutting expenditures in 2003 strengthens the perception that its resolve to lower the debt–GDP ratio is strong, which has certainly contributed to the fall in risk premiums this year. But the markets also observed that the cuts in discretionary

Percent of GDP

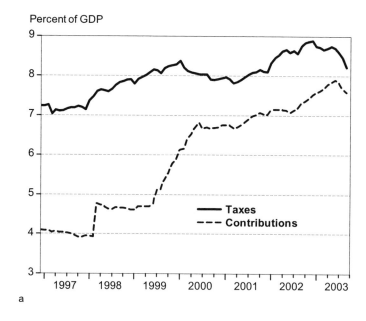

a

Percent of GDP

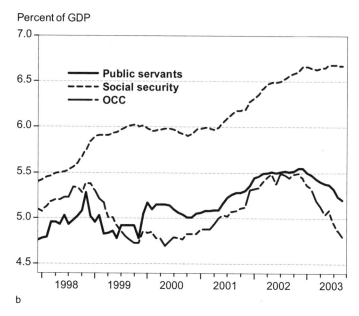

b

Figure 1.8
(a) Taxes and contributions; (b) expenditures—main classification

expenditures (OCC) could not be maintained indefinitely because they include public investments. In part, this problem will be ameliorated in the medium term by economic recovery. The commitment to primary surplus targets makes fiscal policy pro-cyclical: a fall in economic activity, causing revenues to fall as well, obliges a cut in spending, accentuating the economic slowdown. But when the economy recovers, revenues rise, allowing recomposition of discretionary spending while still maintaining the primary surplus target. Expenditures can be recomposed with the recovery of economic activity, but they are on average high already, leading to the need for high taxes. Unless structural reforms reduce expenditures, permitting the easing or elimination of the most distorting taxes, doubts will persist over whether the government will be willing to maintain its commitment to a sustainable public debt, or whether it will choose to renege on it. Or at least the country will continue to endure excessively high taxes.

1.3 Inflation and Monetary Policy

With abandonment of the exchange rate peg in 1999, doubts arose about the country's capacity to control inflation. However, the inflation-targeting regime quickly showed itself effective for keeping a lid on inflation.

In 1999 and 2000, despite the strong exchange rate depreciation during the transition to the new regime, the target for consumer prices was achieved. In 2001, consumer price rises started to surpass the targets. This divergence increased in 2002, but inflation rates started to return to the target from mid-2003 onward. The adherence of inflation rates to the targets is more visible by observing the least volatile series of annualized monthly core inflation rates in figure 1.9.[10]

The divergence from the target in 2001 and 2002 did not derive from a loosening of monetary policy. The various estimations of the central bank's reaction function show that interest rates responded to inflation rates, and that a rise of one percentage point in the inflation rate led to an increase of more than one percentage point in the interest rate (Minella et al. 2002; Fraga, Goldfajn, and Minella 2003). This divergence is due to the magnitude of the exchange rate depreciation, which was stronger in 2002 than in 2001.

Soon after the start of the floating exchange rate regime, we learned that the pass-through of exchange rate depreciation to consumer prices could be low, unlike evidence from the 1995 crisis in Mexico. Based

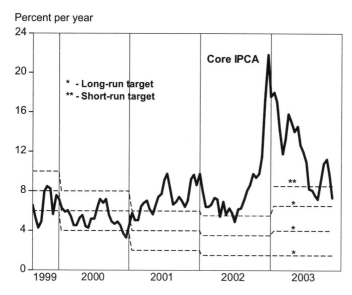

Percent per year

Figure 1.9
Annualized monthly core inflation rates and inflation targets

on a study of panel data, Goldfajn and Werlang (1999) showed that the pass-through to consumer prices should be low at the moment of transition to a floating exchange rate regime. The main reasons pointed out were that (1) the real exchange rate was overvalued at the start of the float, (2) GDP was at a low point in the economic cycle, and (3) although Brazil was a relatively closed economy to foreign trade, its initial inflation was low.

But the evidence from subsequent years shows that the pass-through has remained low even after the transition phase. Based on a VAR model, Belaisch (2003) showed that the exchange rate pass-through to consumer prices in Brazil is low by international standards, although above that of the G7 countries in the short run. This confirms the previous findings of Goldfajn and Werlang that in Brazil it is below the average for Latin American countries, and is consistent with the evidences from Minella et al. (2003). Nevertheless, the data suggest that it has not been constant, being greater in 2002 than in 2001. Figure 1.10 allows visualization of this difference. The exchange rate level appears on the logarithmic scale, on the left.[11] In 2001, the exchange rate depreciated considerably, by around 40 percent from January to October, causing some acceleration in both retail and wholesale prices.

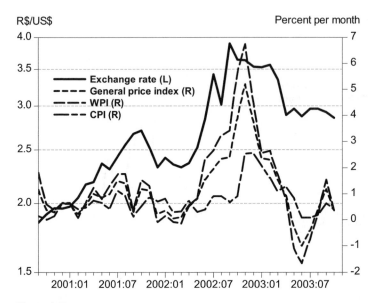

Figure 1.10
Exchange rate (in levels) and monthly inflation rates

Depreciation was even greater in 2002, surpassing 60 percent between January and October. Inflation, both in retail and wholesale prices, rose strongly that year, against a much smaller rise in 2001, even considering the differences in depreciation.

Despite using the dynamic response of prices to the exchange rate estimated by Belaisch (2003), one cannot rule out the hypothesis that the higher pass-through in 2002 derived in part from carryover effects of the depreciation of 2001,[12] the behavior of inflation in response to the exchange rate is roughly consistent with the empirical evidence of Goldfajn and Werlang (1999). During 2001, Brazil experienced an economic slump, caused by moderate rises in interest rates and the effects of the electricity shortage, while in 2002, the economy rebounded soundly, with stable or falling interest rates until the third quarter. Finally, in 2002, the real exchange rate was significantly more depreciated than in 2001. However, since pass-through is endogenous to monetary policy, its behavior is also consistent with the fact that after the success of keeping inflation within the target interval in 1999 and 2000, the credibility of the central bank's commitment to the targets reached its highest point in 2001, which tended to reduce the pass-through. From the start of 2002 inflation rates stayed above the target

Percent per year

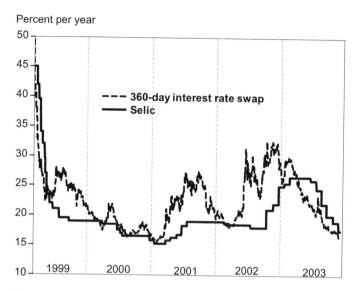

Figure 1.11
Selic and 360-day interest rate swaps

for approximately a year, straying even more from the interval containing the target, tarnishing this credibility.

To stem the contagion from the Argentine crisis, which mainly came from reduced capital flows, the central bank began ratcheting up the Selic rate at the start of 2001 (figure 1.11). However, the Argentine crisis raised not only the risk premiums on sovereign debt, such as the EMBI-Brazil (and depreciated the *real*), but also increased the spreads on the longer-term interest rate swaps, such as the 360-day, touching off a slowdown in industrial output. There is a high positive correlation between the risk premium spreads on sovereign bonds and the spreads on the interest rate swaps over the Selic rate.[13] Economic activity responded quickly to the elevation in the interest rate on longer-term operations, with industrial output contracting for 11 consecutive months starting at the end of 2000, and bottoming out 8 percent below its December 2000 peak.

In 2002, conditions were different. First, although the longer-term interest rate spreads rose quickly again, together with a fall in the exchange rate and rising risk premiums on Brazilian government bonds, the central bank maintained a declining Selic rate for several months, only starting to raise it in October. Concurrently the strong depreciation in the real exchange rate, on top of the fall that had already occurred in 2001, served to stimulate production of tradable goods and boost economic activity.[14] Second, unlike in 2001, when economic activity shrank throughout the year, in 2002 it expanded quickly throughout. Finally, during 2002, the central bank had already shown its concern over excessive exchange rate volatility, which led to stronger inflationary pressures, and started to question to what extent it should avoid migration of this volatility to prices, which accentuated the volatility of both interest rates and economic activity. This preoccupation is certainly one cause for the delayed reaction of the interest rate in 2002.

1.3.1 Temporary Flexibility of the Targets

Faced with a sudden stop in capital flows in 2002, and the significant fall in the exchange rate, the central bank decided to temporarily tolerate deviations from the target set for that year, but without abandoning its long-range inflation target. Instead of calibrating the interest rate in order to maintain inflation within the interval of 2 to 6 percent a year in 2002, that year's target was revised to 8 percent. If with such volatility in the exchange rate the central bank had still tried to meet the previously announced inflation target, it would have raised the volatility of real interest rates and output, causing a deeper recession. However, if it had abandoned the announced target without justification, the central bank would have lost credibility, reducing its capacity to influence the formation of expectations, and to lead to the convergence of inflation to the target, with fewer oscillations of real output. It is clear that in trying to preserve its credibility as much as possible, setting the new target at 8 percent could not be arbitrary. The criterion for this change was revealed by Fraga, Goldfajn, and Minella (2003), and it is roughly consistent with the proposition that faced with a shock that raises inflation, the central bank should accommodate the primary inflationary effects of the shock and calibrate the interest rate to dissipate its inflationary propagation, ensuring a return to the target.

The main argument of Fraga, Goldfajn, and Minella is that in emerging economies, the inflation-targeting framework must be more flexible. In justifying this proposal they analyze not only the sources of this volatility. Their model reproduces in its stylized facts the characteristics of the Brazilian economy that make it not only more sensitive to exchange rate volatility but also to the empirical evidence on the behavior of the standard deviations of inflation rates and output growth in emerging markets and industrialized countries.

Their model assumes two goods—imports and consumer goods—with imports entering as intermediate goods and their prices adjusting to the exchange rate. We have previously seen that the pass-through of exchange rate devaluation to wholesale prices is significantly greater than to retail ones, and raw materials are reflected in wholesale price indexes. Both in this model and the real-world Brazilian economy, inflation is influenced by the exchange rate through intermediate goods. The model also assumes a Philips curve in which the inflation rate at t is influenced by the expectations of future inflation and by the past inflation rate. The capacity of inflation rates is assumed, in turn, to be influenced by policies that change expectations and also by inflationary inertia. The model results confirm intuition: when credibility falls and hence the capacity to influence expectations declines, monetary tightening leads to a very slow fall in inflation and a deep recessive cycle, while with credibility maintained, the fall in inflation is quicker and the sacrifice in terms of output less.

Fraga, Goldfajn, and Minella's empirical evidence also shows that although all countries with inflation targeting have had success in reducing their inflation rates, in emerging countries the volatilities and standard deviations of inflation and output are greater than in industrialized countries. Some of the reasons for this volatility are less developed institutions, a lack of formal central bank independence, worse fiscal policies that increase the risk of sovereign debt, and vulnerability to external shocks.

The best solution to this problem is to have a macroeconomic policy that reduces these volatilities, and since in Brazil the biggest cause comes from fiscal policy, this is what most needs correcting. Although with a bit more complexity, Brazil has the problem Sargent and Wallace (1973) pointed out: faced with an expansionary fiscal policy, the central bank can resist for some time, but not forever. Even though Brazilian fiscal policy over the past few years has ceased being expansionary, the legacy of past fiscal expansion has left its mark in a bloated public debt, whose composition is slanted toward dollar bonds and short-term *real* bonds. The paths to fiscal dominance may be different, acting through growing risk premiums and exchange rate depreciation, but the solution to the problem is the same as the one Sargent and Wallace pointed out, and consists of correcting the fiscal maladjustment.

Fraga, Golfajn, and Minella do not deny this problem, but propose to find a way to live temporarily with its effects on monetary policy.

Faced with a shock such as that of 2002, whether derived mainly from higher risk aversion or from the perception of political risk, if the central bank had tried to stick to the annual target of 4 percent, things would have been very difficult. That would have been due to inflationary inertia, and the primary inflationary effects of the exchange rate shock; certainly the recession would have been deeper. An attempt to meet the target at any cost would have transferred the exchange rate volatility to interest rates and falling GDP. However, what was needed was to preserve credibility as much as possible, and the proposed route was to make this diagnosis explicit, calculating as precisely as possible the potential primary inflation effect of the shock from devaluation, taking into account its propagation by inertia, and clearly explaining the new path to be followed for the inflation rate.

The inflation measured by the IPCA did not stay below the announced target of 8 percent per year. It instead topped 9 percent, rising to 12 percent by the end of the first half of 2002. But since the end of 2002, it has been declining steadily, showing every sign of converging to the 2004 inflation target. In counterpoint, the costs in terms of falling production were very small. In figure 1.12 we compare the intensity and duration of the industrial recession of 2002 to 2003 with

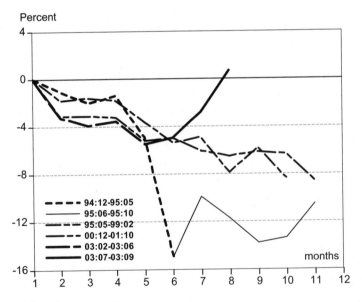

Figure 1.12
Duration of several recessions: Fall in industrial production

three other episodes: after the Mexican devaluation of 1995, after the Russian crisis in 1998, and after the Argentine crisis of 2001. The vertical axis shows the fall of industrial production in percentage points from the peak to the valley and the horizontal axis the duration in months from the previous peak. In the aftermath of the Russian and Argentine cases, Brazilian industrial output fell by an accumulated 8 percent, with this drop lasting for 10 and 11 months, respectively. The deepest and most persistent recession was after Mexico's crisis in 1995, when Brazilian industrial output fell 15 percent before bottoming out, and remained near this level for 11 months. In the 2003 episode in Brazil, the decline lasted five months, with industrial output falling 5 percent from peak to valley. But only eight months later, output had already surpassed this peak.

The success of this experiment was encouraging, but poses a question: How much of this success was due to monetary policy? The rising exchange rate from October 2002 onward was partly influenced by monetary policy, but we are far from able to state that only monetary policy was responsible. One of the reasons for the difficulties encountered in 2002 leading to the exchange rate depreciation is the fiscal fragility analyzed in the previous section. Later in 2002 the exchange rate started to appreciate. This was initially due to the effect of repeated government reassurances that it would maintain a high enough primary surplus to reduce the debt–GDP ratio over a reasonable horizon, backed by a transition agreement with the IMF that contained explicit targets for this surplus. Afterward, the 2002 budget was executed correctly, guaranteeing those targeted surpluses. These actions were fundamental to cutting the risk premiums and restoring capital flows. Similarly the appreciating exchange rate starting in October 2002 benefited from the high international liquidity and the notable fall in the degree of risk aversion, beginning at about the same time as the exchange rate started to rise (as shown in figure 1.4). The low Fed funds rates and the decreased risk aversion encouraged capital inflows and decreased risk premiums not only for Brazil, but for the majority of emerging markets.

We know that inflation targeting is not a regime with rigid rules, like the gold standard or other hard pegs, but rather one of constrained discretion, or simply a monetary policy framework (Bernanke et al. 1999). In this sense it allows for flexibility, and in many ways 2002 was a fortunate year for using this flexibility. But such flexibility has to be used parsimoniously in order to keep successive target changes from causing a loss of credibility of the inflation-targeting regime. The revision of the targets in 2003 can only be justified in a situation of extreme crisis such as the one experienced in 2002, and is far from a blanket recommendation for normal situations. We must remember that Brazil's central bank is not legally independent, and that the true test of its de facto independence occurs when the international scenario is less favorable, and when the vulnerability of the economy derived from its fiscal fragility raises the volatility of the exchange rate.

1.3.2 Interventions in the Foreign Exchange Market

Another instrument for dealing with this volatility is intervention in the foreign exchange market. Brazil has a form of dirty float, with interventions by the central bank in the currency market, both direct (buying and selling dollars on the spot market) and indirect (sales of dollar-denominated bonds and operations with derivatives that alter the supply and demand for dollars by private agents). These interventions were particularly important in 2002.[15] They reduced volatility but, as can be seen from the daily behavior of the exchange rate (figure 1.3), did not stifle it. With this nominal exchange rate behavior, it is hard to characterize Brazil as a victim of fear of floating (Calvo and Reinhardt 2001)[16].

Central bank sales of dollars on the spot market began in June 2002, with the greatest concentrations coming between July and October that year, and reached US$5.8 billion (figure 1.13). There were also auctions of export credit lines with future settlement in *reais*, which injected nearly US$1.5 billion between August and October 2002. This operation has the same effect as selling dollars on the spot market. Finally the Brazilian Treasury practically ceased its dollar purchases in the foreign exchange market, using the international reserves to serve the foreign public debt obligations.

A second form of intervening was for the central bank to sell exchange rate swap contracts, namely contracts traded on the Commodities and Futures Exchange (BM&F) in which investments in *reais* yielding fixed nominal rates for a determined period (30 to 360 days, or more) are exchanged for investment contracts with a yield greater than the exchange rate depreciation.[17] The magnitude of these sales can be inferred from the data in figure 1.6, on the composition of the public debt, which separates within the dollar-denominated debt the portion represented by bonds corrected by the exchange rate, and the portion represented by exchange rate swap contracts. The graph

US$ million

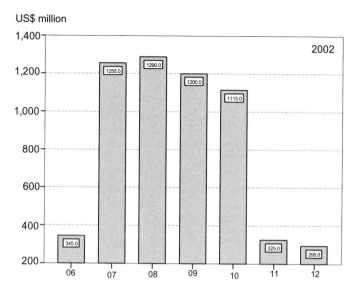

Figure 1.13
Central bank–foreign exchange sales on the spot market

shows that the portion represented by swap contracts exceeded 10 percent of the total internal public debt. We take these values in *reais* since the start of 2000 and convert them into dollars at the closing exchange rate of the month, obtaining the data in figure 1.14, showing the amounts in dollars of the stocks of swap contracts and bonds with exchange rate correction, as well as the sum of the two portions. The value of the stock of swap contracts grew, and quickly reached US$20 billion at the end of 2002. It continued to grow in the first half of 2003, peaking at just under US$40 billion.

The steady supply of exchange rate swap contracts from the central bank reduced the prices and raised the yields of these operations. In reality, as figure 1.15 shows, the yields from these operations held quite steady throughout 2001 but rose in 2002 in quick response to the strong offer of swap contracts. The rise in their yields coincides with strong increase in the stock sold by the central bank.[18] In the third and fourth quarters of 2002, these yields fluctuated between 30 and 40 percent a year.[19]

Commercial banks with access to foreign credit lines could internalize dollars and without exchange rate risk carry out operations with the yields shown in figure 1.15. These offered irresistible profits,

US$ billiion

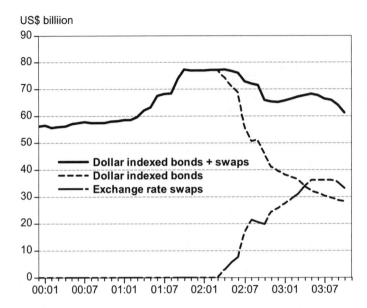

Figure 1.14
Stocks of dollar bonds and exchange rate swaps (US$ billions)

Yield: percent per year

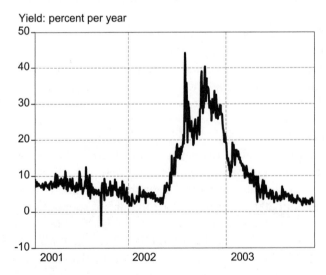

Figure 1.15
Yields of the 360-day exchange rate swaps

Table 1.2
Arbitrage operations (under 360 days)

Issues in 2002	Value (US$ mil)	Issues in 2003	Value (US$ mil)
January	45	January	1075
February	250	February	681
March	5	March	1033
April	19	April	1149
May	30	May	309
June	292	June	360
July	—	July	371
August	—	August	50
September	100		
December	528		

Source: ANBID.

and the banks did not decline the temptation, causing an inflow of short-term capital. There are no official estimates of these inflows, but those of the National Association of Investment and Development Banks (ANBID) serve to give an idea. Table 1.2 shows that between January and April 2003 nearly US$4.5 billion entered the country.

Both direct interventions and those through derivatives helped to push up the *real*,[20] and thus reduced inflationary pressures relative to what would have occurred in their absence.

As in the case of the action discussed in the previous section, this is also a strategy adjusted to an extreme situation such as the one experienced in 2002. It is wrong, however, to assume that in conditions less extreme than those experienced in 2002, the central bank could exploit the foreign exchange channel through this mechanism to reduce inflation, refraining from raising interest rates. If it did so, it would be increasing the proportion of debt in dollars and pushing up the *real*, causing greater current account deficits and overheating the economy. The external vulnerability of the economy would heighten, and the lower interest rates would only not raise inflation more quickly due to the artificial appreciation of the *real*, but this consequence would be inevitable in the longer run.

That conduct was only a temporary response by the central bank. After the cycle of the strong rise in the exchange rate, starting in October 2002, inflation was controlled and a cycle of interest rate cuts has been continuing. The central bank withdrew gradually from selling exchange swaps, and currently has been redeeming nearly all these operations at their maturities.[21]

1.4   The Economic Growth Slowdown

Much of the problems associated with the sustainability of the public debt derive from the high real interest rates and low economic growth rates in Brazil. We show that increases in the real interest rate decelerates economic growth, either by reducing the flow of gross investments and decelerating the growth rate of the capital stock, or by reducing the degree of capital utilization, leading to a decline in the output–capital ratio. But the recent deceleration of economic growth cannot be accounted alone by the real interest rate behavior. It is puzzling that after the adherence to the floating exchange rate regime the real interest rate became lower and less volatile than in the previous exchange rate regime, and although gross investments and the output–capital ratio declined. Such decline can only be accounted by the effects of internal and external shocks, increasing risk perception. In that sense the results of the present section show additional evidences of how the fiscal dominance impinges on economic growth, and potentially reduces the degrees of freedom of the monetary authority.

Gross investments and the output capital ratio are in figures 1.16 and 1.17. Gross investments increased from 1991 through 1996, oscillated widely around a stable level between 1996 and 2000, and declined from 2000 onward. To compute the output capital ratio, we estimated the quarterly capital stock series, K_t.[22]

If the output–capital ratio were constant and equal to its average value ($\bar{\alpha}$) throughout the entire 1991 to 2003 period, the potential output could be estimated by $Y_t^p = \bar{\alpha} K_t$, and would follow the path designed by path A in figure 1.18a. The potential output is also frequently estimated by directly applying a Hodrick-Prescott filter to the quarterly GDP series, leading to the result indicated by path B in figure 1.18, which is almost identical to a third estimate, obtained by assuming that the output–capital ratio can be decomposed into the product of a "trend" (α_t) and the deviations from such trend ξ_t, where α_t is estimated by applying a Hodrick-Prescott filter on $(Y/K)_t$. It becomes clear from the comparison of paths A and B that the deceleration in economic growth since 1996 cannot be explained by the decline in gross investments alone, and is predominantly due to the behavior of the output–capital ratio.

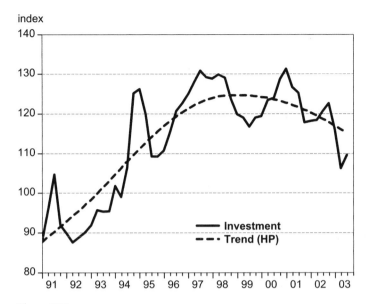

Figure 1.16
Gross investments

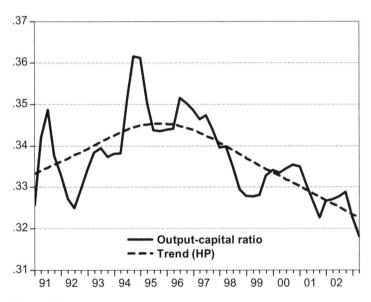

Figure 1.17
Output–capital ratio

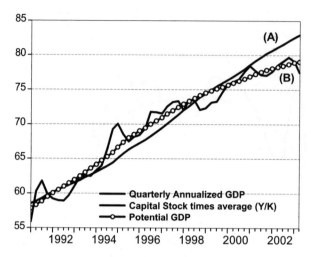

Figure 1.18
Actual and potential output based on quarterly data

Empirically there is a strong positive correlation between the deviations of the gross investments to its trend and the output gap defined by the deviations of actual GDP to the trend represented by path B in figure 1.18, as it can be seen in figure 1.19, and both display a very similar dynamic response to the real interest rate, as it is shown by the two distributed lags models in table 1.3. In those estimates the endogenous variable (either the output gap or the deviations of gross investments from their trend) is regressed by ordinary least squares over the real interest rate and over the one and two quarters lagged values of the respective endogenous variable. The similarity between the coefficients of the two lagged values of the endogenous variable shows that the dynamic response to a once-and-for-all jump in the real interest rate is practically the same, with an adjustment nearly complete in less than two quarters. A fall in the real interest rate, approaching the equilibrium rate, leads to a rise in current output, both because it reduces the output gap and raises gross investment.

The collected evidence thus shows the channels through which shocks and the real interest rate influences the GDP growth rate. An external shock (like the contagion from the Argentine crisis in 2001 or the rise in risk aversion in 2002), or an internal shock (e.g., the electric energy shortage in 2001 or the political uncertainties in 2002), increase risk premiums on the public sector bonds and depreciate the exchange

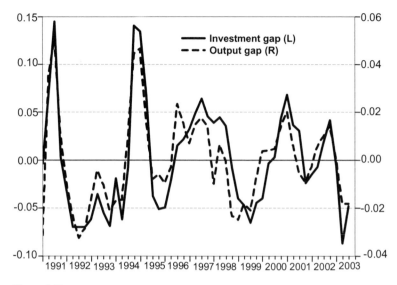

Figure 1.19
Output gap and deviations of real investment from the trend

Table 1.3
Responses to real interest rates of the output gap and deviations of investments from their trend

Coefficient	Output gap using the capital stock	Deviations of investments from their trend
Constant	0.009	0.0351
	(2.904)	(3.293)
Real interest rates	−0.0078	−0.028
	(3.590)	(3.921)
Endogenous variable at $t-1$	0.944	0.948
	(9.688)	(8.243)
Endogenous variable at $t-2$	−0.401	−0.388
	(4.202)	(3.351)
R^2	0.734	0.675
Standard deviation	0.010	0.033
F	40.600	30.486

Note: Numbers in parenthesis below the coefficients are the Student t.

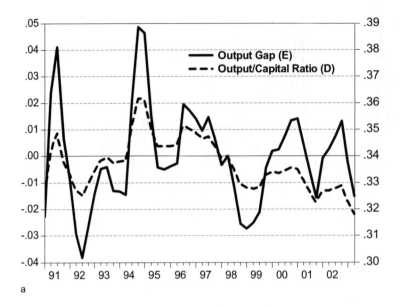

a

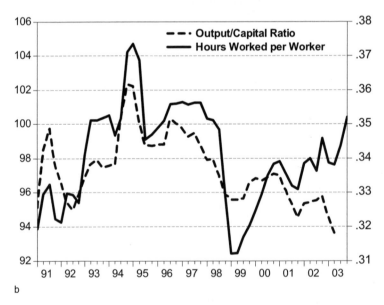

b

Figure 1.20
Output gap–output capital ratio, utilization of installed capacity and hours worked per worker

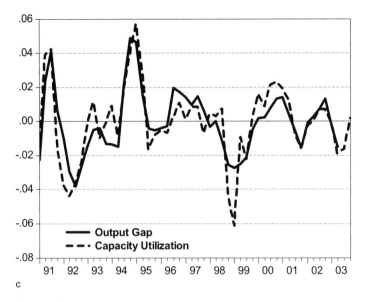

c

Figure 1.20
(continued)

rate, raising the inflation rate. It also increases perceived risks in the returns on fixed capital investments, and given the same real interest rate reduce gross investments. As we saw above, the central bank reacts to all such shocks by hiking the interest rate, which causes a decline in aggregate demand and a widening of the output gap. The widening of the output gap means a reduction in the level of utilization of the actual capital stock, triggering two consequences: (1) a decline in the demand for labor services,[23] which since the marginal costs of changing the level of employment are higher than the marginal cost of changing the hours worked, leads in the short run predominantly to changes in hours worked per worker, and (2) although the level of utilization of the capital stock declines, the actual capital stock rises (but at a slower rate due to the decline in the flow of gross investments), leading to a decline in the ratio of capital services to the actual capital stock, which causes a decline in the output–capital ratio.[24]

    If our description above is correct, we should expect the output–capital ratio to reduce in the short run in response to a rise in the real interest rate, posting a positive correlation between the output–capital ratio and the output gap. Such correlation is shown in figure 1.20a. But the effects of the real interest rate on the output–capital ratio are not a direct one. First, the rise in the real interest rate reduces aggregate demand and, with it, the degree of utilization of the actual stock of capital. An evidence of such effect is possible by comparing our estimate of the output gap with the National Confederation of Industry (CNI) estimate of the level of utilization of the industrial capacity, shown in figure 1.20c.[25] Second, the reduction in the aggregate demand and in the degree of capital utilization contract the demand for labor services, which in the short-run implies a reduction in hours worked per worker. An evidence of that effect is the positive correlation between the CNI's estimate of the hours worked per worker and the output–capital ratio in figure 1.20b.

The variables behind the changes in the short-run economic growth rates are the shocks that hit the Brazilian economy, and the real interest rate. As it was shown in the previous section the central bank has avoided being excessively conservative, and introduced enough flexibility in the execution of the inflation targeting regime to reduce the output volatility in response to shocks, but since the effects of the external shocks are amplified by the uncertainties coming from the fiscal regime, even the use of such flexibility is not enough to avoid a reduction in economic growth.

1.5   Balance of Payments: Expenditure-Switching and Expenditure-Reducing Policies

The flexible exchange rate regime has proved its merits. Combined with inflation targeting, it did not impede inflation control, and it also led to an important adjustment in the current account. The flexible exchange rate regime is also in large part responsible for the mildness of the recession in 2003: real interest rates had to be raised far less than during the shocks under the crawling-peg regime, and the falling exchange rate helped stimulate the output of tradable goods, boosting exports and decreasing imports.

Because of the low pass-through of the exchange rate to consumer prices, shocks to the nominal exchange rate turn into shocks to the real exchange rate, reproducing in Brazil the same phenomenon noted by Mussa (1986) in industrialized countries soon after the start of the floating exchange rate in the 1970s. On the other hand, the response of current account balances to the real exchange rate rejects the hypothesis that in Brazil price adjustments have occurred as predicted by the

models that assume the existence of local currency pricing (LCP) practices. This is in opposition to the view of models that assume producer
currency pricing (PCP) practices, in which the exchange rate adjustments become changes in relative prices (Engel 2002; Obstfeld 2002). A
significant portion of Brazil's exports are in commodities (and imports
as well) whose prices are approximately fixed in dollars, and domestic
prices in *reais*, instantaneously almost fully adjust to the exchange rate
depreciation, producing a strong expenditure-switching effect. The
evidence of this effect appears clearly in the higher pass-through to
wholesale prices (where there is a high proportion of tradable commodities) than to consumer prices (where there is a high proportion of
nontradable services),[26] and also in the current account response to the
real exchange rate. In figure 1.21, we compare current account balances
with the real exchange rate. The positive correlation between the two
series is clear.

Brazil's success in raising exports and producing high trade surpluses has inspired practical persons and politicians alike to propose
that the central bank should set real exchange rate targets, keeping
them depreciated to stimulate production of tradables. There are several arguments against this idea. First, targets for the real exchange
rate reduce the central bank's autonomy to exercise monetary policy,

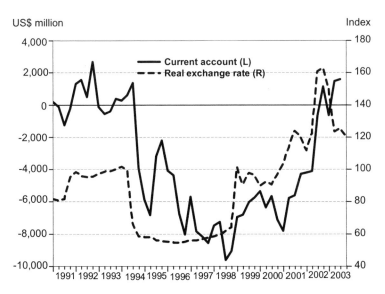

Figure 1.21
Current account balance and real exchange rate based on quarterly data

which is a liability for a country that intends to use it, even if stingily, to smooth out GDP cycles. Second, it generates moral hazard effects, inducing larger dollar liabilities and increasing the demand for dollar-denominated government bonds. The absence of fluctuations induces mismatches between assets and liabilities, discouraging prudent hedging (Velasco 2000). Third, as the experience with the crawling peg showed clearly, faced with external shocks, real interest rates must be used more intensely to defend the exchange rate. This cost could be in part offset if Brazil had large enough reserves to more effectively allow the smoothing of exchange rate volatility, but the monetary effects of such reserves would have to be sterilized, and at an important fiscal cost. The central bank would also be faced with current account surpluses for some consecutive years, to allow the accumulation of these assets. The country would have to resign itself to being an exporter of capital, like Japan and China. But this would not make sense for an economy like Brazil's, since it is facing a scarcity of capital. Fourth, soft-peg or hard-peg regimes are subject to exchange rate crises. Finally, as Milton Friedman says, "there is no such thing as a free lunch." The empirical evidence shows that a depreciating exchange rate has expenditure switching effects as well as expenditure reduction effects.

We know ex post that the current account surplus is equal to the excess of output over absorption, and that the dominant portion of absorption is household consumption. In figure 1.22 we show the strong inverse correlation between consumption and current account balances, demonstrating that contracting absorption, or better, contracting consumption, contributed to the adjustment in the current accounts.[27]

This result is not surprising based on the dependent economy model put forward by Dornbusch (1976), in which exchange rate depreciation reduces real wages, lowering real available income. It is not our purpose here to estimate the path of consumption, but we can mention some interesting indications. The National Confederation of Industry puts out an estimate of the national industrial payroll in real terms. This is admittedly only a partial estimate of income, because it covers only one sector of the economy. But there is a strong positive correlation between this payroll estimate and the real exchange rate, and also a strong positive correlation between the deviations of consumption from their linear trend and industrial wages (figure 1.23).

As was stated earlier, there is no evidence that a contractionary devaluation occurred in Brazil, as it did in Southeast Asian countries during the 1997 crisis (Goldfajn and Olivares 2001). But there is evi-

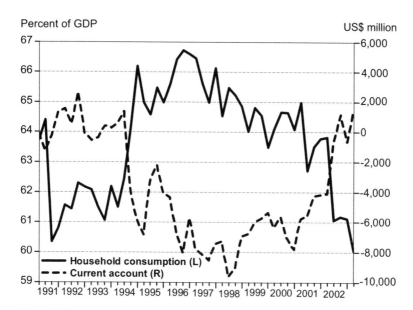

Figure 1.22
Current account balance and consumption

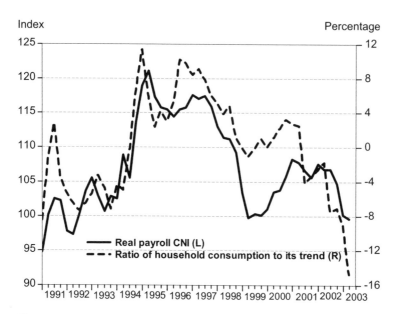

Figure 1.23
Consumption and real industrial payroll

dence that the exchange rate depreciation cut consumption, and in turn helped reduce absorption relative to output. We are not saying that this is the only cause of this contraction. After all, between 1996 and 2002, the tax burden grew from 26 to 36 percent of GDP, which certainly reduced real income available for consumption. But one may not reject the hypothesis that besides an expenditure-switching tendency, the exchange rate depreciation also had an expenditure-reducing effect.

This result suggests that we should take with a grain of salt the proposal that the central bank set exchange rate targets and intervene in the exchange market more often to meet them. It is clear that an overvalued currency is costly for a country, as proven by the experience of 1994 to 1998. But it is also clear that an undervalued currency has its own costs: to encourage production of tradable goods, the country has to tolerate reduced consumption. And more than this, the country will be reducing its overall savings, and to the extent that this undervaluation leads to current account surpluses, it will be exporting capital.

Notes

1. The simple correlation coefficients in the period January to December 2002 between the EMBI for Brazil and various other emerging markets are Argentina 0.867, Bulgaria −0.458, Colombia 0.878, Ecuador 0.896, Philippines 0.721, Morocco 0.840, Mexico 0.922, Nigeria 0.899, Panama 0.928, Peru 0.969, Poland 0.842, Russia 0.229, Turkey 0.860, Ukraine 0.080, and Venezuela 0.448.

2. Megale (2003) estimated the risk premiums for Brazil in response to domestic and international variables. After controlling for domestic variables, such as the public debt size, the behavior of current accounts, and economic growth, among other factors, the risk premiums varied directly with the Fed funds rates, as long as the spreads on high-yield bonds were included in the equation as a proxy for the level of risk aversion, whose increase significantly raised the risk premiums for Brazil.

3. We will discuss the evidence on the pass-through later. For now it is enough to note that based on monthly data, between January 1999 and October 2003, the simple correlation coefficients between the logarithms of the nominal and real exchange rates in relation to the dollar and to the basket of currencies are 0.9818 and 0.9974 respectively, when calculated in levels, or 0.9974 and 0.6405 when calculated in first differences.

4. The agreement was concluded before the results of the elections were known, but all candidates were informed of the agreement.

5. The real interest rate was calculated by "deflating" the Selic rate by inflation, as measured by the IPCA accumulated over the past 12 months.

6. Another source of this rise was the recognition of debts that previously were not included in the public debt statistics. See Goldfajn (2003).

7. This figure also excludes the external public debt.

8. Recent changes have started to address the solution to this bias.

9. The Brazilian government sets a minimum monthly salary for full-time workers rather than a minimum wage per se. The most important feature of this is that social security benefits are tied to the minimum salary, making it difficult to boost pay without impacting nondiscretionary public spending.

10. The core inflation in figure 1.9 was constructed by trimmed means *cum* smoothing of the administered prices readjustments, as suggested by Bryan and Cecchetti (2001). In the Brazilian case, since the readjustment of administered prices occurs with low frequency, they tend to cluster in the right tail of the distribution of price monthly variations, and they would be eliminated from the inflation computation if the tails are trimmed prior to their distribution within the year (the "smoothing"), introducing a downward bias in the measure of core inflation.

11. On a logarithmic scale, equal distances represent equal rates.

12. For example, she estimates that for consumer prices, the pass-through for three months is 3 percent, for 12 months is 17 percent, and for 16 months is 20 percent. The respective pass-through values for the general price index are 27 percent, 53 percent, and 60 percent.

13. Indeed, there is a high pairwise positive correlation between three variables: the sovereign bonds spreads, the premiums of the interest rate swaps over the Selic rate, and the exchange rate. In the period January 1999 to October 2003, the simple correlation coefficient based on daily data between the Brazil EMBI and the 360-day interest rate swaps was 0.62.

14. Neither at the moment of initial exchange rate depreciation, in January 1999, nor during the period 2001 to 2002 is it possible to find evidence in Brazil of the type of contractionary devaluation that occurred in the majority of Southeast Asian countries in 1997. This conclusion is, for example, in Goldfajn and Olivares (2001). Although the private sector had liabilities in dollars being a victim of a form of original sin (Eichengreen, Hausmann, and Panizza 2003), the public sector supplied the hedge with sales of bonds corrected by the exchange rate and of exchange rate swaps. What could have turned into a contractionary devaluation became instead a growing debt–GDP ratio.

15. During 2001 the interventions followed a rigid and explicit rule. A reduction in the minimum reserve level was negotiated with the IMF, and this freed the central bank to sell US\$50 million per day, without alterations.

16. Goldfajn and Olivares (2000) showed that in 1999–2000 the exchange rate volatility in Brazil was significantly smaller than the dollar–euro volatility. In 2001 and 2002 such volatility increased in Brazil and the central bank reacted by raising the interest rate and intervening in the foreign exchange market. But rather than attributing such behavior to the fear of float, Goldfajn and Olivares attribute it to the fear of inflation. Even if the pass-through of the exchange rate depreciation to consumer prices is low for the international standards, it is larger than in the G7 countries, and such exchange rate depreciation would drive the inflation rate out of the interval for the inflation target, requiring stronger actions for a central bank still establishing its reputation than for truly independent central banks in countries with a long history of success in controlling inflation.

17. There are two types of contracts widely traded on the BM&F. The first is the contract to swap DI (daily interbank interest rates, which follow the overnight rate) for fixed nominal rates (for 30 days, 60 days, etc., up to more than 360 days); the second is the contract to swap fixed nominal rates for others with rates above the exchange rate depreciation, which also involves contracts of 30 to more than 360 days. This second contract is what we call exchange rate swaps. The relationship between these two contracts for a determined duration gives the quotation of the future exchange rate for that period.

18. There was, however, a certain asymmetry in the falling phase of exchange rate swaps. When the exchange rate started to rise, the central bank began a gradual process of reducing the proportion of debt in dollar swaps rolled over until it started redeeming all that debt coming due in 2003. The value of the stock of debt did not decline immediately, despite the fall in the number of contracts, even after the redemptions began. This is because the decline in yields raised the prices of the swaps contracts, and the central bank marks to market its stock of debt.

19. We take two swap contracts with the same term, say 360 days: the first DI for fixed interest rates, and the second fixed-yield investments for those paying interest above the exchange rate depreciation. The ratio between these two contracts determines the futures exchange rate 360 days ahead. The rise in the yields on 360-day swap contracts was so great that the exchange rates in the futures market for 360 days fell below those on the spot market.

20. It is clear we are not attributing the power to put strong upward pressure on the *real* only to these inflows, which occurred after October 2002. To this factor we must add the other capital inflows, the sharp reversion of current account balances, and the direct selling of dollars by the central bank. And surely we cannot ignore the role of rising interest rates beginning in October 2002 as well.

21. With shorter term exchange coupons (30 and 60 days) currently near zero, arbitragers have been selling the swaps, which are redeemed by the central bank to avoid a fall in their prices and elevation of their coupons, and buying dollars in the foreign exchange market to settle the external part of the operation. With this, the proportion of debt in dollars out of the total public debt has been falling, lessening the external vulnerability of the Brazilian economy.

22. We start from a perpetual inventory model, expressing $K_t = (1 - \delta')K_{t-1} + I_{t-1}$, where K_t and I_t are the stock of capital and the investments, and δ' is the quarterly rate of economic depreciation of the stock of capital. Substituting successively $K_{t-1}, K_{t-2}, \ldots,$ $K_{t-n} = K_0$ gives $K_t = \sum_{j=0}^{n-1} (1 - \delta')^j I_{t-j} + (1 - \delta')^n K_0$. The K_0 and δ' values were taken from Gomes, Pessoa, and Velloso (2003): K_0 is their estimate of the capital stock for 1990, and δ' corresponds to their annual rate of economic depreciation ($\delta = 0.035$), being given by $\delta' = \exp[\log(1 + \delta)/4] - 1 = 0.0086$.

23. This is a consequence of both: (1) the decline in the aggregate demand, triggering a reduction in the derived demand for labor services, and (2) to the fact that in the production function $Y = f(K^s, N^s)$ capital services (K^s) and labor services (N^s) are "gross substitutes," meaning $\partial/\partial N^s [\partial Y/\partial K^s] > 0$.

24. Assuming that $Y = f(K^s, N^s)$ is homogeneous of degree one, and since in the short-run the effects of changes in technical progress and the quality in human capital can be ignored, the output–capital ratio is given by $Y/K = (K^s/K) f(1, N^s/K^s)$. The output–capital ratio declines with a fall in the degree of utilization of the actual capital stock (K^s/K).

25. CNI's estimates are restricted to the industrial sector, which would tend to reduce the correlation with the GDP output gap. The series in figure 1.20c are the deviations of the CNI capacity utilization index to its trend, also estimated by a Hodrick-Prescott filter.

26. This makes the real exchange rate estimated by $Q = (SP^*)/P$, where S is the spot exchange rate, P^* is the wholesale price index of the United States, and P is the consumer price index in Brazil, have a high correlation in the low-frequency movements with the quotient WPI/CPI. WPI and CPI are the wholesale price index and consumer price index in Brazil.

27. Indeed such inverse correlation occurs between the current account balance and the excess of absorption $(C + I + G)$ over income, but C is the dominant component of the absorption. Looking to the problem from another angle, the current account balance can be expressed as the excess of private investments over private savings plus the fiscal deficit, or $(M - X) = (I - S) + (G - T)$. The relevant measure of $(G - T)$ is equal to the primary balance plus the real interest payments (total interest payments minus its monetary correction), turning it very close to the concept of the operational surplus. The rise in the primary fiscal surplus lead to a shrinkage of the operational deficit, and as a consequence the fiscal adjustment was also partly responsible for the improvement in the current account balance. But as it was shown above, the bulk of the fiscal adjustment was produced by a rise in T, and not by a decline in G, which lead to a reduction in income after taxes, provoking a crowding-out of the private consumption.

References

Belaisch, A. 2003. Exchange rate pass-through in Brazil. IMF Working Paper.

Bernanke, B., T. Laubach, F. S. Mishkin, and A. S. Posen. 1999. *Inflation Targeting: Lessons from the International Experience.* Princeton: Princeton University Press.

Bryan, M. F., and S. Cecchetti. 2001. A note on the efficient estimation of inflation in Brazil. Working Paper Series 11. Brazilian Central Bank, March.

Calvo, G., and C. Reihardt. 2000. *Fear of Floating.* B: NBER Working Paper 9118.

Dornbusch, R. 1980. *Open Economy Macroeconomics.* New York: Basic Books, ch. 6.

Eichengreen, B., R. Hausmann, and U. Panizza. 2003. Currency mismatches, debt intolerance and original sin: Why they are not the same and why it matters. NBER Working Paper 10036.

Engel, C. 2002. Expenditure switching and exchange rate policy. *NBER Macroeconomics Annual.*

Frankel, J., S. Schmukler, and L. Servén. 2000. Global transmissions of interest rates: Monetary independence and currency regimes. Mimeo. World Bank.

Fischer, S. 2002. Financial crises and reform of the international financial system. NBER Working Paper 9297.

Fraga, A. I. Goldfajn, and A. Minella. 2003. Inflation targeting in emerging market economies. NBER Working Paper.

Freund, C. 2000. Current account adjustments in industrialized countries. International Finance Discussion Papers 692. Board of Governors of the FRB.

Froot, K., and K. Rogoff. 1995. Perspectives on PPC and long-run real exchange rates. In G. Grossman and K. Rogoff, eds., *Handbook of International Economics*, Vol. 3. Amsterdam: North Holland.

Goldfajn, I., and R. O. Valdés. 1996. The aftermath of depreciations. NBER Working Paper.

Goldfajn, I., and G. Olivares. 2001. Can flexible exchange rates still "work" in financially open economies? G-24 Discussion Paper 8.

Goldfajn, I. 2002. Are there reasons to doubt fiscal sustainability in Brazil? Bank of International Settlements.

Goldfajn, I., and S. R. da Costa Werlang. 1999. The pass-through from depreciation to inflation: A panel study. Banco Central do Brazil, Working Paper Series 5.

Gomes, V., S. Pessoa, and F. A. Velloso. 2003. Evolução da Produtividade Total dos Fatores na Economia Brasileira: Uma análise Comparativa. Mimeo.

Megale, C. 2003. Fatores Externos e Risco País. Dissertação de Mestrado, PUC-RIO.

Minella, A., P. S. de Freitas, I. Goldfajn, and M. K. Muinhos. 2003. Inflation targeting in Brazil: Constructing credibility under exchange rate volatility. Brazilian Central Bank Discussion Paper.

Mussa, M. 1986. Nominal exchange rate regimes and the behavior of the real exchange rate: Evidence and implications. Carnegie-Rochester Conference Series on Public Policy.

Obstfeld, M. 2002. Exchange rates and adjustment: Perspectives from the new open economy macroeconomics. NBER Working Paper 9118.

Velasco, A. 2000. Exchange rate policies for developing countries: What have we learned? What do we still not know? G-24 Discussion Paper Series 5. United Nations Conference on Trade and Development, Geneva.

Comment on Chapter 1

Pedro S. Malan

Like Pastore and Pinotti, I believe that both fiscal policy and monetary policy influence aggregate demand, exchange rates, real interest rates, and asset prices. Like them, I believe that so-called initial conditions are very important, especially for debates about debt sustainability, the initial debt level, and its composition. Like them, I believe in Keynes's insistence that a monetary economy is essentially one in which changing views about the future are capable of influencing the quantity of employment and not merely its direction. Like them, I believe that the key practical macroeconomic policy issue is the interaction and the consistency among the fiscal, monetary, and exchange rate regimes.

I had the privilege to attend the conference at which the papers collected in this book were presented and discussed. I noticed the importance many of the presentations attached to the application of the Woodford-Sims fiscal theory of the price level to Brazil, as well as to the "fiscal dominance" hypothesis, which explores the extent to which debt intolerance or perceptions of default risk can negatively affect monetary policy. Some considered the conditions under which, for a given initial stock of debt (and perceptions about its sustainability), a certain monetary policy could have adverse effects on inflation, output, and expectations in the future.

In this respect Pastore and Pinotti make an important contribution to the understanding of Brazil's current dilemma. Let me try to explain why in this rather brief and necessarily selective comment, which will surely not do justice to many of the fine points presented in the chapter.

The first section on fiscal policy and public debt shows how fiscal policy in Brazil is affected by what is perceived as a relatively large public debt (consolidated, domestic and external, net public debt of

the federal, state, and local governments and all their public enterprises, stood at around 58 percent of GDP at year-end 2003). Pastore
and Pinotti show that the dynamics of such debt is determined not
only by the traditional debt-model variables of closed economies (real
interest rate, real GDP growth, initial debt level, size of primary fiscal
surpluses) but also in a very relevant sense by the exchange rate.

The reason is straightforward: consolidated public debt includes
(1) external debt denominated and settled in foreign exchange, (2) public debt that, despite being denominated in local currency and settled
in local currency, is indexed to the exchange rate, and (3) the debt expressed by the value in local currency of the exchange rate swap contracts sold by the central bank.

Therefore the dynamics of Brazil's public debt becomes dependent
on the traditional debt-models variables, the exchange rate, or more
precisely on assumptions about their expected future course. These
variables in turn are dependent on general risk aversion in international financial markets, self-fulfilling prophecies, views concerning
fundamentals and expectations about government's policies—including uncertainties about a future government's possible policies.

As Pastore and Pinotti clearly put it: "doubts about the government's commitment to primary surpluses high enough to stabilize the
public debt cause risk premiums to rise and the real exchange rate to
fall, validating the expectation of high debt." They rightly note that
this was largely the cause of the crisis experienced in the run-up to the
2002 October elections in Brazil. In less than six months prior to election date, the exchange rate overshot from 2.4 to nearly 4.0 *reais* to the
US dollar and so-called Brazil's risk moved from around 700 to 2,400
basis points. This is not the place to discuss the reasons behind this
"market hysteria," as Pastore and Pinotti call it, or whether there was
any justification for the underlying expectations—which have so far
proved wrong—about a new government's shifts in macroeconomic
policies away from fiscal responsibility, inflation control, and sensible relations with the international financial community. Someday the
story of the Cardoso-Lula transition will be told in full.

What matters most, I think, is that it was a civilized transition, indicating a certain stage of political and institutional maturity and that, in
the process, the debate about macroeconomic policy issues acquired a
slightly higher degree of economic rationality.

To probe deeper into "fiscally dominant" themes, one will need to
add to arcane macroeconomic debates the more "microeconomic" and

"institutional" issues related not to aggregate levels of expenditure and taxation but to the structure and composition of spending and taxing and the efficiency of both in promoting economic growth, investment, employment, financial intermediation, and total factor productivity of the Brazilian economy. This is of course a huge, never fully finished agenda.

The second section on inflation and monetary policy in the chapter deals essentially with the period after the adoption of the inflation-targeting regime in early 1999. The former crawling-peg regime, as rightly called by the authors, had been replaced by floating and the new monetary regime was an essential ingredient of the change.

Pastore and Pinotti support, convincingly, the view that the inflation-targeting regime in Brazil has functioned reasonably well since 1999 (and weathered the shocks of 2002) given the flexibility in actual implementation, associated, like anywhere else, from learning from experience, continuously improved empirical research and close following of international debate about the subject.

It is important to note that they fully recognize the serious efforts of the Brazilian central bank in explaining the technical reasons for the adoption of a higher degree of flexibility in implementation of what in fact is a regime of "constrained discretion" or a framework for monetary policy. Pastore and Pinotti recognize that the central bank went well beyond the general assertion that standard deviations of inflation rates and real output growth are larger in emerging markets, and that characteristics of the Brazilian economy make it relatively more sensitive to exchange rate volatility.

These aspects have been given, gradually, operational content in Brazil. For instance, the technical argument that one should accommodate the primary inflationary effect of a shock and concentrate on containing its propagation comes out of legitimate concern with avoiding to raise, unnecessarily, volatility of real interest rates and real output. Likewise the reaction function of the central bank is essential in that it should ensure a return to the inflation target over a relevant time horizon—which surely should be longer than twelve months. The central bank of Canada, for instance, has chosen an eighteen to twenty-four month horizon for achieving the inflation target. Others (e.g., Mishkin) believes that even this apparently long time horizon may be too short if shocks drive inflation substantially away from its long-run target (in itself a controversial issue in Brazil).

What is needed, and I entirely agree with Pastore and Pinotti, is to preserve credibility as much as possible and therefore the diagnosis must be made explicit, the shock's primary inflationary effect and its propagation calculated, and the new proposed path for the inflation rate clearly explained.

The authors' words of caution are well taken: "We must remember that Brazil's central bank is not legally independent, and that the fine test of its de facto independence occurs when the international scenario is less favorable and when the vulnerability of the economy derived from its fiscal fragility raises the volatility of the exchange rate."

For purposes of this conference, Pastore and Pinotti went beyond the call of duty, presenting two short final sections. The first of these is a brief preliminary assessment of the extent to which "excessive orthodoxy" of the central bank could have been responsible for Brazil's sluggish aggregate growth performance of the recent past, by reducing gross investment in real terms. The authors find that this is only part of the story, since more important than the slowing growth of capital stock has been the increase in the capital–output ratio (in explaining the slowdown in real GDP growth). This raises a set of issues going well beyond interest rates, and further research is needed on this important subject.

The rather short last section on balance of payments is essentially a reminder addressed to advocates of an active exchange rate policy designed to set the exchange rate at a sufficiently depreciated level in order to stimulate production of tradables: an expenditure-switching policy. The authors remind those advocates that a depreciating exchange rate may have also expenditure-reducing effects by reducing real wages and real disposable income. In short, there are costs in both, overvaluation and undervaluation, and the debate will go on. On this and most of the other issues raised in this valuable chapter we have a most welcome contribution to this debate.

II

Inflation Targeting and Fiscal Policy

2

Fiscal Dominance and Inflation Targeting: Lessons from Brazil

Olivier Blanchard

2.1 Introduction

A standard proposition in open economy macroeconomics is that an increase in the real interest rate engineered by the central bank makes domestic government debt more attractive and leads to a real appreciation. If, however, the increase in the real interest rate also increases the probability of default on the debt, the effect may be instead to make domestic government debt less attractive, and to lead to a real depreciation. That outcome is more likely the higher the initial level of debt, the higher the proportion of foreign-currency-denominated debt, and the higher the price of risk.

Inflation targeting under that outcome can clearly have perverse effects: an increase in the real interest in response to higher inflation leads to a real depreciation. The real depreciation leads in turn to a further increase in inflation. In this case fiscal policy, not monetary policy, is the right instrument to decrease inflation. In this chapter, I argue that this is precisely the situation of the Brazilian economy in 2002 and 2003.

In 2002 the increasing probability that the left-wing candidate, Luiz Inacio Lula da Silva, would be elected, led to an acute macroeconomic crisis in Brazil. The rate of interest on Brazilian government dollar-denominated debt increased sharply, reflecting an increase in the market's assessment of the probability of default on the debt. The Brazilian currency, the *real*, depreciated sharply against the dollar. The depreciation led in turn to an increase in inflation.

In October 2002 Lula was elected. Over the following months his commitment to a high target for the primary surplus, together with the announcement of a reform of the retirement system, convinced financial markets that the fiscal outlook was better than they had feared.

This in turn led to a decrease in the perceived probability of default, an appreciation of the *real*, and a decrease in inflation. In many ways, 2003 looked like 2002 in reverse.

While the immediate danger has passed, there are general lessons to be learned. One of them has to do with the conduct of monetary policy in such an environment. Despite its commitment to inflation targeting, and an increase in inflation from mid-2002 on, the Central Bank of Brazil did not increase the real interest rate until the beginning of 2003. Should it have? The answer given in the chapter is that it should not have. In such an environment the increase in real interest rates would probably have been perverse, leading to an increase in the probability of default, to further depreciation, and to an increase in inflation. The right instrument to decrease inflation was fiscal policy, and in the end, this is the instrument that was used.

The theme of fiscal dominance of monetary policy is an old theme, running in the modern literature from Sargent and Wallace (1981) "unpleasant arithmetic" to Woodford's "fiscal theory of the price level" (2003, with an application of Woodford's theory to Brazil by Loyo 1999). The contribution of this chapter is to focus on a specific incarnation, to show its empirical relevance, and to draw its implications for monetary policy in general, and for inflation targeting in particular.

In section 2.2, I formalize the interaction between the interest rate, the exchange rate, and the probability of default, in a high-debt, high-risk-aversion economy such as Brazil in 2002 and 2003. In section 2.3, I estimate the model using Brazilian data. I conclude that in 2002 the level and the composition of Brazilian debt, together with the general level of risk aversion in world financial markets, were indeed such as to imply perverse effects of the interest rate on the exchange rate and on inflation.

2.2   A Simple Model

In standard open economy models, a central bank engineered increase in the real interest rate leads to a decrease in inflation through two channels. First, the higher real interest rate decreases aggregate demand, output, and, in turn, inflation. Second, the higher real interest rate leads to a real appreciation. The appreciation then decreases inflation, both directly and indirectly through the induced decrease in aggregate demand and output.

The question raised by the experience of Brazil in 2002 and 2003 is about the sign of the second channel. It is whether and when, once one takes into account the effects of the real interest rate on the probability of default on government debt, an increase in the real interest rate may lead instead to a real depreciation. This is the question taken up in this model, and in the empirical work that follows. The answer is clearly only part of what we need to know to assess the overall effects of monetary policy, but it is a crucial part of it. A discussion of the implications of the findings for overall monetary policy is left to the concluding section of the chapter.

The model is a one-period model. The economy has (at least) three financial assets:

• A one-period bond, free of default risk, with nominal rate of return i. Inflation, π, will be known with certainty in the model, so there is no need to distinguish between expected and actual inflation. The real rate of return r on the bond (in terms of Brazilian goods) is given by

$$(1 + r) \equiv \frac{1 + i}{1 + \pi}.$$

One can think of r as the rate controlled by the central bank (the model equivalent of the Selic in Brazil).

• A one-period government bond denominated in domestic currency (*real*), with stated nominal rate of return in *real* of i^R.

Conditional on no default, the real rate of return on this bond, r^R, is given by

$$(1 + r^R) \equiv \frac{1 + i^R}{1 + \pi}.$$

Let p be the probability of default on government debt (default is assumed to be full, leading to the loss of principal and interest). Taking into account the probability of default, the expected real rate of return on this bond is given by

$$(1 - p)(1 + r^R).$$

• A one-period government bond denominated in foreign currency (dollars), with stated nominal rate of return in dollars of $i^\$$.

Conditional on no default, the real rate of return (in terms of US goods) on this bond, $r^\$$, is given by

$$(1+r^{\$}) \equiv \frac{1+i^{\$}}{1+\pi^{*}},$$

where stars denote foreign variables, so π^{*} is foreign (US) inflation.

Conditional on no default, the gross real rate of return in terms of Brazilian goods is given by

$$\frac{\varepsilon'}{\varepsilon}(1+r^{\$}),$$

where ε denotes the real exchange rate, and primes denote next-period variables.

Because of the probability of default, the gross expected real rate of return on this bond is given by

$$(1-p)\frac{\varepsilon'}{\varepsilon}(1+r^{\$}).$$

2.2.1 Equilibrium Rates of Return

We need a theory for the determination of r^{R} and $r^{\$}$ given r. I will stay short of a full characterization of portfolio choices by domestic and foreign residents, and simply assume that both risky assets carry a risk premium over the riskless rate. Their expected return is given by

$$(1-p)(1+r^{R}) = (1+r) + \theta p \qquad (1)$$

and

$$(1-p)\frac{\varepsilon'}{\varepsilon}(1+r^{\$}) = (1+r) + \theta p. \qquad (2)$$

Both assets are subject to the same risk, and so carry the same risk premium. The parameter θ reflects the average degree of risk aversion in the market. The probability of default p proxies for the variance of the return. For empirically relevant values of p, the variance is roughly linear in p, and using p simplifies the algebra below.[1]

Note the two roles of the probability of default in determining the stated rate on government debt. First, a higher stated rate is required to deliver the same expected rate of return; this is captured by the term $(1-p)$ on the left in both equations. Second, if investors are risk averse, a higher expected rate of return is required to compensate them for the risk; this is captured by the term θp on the right in both equations.

2.2.2   Capital Flows and Trade Balance

The next step is to determine the effect of the probability of default, p, and of the real interest rate, r, on the real exchange rate, ε. To do so requires looking at the determinants of capital flows.

Let the nominal interest rate on US bonds be i^*, so the gross expected real rate of return (in terms of US goods) on these bonds is $(1 + r^*) \equiv (1 + i^*)/(1 + \pi^*)$. Assume that foreign investors are risk averse, and choose between Brazilian dollar bonds and US government dollar bonds. Capital flows are given by

$$CF = C\left(\frac{\varepsilon'}{\varepsilon}(1 - p)(1 + r^\$) - \frac{\varepsilon'}{\varepsilon}(1 + r^*) - \theta^* p\right), \qquad C' > 0.$$

The first two terms are the expected rates of return on Brazilian and US dollar bonds respectively, both expressed in terms of Brazilian goods. The third term reflects the adjustment for risk on Brazilian dollar bonds: the parameter θ^* reflects the risk aversion of foreign investors, and p proxies, as before, for the variance of the return on Brazilian dollar bonds. The higher is the expected return on Brazilian dollar bonds, or the lower is the expected return on US dollar bonds, or the lower is the risk on Brazilian bonds, the larger are the capital inflows.

Using the arbitrage equation between risk-free domestic bonds and domestic dollar bonds derived earlier, we can rewrite the expression for capital flows as

$$CF = C\left((1 + r) - \frac{\varepsilon'}{\varepsilon}(1 + r^*) + (\theta - \theta^*)p\right).$$

Whether an increase in the probability of default leads to a decrease in capital flows depends therefore on $(\theta - \theta^*)$, the difference between average risk aversion and the risk aversion of foreign investors. If the two were the same, then the increased probability of default would be reflected in the equilibrium rate of return, and foreign investors would have no reason to reduce their holdings.

The relevant case appears to be, however, the case where $\theta^* > \theta$. This is the case where foreign investors have higher risk aversion than the market, so an increase in risk leads both to an increase in the stated rate and to capital outflows. This is the assumption I will make here. A simple way of capturing this discussion is to assume that θ and θ^* satisfy

$$\theta = \lambda\theta^*, \qquad \lambda \le 1. \tag{3}$$

In words, the average risk aversion in the market increases less than one for one with the foreign investors' risk aversion.[2] Under this assumption capital flows are given by

$$CF = C\left((1+r) - \frac{\varepsilon'}{\varepsilon}(1+r^*) - (1-\lambda)\theta^*p\right).$$

Turn now to net exports. Assume net exports to be a function of the real exchange rate:

$$NX = N(\varepsilon), \qquad N' > 0.$$

Then the equilibrium condition that the sum of capital flows and net exports be equal to zero gives

$$C\left((1+r) - \frac{\varepsilon'}{\varepsilon}(1+r^*) - (1-\lambda)\theta^*p\right) + N(\varepsilon) = 0.$$

In a dynamic model, ε' would be endogenously determined. In this one-period model, a simple way to proceed is as follows: Normalize the long-run equilibrium exchange rate (equivalently the pre-shock exchange rate) to be equal to one. Then assume

$$\varepsilon' = \varepsilon^\eta$$

with η between zero and one. The closer η is to one, the more the future exchange rate moves with the current exchange rate, and by implication the larger the real depreciation needed to achieve a given increase in capital flows.

Replacing ε' in the previous equation gives us the first of the two relations between ε and p that we need:

$$C((1+r) - \varepsilon^{\eta-1}(1+r^*) - (1-\lambda)\theta^*p) + N(\varepsilon) = 0. \tag{4}$$

This first relation between the exchange rate and the probability of default is plotted in figure 2.1.

An increase in the probability of default increases risk. This increase in risk leads to an increase in the exchange rate—to a depreciation: The locus is upward-sloping.[3] The slope depends, in particular, on the degree of risk aversion, θ^*. Two loci are drawn in the figure. The flatter one corresponds to low risk aversion; the steeper one corresponds to high risk aversion.

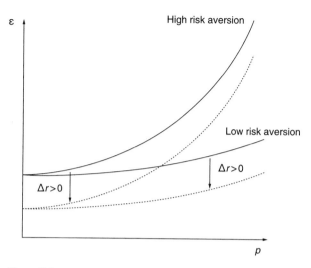

Figure 2.1
The exchange rate as a function of the probability of default

For a given probability of default, an increase in the interest rate leads to a decrease in the exchange rate, to an appreciation—the standard channel through which monetary policy affects the exchange rate. To a first approximation, the vertical shift in the locus does not depend on risk aversion. The two dotted lines show the effects of an increase in the interest rate on the equilibrium locus.

2.2.3   Debt Dynamics and Default Risk

The next step is to determine the effect of the real exchange rate, ε, and the interest rate, r, back on the probability of default, p. This requires us to look at debt dynamics.

Assume that the government finances itself by issuing the two types of bonds we have described earlier, some in *real*, some in dollars, and both subject to default risk.

Denote by $D^\$$ the amount of dollar-denominated debt (measured in US goods) at the start of the period. Given the current real exchange rate ε, the current real value (in Brazilian goods) of this dollar debt is $D^\$\varepsilon$. Absent default, the real value (again, in Brazilian goods) of the dollar debt at the start of the next period is $(D^\$(1 + r^\$)\varepsilon')$.

Denote by D^R the amount of *real*-denominated debt (measured in Brazilian goods) at the start of the period. Then, absent default, the real value of this *real*-denominated debt at the start of next period is $D^R(1+r^R)$.

Conditional on no default, debt at the start of next period is thus

$$D' = D^\$(1+r^\$)\varepsilon' + D^R(1+r^R) - X,$$

where X is the primary surplus. Using equations (1) and (2) to eliminate $(1+r^\$)$ and $(1+r^R)$, and equation (3) to replace θ by $\lambda\theta^*$, gives

$$D' = \left(\frac{1+r}{1-p} + \frac{\lambda\theta^*p}{1-p}\right)[D^\$\varepsilon + D^R] - X.$$

For convenience (so that we can discuss composition versus level effects of the debt), define μ as the proportion of dollar debt in total debt at the equilibrium long-run exchange rate (normalized earlier to be equal to one). So $\mu \equiv D^\$/D$, where $D = (D^\$ + D^R)$. The equation above becomes

$$D' = \left(\frac{1+r}{1-p} + \frac{\lambda\theta^*p}{1-p}\right)[\mu\varepsilon + (1-\mu)]D - X.$$

A higher probability of default affects next-period debt through two channels. It leads to a higher stated rate of return on debt so as to maintain the same expected rate of return; this effect is captured through $1/(1-p)$. And, if risk aversion is positive, the higher risk leads to a higher required expected rate of return; this effect is captured through $\lambda\theta^*p$.

The last step is to relate the probability of default to the level of debt next period. If we think of the probability of default as the probability that debt exceeds some (stochastic) threshold, then we can write

$$p = \psi(D'), \qquad \psi' > 0.$$

We can think of the function $\psi(.)$ as a cumulative probability distribution, low and nearly flat for low values of debt, increasing rapidly as debt enters a critical zone, and then flat again and close to one as debt becomes very high.

Putting the last two equations together gives us the second relation between the probability of default and the exchange rate that we need:

$$p = \psi\left(\left(\frac{1+r}{1-p} + \frac{\lambda\theta^*p}{1-p}\right)[\mu\varepsilon + (1-\mu)]D - X\right). \tag{5}$$

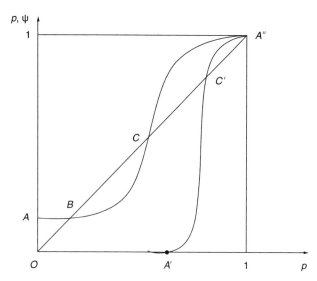

Figure 2.2
The probability of default as a function of itself

Note that p depends on itself in a complicated, nonlinear fashion. This relation is explored in figure 2.2. In the figure the right- and the left-hand sides of the equation are plotted, with p on the horizontal axis and both p and $\psi(.)$ on the vertical axis, for given values of the other variables, including the exchange rate. The left-hand side, p, as a function of p, is given by the 45 degree line. The shape of ψ as a function of p depends on whether the underlying distribution has infinite or finite support:

• If p has infinite support, then the shape of ψ is as shown by the locus AA''. For any level of debt, there is a positive probability of default, however small. Thus, even for $p = 0$, ψ is positive. As p increases, so does D', and so does ψ. As p tends to one, $1/(1 - p)$ tends to infinity; so does D', and ψ tends to one.

• If p has finite support, then the shape of ψ is as shown by the locus $OA'A''$. In this case, there is a critical value of next-period debt below which the probability of default is zero. So long as initial debt, the interest rate, and the primary surplus are such that next-period debt remains below the critical value, increases in p do not increase ψ, which remains equal to 0. For some value of p, the probability of default becomes positive. And, as before, as p tends to one, ψ tends to one.

58

O. Blanchard

This discussion implies that there are typically three equilibria (B, C, and A'' in the case of infinite support, and O, C', and A'' in the case of finite support). (If debt is high enough, there may be no equilibrium except $p = 1$; I leave this standard case of credit rationing aside here.) Standard comparative statics arguments eliminate the middle equilibrium (C or C'). The equilibrium with $p = 1$ is present in any model and is uninteresting. I will assume in what follows that the relevant equilibrium is the lower equilibrium (O or B) and that such an equilibrium exists. Under this assumption, we can draw the relation between p and ε implied by equation (5):

If there is no dollar debt ($\mu = 0$), then the locus is horizontal: p may be positive but is independent of the exchange rate.

If there is dollar debt, then the locus is either flat (if the support is finite, and the exchange rate is such that next-period debt remains below the critical level), or is upward-sloping (if the exchange rate is such that the probability of default becomes positive.) If it is upward-sloping, its slope is an increasing function of the proportion of dollar debt, and an increasing function of total initial debt. Figure 2.3 shows two loci, one with a flat segment, corresponding to low initial debt, the other upward-sloping and steeper, corresponding to higher initial debt.

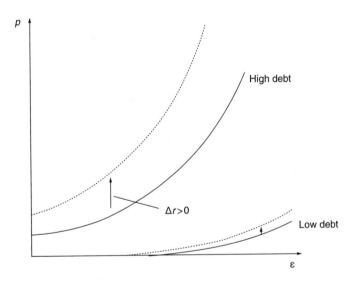

Figure 2.3
The probability of default as a function of the exchange rate

The effect of an increase in the interest rate is then either to leave the probability of default unchanged (if next-period debt remains below the critical level), or to increase the probability of default. The effect is again stronger the higher the initial level of debt. Figure 2.3 shows the effects of an increase in the interest rate on each of the two loci.

2.2.4 The Effects of the Interest Rate on Default Risk and the Real Exchange Rate

To summarize: The economy is characterized by two equations in p and ε, for given values of monetary and fiscal policies, r, r^*, D, X, and given parameters $\eta, \theta^*, \mu, \lambda$:

$$C((1+r) - \varepsilon^{\eta-1}(1+r^*) - (1-\lambda)\theta^* p) + N(\varepsilon) = 0, \tag{6}$$

$$p = \psi\left(\left(\frac{1+r}{1-p} + \frac{\lambda\theta^* p}{1-p}\right)[\mu\varepsilon + (1-\mu)]D - X\right). \tag{7}$$

For lack of better names, call the first the "capital flow" relation, and the second the "default risk" relation.

The question we want to answer is: Under what conditions will an increase in the interest rate lead to a depreciation rather than to an appreciation?

From the two equations, the answer is straightforward: The higher the level of the initial debt, or the higher the risk aversion of foreign investors, or the higher the proportion of dollar debt in total government debt, then the more likely it is that an increase in the interest rate will lead to a depreciation rather than an appreciation of the exchange rate. This is shown in the three panels of figure 2.4:

• Figure 2.4a looks at the case where the government has *no dollar debt outstanding*, so the probability of default is independent of the real exchange rate, and the default risk locus is vertical (it was horizontal in figure 2.3, but the axes are reversed here). The equilibrium is shown for *two different levels of debt*, and thus two different probabilities of default. From figure 2.1, the capital flow locus is upward-sloping. The equilibrium for low debt is at A; the equilibrium for high debt is at B.

In this case, an increase in the interest rate shifts the capital flow locus down: A higher interest rate leads to a lower exchange rate. The increase in the interest rate also shifts the default risk locus to the right: A higher interest rate increases the probability of default. The size of the shift is proportional to the initial level of debt. So the larger the

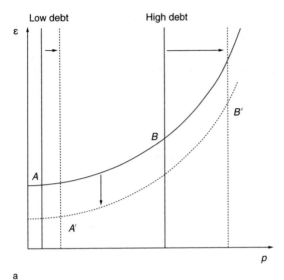

a

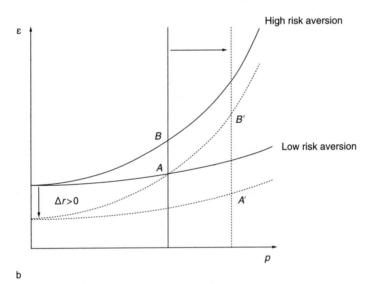

b

Figure 2.4
Effects of an increase in the interest rate on the exchange rate

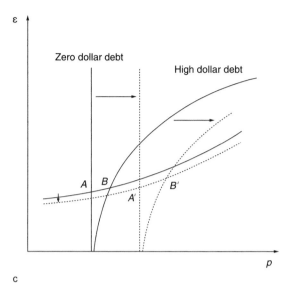

Figure 2.4
(continued)

initial debt is, the more likely it is for the increase in the interest rate
to lead to a depreciation. As drawn, at low debt, the equilibrium goes
from A to A', and there is an appreciation; at high debt, the equilibrium goes from B to B', and there is a depreciation.

• Figure 2.4b still looks at the case where the government has *no dollar
debt outstanding* and the default risk locus is vertical. It shows the equilibrium for *two different values of risk aversion*, and thus two different
slopes of the capital flow locus. In response to an increase in the interest rate, the capital flow locus shifts down; the size of the shift is approximately independent of the degree of risk aversion.

   So, under low risk aversion, the equilibrium goes from A to A', with
an appreciation. Under high risk aversion, the equilibrium goes from B
to B', with a depreciation. Again, in this second case, the indirect effect
of the interest rate, through the increase in the probability of default
and the effect of the probability of default on capital flows, dominates
the direct effect of the interest rate on the exchange rate.

• Figure 2.4c compares two cases, one in which the proportion of dollar
debt μ is equal to zero and one in which μ is high. The equilibrium for
low dollar debt is at A; the equilibrium for high dollar debt is at B.

   An increase in the interest rate shifts the capital flow locus down.
It shifts the default risk locus to the right, and the shift is roughly

independent of the value of μ. For the low value of μ, the equilibrium moves from A to A', with an appreciation. But for a high value of μ, the equilibrium moves from B to B', with a depreciation.[4]

In short: *High debt, high risk aversion on the part of foreign investors, or a high proportion of dollar debt can each lead to a depreciation in response to an increase in the interest rate.*

All these factors were indeed present in Brazil in 2002. The next question is thus to get a sense of magnitudes. This is what we do in the next section.

2.3 A Look at the Empirical Evidence

Our purpose in this section is to look at the evidence using the model of section 2.2 as a guide. More specifically, we want to estimate the two relations between the exchange rate and the probability of default suggested by the model, and look at whether, under conditions such as those faced by Brazil in 2002, an increase in the interest rate is likely to lead to an appreciation or, instead, to a depreciation.[5]

The first step is to obtain a time series for the probability of default, p. We can then turn to the estimation of the two basic equations.

2.3.1 From the EMBI Spread to the Probability of Default
A standard measure of the probability of default is the EMBI spread, the difference between the stated rate of return on Brazilian dollar-denominated and US dollar-denominated government bonds of the same maturity. However, the EMBI spread reflects not only the probability of default but also the risk aversion of foreign investors, and we know that their degree of risk aversion (or its inverse, their "risk appetite") varies substantially over time. The question is whether we can separate the two and estimate a time series for the probability of default.

To make progress, go back to the capital flow equation and rewrite it as

$$C\left(\frac{\varepsilon'}{\varepsilon}[(1-p)(1+r^\$) - (1+r^*)] - \theta^* p\right) = -N(\varepsilon). \tag{8}$$

Invert $C(.)$ and reorganize to get

$$(1-p)(1+r^\$) - (1+r^*) = \frac{\varepsilon}{\varepsilon'}\theta^* p + \frac{\varepsilon}{\varepsilon'}C^{-1}(-N(\varepsilon)).$$

Define the Brazil spread as[6]

$$S \equiv 1 - \frac{1+r^*}{1+r^\$} = \frac{r^\$ - r^*}{1+r^\$}.$$

Equation (8) can then be rewritten to give a relation between the spread, the probability of default, and the exchange rate:

$$S = p + \left(\frac{\varepsilon}{\varepsilon'}\frac{1}{1+r^\$}\right)\theta^* p + \left(\frac{\varepsilon}{\varepsilon'}\frac{C^{-1}(-N(\varepsilon))}{1+r^\$}\right). \qquad (9)$$

The interpretation of equation (9) is straightforward. Suppose investors were risk neutral so that $\theta^* = 0$ and $C' = \infty$. Then $S = p$. The spread (as defined above, not the conventional EMBI spread itself) would simply give the probability of default—the first term on the right. If investors are risk averse, however, then two more terms appear. First, on average, investors require a risk premium for holding Brazilian dollar-denominated bonds. This risk premium is given by the second term on the right. Second, as the demand for Brazilian dollar-denominated bonds is downward-sloping, the rate of return on these bonds must be such as to generate capital flows equal to the trade deficit. This is captured by the third term on the right. If capital flows are very elastic, then changes in the rate of return required to generate capital flows are small, and this third term is small.

We can now turn to the econometrics.

A good semilog approximation to equation (9), if θ^* and p are not too large, is given by

$$\log S = \log p + a\theta^* + u,$$

where $a = 1/(1+\overline{r^\$})$, and u is equal to the last term in equation (9) divided by $1 + C^{-1}(.)/(1+r^\$)$.

We clearly do not observe θ^*, but a number of economists have suggested that a good proxy for θ^* is the Baa spread, meaning the difference between the yield on US Baa bonds and US T-bonds of similar maturities. (In other words, their argument is that most of the movements in the Baa spread reflect movements in risk aversion, rather than movements in the probability of default on Baa bonds). If we assume that the Baa spread is linear in θ^*, this suggests running the following regression:

$$\log S = c + b \, \text{Baa spread} + \text{residual}$$

Table 2.1
Estimating the probability of default

	Sample	$\hat{b}$ (t-statistic)	DW	ρ	$\overline{R^2}$
OLS	1995:2–2004:1	0.37 (9.5)	0.34		0.46
AR(1)	1995:2–2004:1	0.31 (3.6)		0.84	0.89
AR(1)	Baa spread < 3.0%	0.16 (1.7)		0.85	0.89
AR(1)	Baa spread < 2.5%	0.15 (0.9)		0.88	0.90

and recovering the probability of default as the exponential value of c plus the residual. This procedure, however, raises two issues:

· First, the residual gives us at best $(\log p + u)$, not $(\log p)$. Approximating the log probability in this way will thus be approximately correct only if u is small relative to changes in probability. This will in turn be true if capital flows are relatively elastic. As there does not seem to be a simple way out, I will maintain this assumption.

· Second, the estimate of b, and by implication, the estimate of $(\log p)$ will be unbiased only if the Baa spread and the residual are uncorrelated. This is unlikely to be true. Recall that the residual includes the log of the probability of default. As we saw earlier, an increase in risk aversion, which increases the Baa spread, is also likely to increase the probability of default. Again, there is no simple way out, no obvious instrument. As the effect of risk aversion on the probability of default is nonlinear, however, and likely to be most relevant when θ^* (and, by implication, the Baa spread) is high, this suggests estimating the relation only over subsamples where the Baa spread in relatively low. This is what I do next.

Table 2.1 reports the results of regressions of the log spread on the Baa spread, using monthly data. All data here and below, unless otherwise noted, are monthly averages. The spread is defined as described above, based on the spread of the Brazilian C-bond over the corresponding T-bond rate. The Baa spread is constructed as the difference between the rate on Baa bonds and the ten-year Treasury bond rate.

The first line reports OLS results for the longest available sample, 1995:2 to 2004:1. The estimated coefficient $\hat{b}$ is equal to 0.37. The change in exchange and monetary regimes that took place at the start of 1999, with a shift from crawling peg to floating rates and inflation targeting, raises the issue of subsample stability. One might expect this regime change to have modified the relation of the Brazil spread to

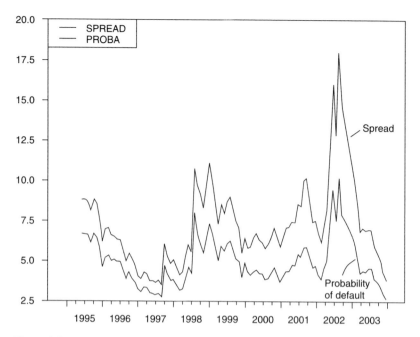

Figure 2.5
The evolution of the EMBI spread, and the estimated probability of default

the Baa spread; results using the smaller sample 1999:1 to 2004:1 give, however, a nearly identical estimate for b. So I keep the longer sample.

The second line shows the results of AR(1) estimation. The estimated coefficient $\hat{b}$ is nearly identical. To explore the potential role of simultaneity bias, the next two lines look at two subsamples. In the first are eliminated all months for which the Baa spread is above 3.0 percent; this removes all observations from 2001:9 to 2001:11, and from 2002:6 to 2003:3. In the second are eliminated all months for which the Baa spread is above 2.5 percent; this removes all observations from 1998:10 to 1999:1 (the Russian crisis), and from 2000:9 to 2003:4. As expected, the coefficient on b decreases, from 0.32 to 0.16 in the first case and to 0.15 in the second case.

In what follows, I use a series for p constructed by using an estimated coefficient $\hat{b} = 0.16$. (Results below are largely unaffected if I use one of the other values for $\hat{b}$ in table 2.1 instead.) Figure 2.5 shows the evolution of the EMBI spread, and the constructed series for p. The two series move fairly close together, except for mean and amplitude. The main difference between the spread and probability series takes place from early 1999 to early 2002. While the spread increases slightly, the increase of the spread is largely attributed to an increase in risk aversion, and the estimated probability of default decreases slightly during the period.

2.3.2 Estimating the Capital Flow Relation

We can now turn to the estimation of the two relations between the exchange rate and the probability of default.

The first is the "capital flow" relation, which gives us the effect on the exchange rate of a change in the probability of default. A good semilog approximation to equation (6) is given by

$$\log \varepsilon = a - b(r - r^*) + c(p\theta^*) + u_\varepsilon. \tag{10}$$

The real exchange rate between Brazil and the United States is a decreasing function of the real interest differential, and a decreasing function of the risk premium—the product of the probability of default times the degree of risk aversion of foreign investors. The error term captures all other factors.

The main statistical fact here is the strong relation between the risk premium and the real exchange rate. This is shown in figure 2.6, which plots the real exchange rate against the risk premium for the period 1999:1 to 2004:1 (the period of inflation targeting and floating exchange rate). The real exchange rate is constructed using the nominal exchange rate and the two CPI deflators. The risk premium is constructed by multiplying estimated p and θ^* from the previous subsection. (Using the EMBI spread instead of $p\theta^*$ would give a very similar picture.) The two series move surprisingly close together.

I estimate two different specifications of equation (10). The first uses the nominal exchange rate and nominal interest rates; the second uses the real exchange rate and real interest rates. The only justification for the nominal specification is that it involves less data manipulation (no need to choose between deflators, nor to construct series for expected inflation to get real interest rates).[7]

The results from using the nominal specification are presented in the top part of table 2.2. The nominal exchange rate is the average exchange rate over the month. The nominal interest rate differential is constructed as the difference between the average Selic rate and the average federal funds rate over the month, both measured at annual rates.

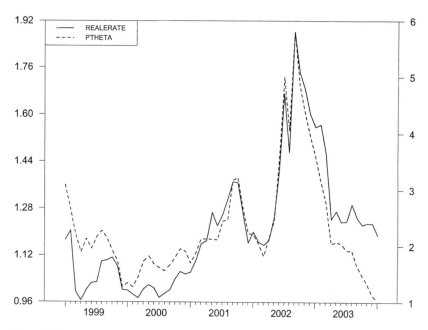

Figure 2.6
The real exchange rate and the risk premium

Table 2.2
Estimating the capital flow relation

		$\log e\,(i - i^*)$	$p\theta^*$	DW	ρ	$\overline{R^2}$
1	OLS	0.73 (1.8)	15.35 (6.1)	0.05		0.43
2	AR(1)	−0.21 (−0.9)	12.43 (13.1)		0.99	0.98
3	IV AR(1)	0.74 (1.3)	10.99 (2.4)		0.99	0.97
		$\log \varepsilon\,(r - r^*)$	$p\theta^*$	DW	ρ	$\overline{R^2}$
4	OLS	−0.05 (−0.2)	14.08 (11.6)	0.15		0.70
5	AR(1)	−0.08 (−0.4)	12.41 (12.5)		0.94	0.96
6	IV AR(1)	0.47 (0.6)	9.04 (4.3)		0.72	0.99

Note: Period of estimation: 1999:1 to 2004:1. Instruments: Current and one-lagged value of the federal funds rate and of the Baa spread.

Line 1 gives OLS results. The risk premium is highly significant; the interest rate differential is wrong signed and insignificant. The residual has high serial correlation. Thus line 2 gives results of estimation with an AR(1) correction. The risk premium remains highly significant; the interest differential is correctly signed, but insignificant.

Factors left in the error term may, however, affect p and by implication $p\theta$ and, to the extent that the central bank targets inflation, also affect i. To eliminate this simultaneity bias, there are two natural instruments. The first is the US federal funds rate, i^*, which should be a good instrument for the interest differential; the second is the foreign investors' degree of risk aversion, θ^* (the Baa spread), which should be a good instrument for $p\theta^*$.[8] Events in Brazil are unlikely to have much effect on either of the two instruments. Line 3 presents the results of estimation using current and one lagged values of each of the two instruments. The risk premium remains highly significant. The interest rate differential remains wrong signed.

Results using the real specification are given in the lower panel of table 2.2. The real exchange rate is constructed using CPI deflators. The real interest rate for the United States is constructed by using the realized CPI inflation rate over the previous six months as a measure of expected inflation. For Brazil, I constructed two series. The first is constructed in the same way as for the United States. The second takes into account the fact that, since January 2000, the Central Bank of Brazil has provided a daily forecast for inflation over the next 12 months, based on the mean of daily forecasts of a number of economists and financial market participants. These forecasts can differ markedly from lagged inflation. This was indeed the case in the wake of the large depreciation of the *real* in 2002. Inflation forecasts took into account the prospective effects of the depreciation on inflation, something that retrospective measures obviously miss. Thus the second series is constructed using the retrospective measure of inflation until December 1999, and the monthly average of the inflation forecast for each month after December 1999. The results of estimation using either of the two measures for expected inflation in Brazil are sufficiently similar that I present only the results using the second series in table 2.2.

Results from lines 4 to 6 are rather similar to those in lines 1 to 3. The risk premium is highly significant. The interest rate differential is correctly signed but insignificant in the first two lines, wrong signed and insignificant in the last line.

Because of the importance of the sign and the magnitude of the direct interest rate effect on the exchange rate, I have explored further whether these insignificance results for the interest differential were robust to alternative specifications, richer lag structures for the variables, or the use of other instruments. The answer is that they appear to be. Once one controls for the risk premium, it is hard to detect a consistent effect of the differential on the exchange rate.

The specification in equation (10) reflects, however, the theoretical shortcut taken earlier, where we assumed that movements in the expected exchange rate are a constant elasticity function of movements in the current exchange rate. I have also explored a specification that does not make this assumption, and allows the exchange rate to depend on the expected exchange rate:

$$\log(\varepsilon) = a + dE[\log \varepsilon'] - b(r - r^*) + c(p\theta^*) + u_\varepsilon. \tag{11}$$

Equation (11) can be estimated using the realized value of ε' and using the same instruments as before, as they also belong to the information set at time t. The empirical problem is the usual problem of obtaining precise estimates of d versus the degree of serial correlation of the error term. To get around this problem, I show, in figure 2.7, the coefficients on the interest differential and the risk premium conditional on values of d ranging from 0.8 to 1.0. For each value of d, estimation is carried out, using the real specification, with an AR(1) correction and the list of instruments listed earlier. The bands are two-standard-deviation bands. The future exchange rate is taken to be the exchange rate six months ahead. (Shifting the exchange rate anywhere from one month to nine months ahead makes little difference to the results. Shifting the exchange rate more than nine months ahead eliminates some of the months corresponding to the crisis, and thus drops a lot of the information from the sample.) The figure reports the results of estimation using the nominal exchange rate and nominal interest rate specification; the results using the real specification are quite similar.

The lesson from the figure is that the coefficient on the risk premium remains consistently positive. The coefficient on the interest differential is consistently wrong-signed.

In short, the empirical evidence strongly supports the first central link in our theoretical argument, the effect of the probability of default on the exchange rate. In contrast (and as is often the case in the estimation of interest parity conditions), there is little empirical support for

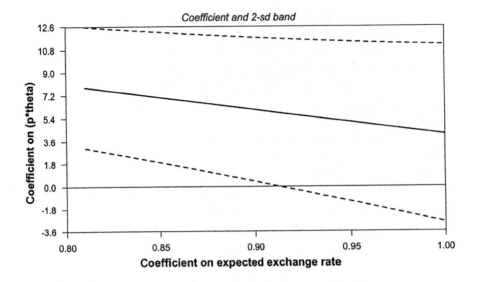

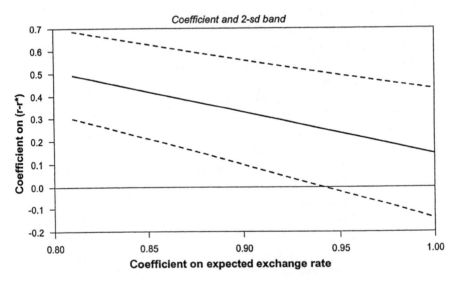

Figure 2.7
Estimated effects of the risk premium and the interest rate differential on the exchange rate, as a function of the coefficient on the expected exchange rate

the conventional effect of the interest rate differential effect on the exchange rate.

2.3.3   Estimating the Default Risk Relation

The second relation we need to estimate is the default risk relation. This relation gives the probability of default as a function of the expected level of debt, which itself depends on the exchange rate, the interest rate, and the current level of debt, among other factors.

The relation we need to estimate is

$$p = \psi(ED') + u_p, \tag{12}$$

where, in contrast to the theoretical model, we need to recognize that next-period debt is uncertain even in the absence of default, and that there may be shifts in the threshold (e.g., a lower threshold if a leftist government is elected). These shifts are captured by u_p.

The theory suggests assuming a distribution for the distance of next-period debt from the threshold, and using it to parameterize $\psi(.)$. I have not explored this, since there is not enough variation in the debt–GDP ratio over the sample to allow us to estimate the position of the cumulative distribution function ψ function precisely. So I specify and estimate a linear relation:

$$p = \psi\, ED' + u_p.$$

Next period debt is itself given by the equation

$$D' = \left(\frac{1+r}{1-p} + \frac{\lambda\theta^*p}{1-p}\right)[D^\$\varepsilon + D^R] - X.$$

This equation does not need, however, to be estimated.

In estimating equation (12), I consider three different proxies for ED':

• The first is simply D, the current level of the net debt–GDP ratio. The strong relation between D and p is shown in figure 2.8, in which the estimated probability of default p is plotted against the current debt–GDP ratio for the period 1990:1 to 2004:1.

That expectations of future debt matter beyond the current level of debt is also made clear, however, by the partial breakdown of the relation during the second half of 2003. Debt was stabilized, but did not decrease further. In contrast, the estimated probability of default, continued to decrease. From what we know about that period, the likely

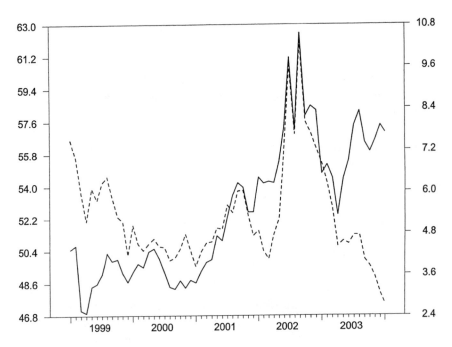

Figure 2.8
The relation of the estimated probability of default to the debt–GDP ratio

explanation is the growing belief by financial markets that structural
reforms, together with a steady decrease in the proportion of dollar
debt,[9] would improve the fiscal situation over the long run despite the
current debt situation. For this reason, I explore two alternative measures of ED'.

• The first measure of ED' is the mean forecast of the debt–GDP ratio
one year ahead. Since January 2000, the Central Bank of Brazil has collected daily forecasts of the debt ratio for the end of the current year
and for the end of the following year. Using average forecasts over
the month, we can construct one-year ahead forecasts of the ratio by
applying the appropriate weights on the current and the following
end-of-year forecasts. For example, the one-year ahead forecast as of
February 2000 is constructed as 10/12 times the forecast for debt at the
end of 2000, plus 2/12 times the forecast for debt at the end of 2001. (It
turns out that, during 2003, this measure of expected debt does not
move very differently from current debt, and so still does not explain
the decrease in p during the second half of 2003. A forecast of debt

Table 2.3
Estimating the default risk relation

	p on	D	D' forecast	D' actual	DW	ρ	$\overline{R^2}$
1	OLS	0.15 (3.4)			0.23		0.15
2	OLS		0.18 (3.7)		0.41		0.21
3	AR(1)	0.42 (10.4)				0.99	0.89
4	AR(1)		0.02 (0.2)			0.86	0.75
5	IV	0.23 (3.4)			0.17		0.11
6	IV		0.23 (3.8)		0.41		0.18
7	IV			0.21 (3.1)	0.48		0.02
8	IV AR(1)	0.38 (3.4)				0.98	0.88
9	IV AR(1)		0.22 (0.8)			0.96	0.73
10	IV AR(1)			−0.28 (−1.4)		0.97	0.65

Note: Period of estimation: 1999:1 to 2004:1. Instruments: Current and four lagged values of the Baa spread.

many years ahead might do better, but such a time series does not exist.)

• The second measure of ED' is the realized value of the debt-GDP six months ahead, instrumented by variables in the information set at time t. The results are farily similar if the realized values used are from one to nine months ahead. (As with exchange rates earlier, we want to avoid using values more than nine months ahead, since this eliminates important crisis months from the sample.) I will discuss the choice of instruments below.

The estimation results are given in table 2.3. Lines 1 and 2 report the results of OLS regressions using either current or forecast debt. They confirm the visual impression of a strong relation between debt and the probability of default. There is evidence of high serial correlation, so lines 3 and 4 report AR(1) results. The relation becomes stronger when current debt is used, weaker when forecast debt is used.

OLS and AR(1) results are likely, however, to suffer from a simultaneity bias. Any factor other than debt that affects the probability of default will in turn affect expected debt. For example, financial markets may have concluded that the election of Lula would both lead to higher debt, and a higher probability of default at a given level of debt. A natural instrument here is again the Baa spread, which affects expected debt, but is unlikely to be affected by what happens in Brazil.[10] The same instrument can be used when using the realized value of debt six months ahead (the third measure of debt I consider), as it is in the information set at time t. The next six lines report results of estimation using the current and four lagged values of the Baa spread as instruments.

Lines 5 to 7 report the results of IV estimation without an AR correction. The coefficients are largely similar across the three measures of debt, and significant. Lines 8 to 10 give the results of IV estimation with an AR(1) correction. The results using the first two measures of debt are roughly unchanged by the AR(1) correction. The results of estimation using six months ahead debt (instrumented) give a negative and insignificant coefficient. It is the only negative coefficient in the table.

In short, the empirical evidence strongly supports the other central link in the theoretical model, the link from expected debt to the probability of default. This in turn implies that any factor that affects expected debt, from the interest rate to the exchange rate, to the initial level of debt, affects the probability of default.

2.3.4 Putting Things Together

From our two estimated relations, we can determine whether and when an increase in the domestic interest rate will lead to an appreciation—through the conventional interest rate channel—or rather to a depreciation—through its effect on the probability of default.

In a way we already have the answer, at least as to the sign. In most of the specifications of the capital flow relation, we found the effect of the interest rate differential to be either wrong signed or correctly signed but insignificant. If this is indeed the case, only the second channel remains, and an increase in the interest rate will always lead to a depreciation. However, to give a chance to both channels, I use, for the capital flow equation, the specification that gives the strongest correctly signed effect of the interest rate on the exchange rate, line 2 of table 2.2:

$$\log \varepsilon = \text{constant} - 0.21(r - r^*) + 12.43(\theta^* p).$$

For the default risk equation, we then use line 6 of table 2.3, which is representative of the results in the table:

$$p = \text{constant} + 0.23 ED'$$

$$= \text{constant} + 0.23 \left[\left(\frac{1+r}{1-p} + \frac{\lambda \theta^* p}{1-p} \right) [\mu \varepsilon + (1-\mu)]D - X \right].$$

• The direct effect of an increase in the interest rate on the exchange rate is given by the coefficient on $(r - r^*)$. Thus, given the probability of default, an increase in the Selic of 100 basis points leads to an appreciation of 21 basis points.

• The increase in the interest rate, however, also leads to an increase in expected debt, and thus to an increase in the probability of default, which leads to a depreciation.

The strength of this indirect effect depends on the risk aversion of foreign investors, θ^*, the initial debt–GDP ratio, D, and its composition, μ, and the relation between the market and foreign investors' risk aversion, λ. For the first three parameters, I use as benchmark values the average values of these three variables for the period 1999:1 to 2004:1: $D = 0.53$, $\mu = 0.50$, and $\theta^* = 0.56$. For the last, I use a value of $\lambda = 0.50$ (While one may choose a different value, it turns out that the specific value of λ does not have much effect on the results.)

Under these assumptions, the equations above imply an indirect effect on the exchange rate of 279 basis points. The net effect of an increase in the interest rate of 100 basis points is therefore to lead to a *depreciation* of 258 basis points.

Table 2.4 gives a sense of the sensitivity of the effect to values of $D, \mu,$ and θ^*. Benchmark values are boldfaced.

The first set of columns show the effects of different initial debt levels (while keeping the other parameters equal to their benchmark values). For debt–GDP ratios of 13 percent, the effect of an increase in the interest rate on the exchange rate is roughly equal to zero: the direct and indirect effects roughly cancel. The indirect effect rapidly increases with the debt ratio. With a debt ratio of 63 percent, the effect of a one percentage point increase in the interest rate is a depreciation of 8.57 percent. For debt ratios above 70 percent, we are in the case discussed in the theoretical section, where there is no longer an

Table 2.4
Effects of an increase in the Selic of one percentage point on the exchange rate, for different values of $D, \mu,$ and θ^*

	$\Delta \log \varepsilon$ (%)		$\Delta \log \varepsilon$ (%)		$\Delta \log \varepsilon$ (%)
$D = 0.13$	0.00	$\mu = 0.00$	0.91	$\theta^* = 0.10$	−0.03
$D = 0.33$	0.59	$\mu = 0.30$	1.48	$\theta^* = 0.20$	0.22
$D = 0.53$	2.58	$\mu = 0.50$	2.58	$\theta^* = 0.56$	2.58
$D = 0.63$	8.57	$\mu = 0.70$	12.11	$\theta^* = 0.80$	21.2

equilibrium. The interactions between the probability of default and the debt are too strong. (This may explain the high volatility in the EMBI and the nervousness of foreign investors in 2002.)

The next two columns show the effects of different proportions of dollar-denominated debt (while keeping the other parameters equal to their benchmark value). With no dollar-denominated debt, the exchange rate barely moves in response to the interest rate. As the proportion increases, however, the effect increases rapidly. For $\mu = 0.7$, the depreciation reaches 12.11 percent. And for values above 0.8, there is no longer an equilibrium. The fact that the Brazilian government has steadily reduced μ in 2003 may help explain why the estimated probability of default decreased steadily while the level of debt remained relatively high.

The last two columns show the effect of different degrees of risk aversion on the part of foreign investors. For low risk aversion, the exchange rate actually appreciates, but by very little. Again, however, as the degree of risk aversion increases, the exchange rate depreciates. As risk aversion reaches 0.8, the depreciation reaches 21.2 percent. And for risk aversion slightly higher than 0.8, the equilibrium is lost.

2.4   Conclusions and Extensions

The model and the empirical work presented in this chapter lead to a clear conclusion. When fiscal conditions are wrong—that is, when debt is high, when a high proportion of debt is denominated in foreign currency, and when the risk aversion of investors is high—an increase in the interest rate is likely to lead to a depreciation rather than to an appreciation. And fiscal conditions were indeed probably wrong, in this specific sense, in Brazil in 2002.

The limits of the argument should be clear as well. To go from this model and these conclusions to a characterization of optimal monetary and fiscal policy in such an environment requires a number of additional steps:

• The model should be made dynamic. The basic mechanisms will be the same. But this will allow for a more accurate mapping to the data. In a dynamic model, the probability of default will depend on the distribution of the future path of debt, not just "next-period debt."

• The model should be nested in a model with an explicit treatment of nominal rigidities. This is needed for two reasons: To justify the assumption that the central bank indeed controls the real interest rate, and to derive the effect of changes in the real exchange rate on inflation.

• The model focused on the effects of the interest rate on inflation through the real exchange rate. There is obviously another and more conventional channel through which a change in the interest rate affects inflation, namely through its effect on demand and output.

When and whether this second channel dominates the first is an empirical issue. I speculate that in the case of Brazil, this second channel may not be very strong. The safe real interest rate has been very high for the last three or four years, remaining consistently above 10 percent. The real rate at which firms and consumers can borrow has been much higher than the safe real rate, averaging 30 to 40 percent over the same period. At that rate, few firms and consumers borrow, and the demand from those who borrow may not be very elastic. In effect, the main borrower in the economy is the government, and the effect of the interest rate may fall primarily on fiscal dynamics. The issue, however, can only be settled by extending the model and estimating the strengths of the different channels.

Turning to another set of issues: It was not the aim of this chapter to characterize the monetary policy that was followed in Brazil in 2002–2003. Although the argument developed here is about a mechanism rather than an episode, how monetary policy was conducted is of interest, and it helps us understand the behavior of a central bank in such an environment.

To give a sense of policy during that period, and given that the main instrument of monetary policy is the Selic rate, figure 2.9 plots forecast inflation and the real interest rate over the period 2002:1–2004:1. Forecast inflation is the mean forecast of CPI inflation over the following 12 months, described earlier. The real interest rate is constructed by subtracting forecast inflation from the Selic rate.

The figure tells a clear story. Until September 2002, forecast inflation remained low, and the central bank continued its policy of allowing for a slow decrease in the Selic rate, both nominal and real. As the currency depreciated further and forecast inflation increased, the central bank increased the Selic rate, first in October (before the elections) and then again in November and December. These increases were smaller, however, than the increase in the inflation forecast, resulting in a further small decline in the real interest rate. All changed, starting in early

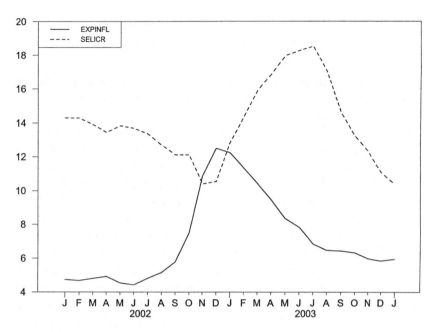

Figure 2.9
Forecast inflation and real interest rate

2003. Throughout the first half of the year, increases in the Selic combined with a steady decrease in the inflation forecast to effect a large increase in the real interest rate, from 10 percent in late 2002 to 18 percent in mid-2003. Since then, decreases in the Selic have led to a steady decrease in the real interest rate, which is now close to 10 percent, its 2002 low.

Why did the central bank allow for a decrease in the real rate until the end of 2002, before increasing the real rate strongly during the first half of 2003? The rationale explored in this chapter, the effect of higher real rates on fiscal dynamics, could have played a role. The reluctance to take an unpopular measure in the middle of an electoral campaign could have been another factor—although the first increase in the Selic took place before the election. The rationale given by the central bank itself is that it initially believed that inflation would turn around faster and subsequently realized that tighter monetary policy was needed to achieve lower inflation in 2003 (Banco Central do Brazil 2003).

Whatever the reasons, it is the case that, in contrast to the conceptual experiment discussed in this chapter, monetary policy did not lead to a higher real interest rate in 2002. By the time the real interest rate was

increased, in 2003, the commitment to fiscal austerity by the new government dominated any potentially perverse effects of higher real interest rates on debt dynamics.

Notes

MIT and NBER; Visiting Scholar, Russell Sage Foundation. I thank Eliana Cardoso, Francesco Giavazzi, Ilan Goldfajn, Charles Wyplosz, and Santiago Herrera for many useful
discussions. I also thank Ricardo Caballero, Arminio Fraga, Marcio Garcia, and Eduardo
Loyo for comments. The chapter has also benefited from discussions with staff members
at the central bank, and the Ministry of Finance of Brazil. The data and programs used
in the chapter are available on my Web site *econ-www.mit.edu/faculty/index.htm?prof_id=*
blanchar.

1. The variance is given by $V \equiv p(1 - p)(1 + r^R)^2$. So using equation (1), with pV replacing $p\theta$, the variance is implicitly defined by $V(1 - p) = p((1 + r) + \theta V)^2$, and depends
on $p, r,$ and θ. For small values of p (e.g., p less than 0.2), $V \approx p$.

2. Whether sharp changes in capital flows (so-called sudden stops) reflect changes in risk
aversion on the part of foreign investors, or other factors (factors generally referred to as
"liquidity"), is not important here (for an approach based on liquidity shocks, see Caballero and Krishnamurthy 2002). All these changes can be captured by changes in θ^*. What
is important is that the shifts affect foreign investors more than the average investor in
the market.

3. If $C(.)$ and $N(.)$ are linear, then the locus is convex. I draw it as convex, but the results
below do not depend on convexity.

4. In this case the convexity and concavity of the two loci suggest the potential existence
of another equilibrium with higher p and ε. I have not looked at the conditions under
which such an equilibrium might exist. I suspect that if it does, it has unappealing comparative statics properties.

5. For readers wanting more background, two useful descriptions and analyses of events
in 2002 and 2003 are given by Pastore and Pinotti (2003) and Cardoso (2004). For an
insightful analysis of the mood and the actions of foreign investors, see Santiso (2004).

6. This definition turns out to be more convenient than the conventional EMBI spread.
For empirically relevant values of $r^\$$, the two move closely together.

7. Capital flows can be expressed as a function of the real exchange rate and real interest
rates, or as a function of the nominal exchange rate and nominal interest rates. But the
trade balance is a function of the real exchange rate. Thus the nominal specification is,
stricto sensu, incorrect.

8. Note that p and θ^* are uncorrelated by construction. But $p\theta^*$ and θ^* are correlated.

9. The proportion of dollar debt, net of swap positions, has decreased from 37 percent in
December 2002 to 21 percent in January 2004.

10. The reader may wonder how the Baa spread can be used as an instrument in both the
capital flow and the default risk equations. It is because the spread enters multiplicatively
(as θ^* in $p\theta^*$) in the capital flow equation, and can therefore be used as an instrument for
$p\theta^*$ in that equation.

References

Banco Central do Brazil. 2003. Open letter from the governor of the central bank to the minister of finance. January. Brazilia.

Caballero, R., and A. Krishnamurthy. 2002. A dual liquidity model for emerging markets. Mimeo. MIT.

Cardoso, E. 2004. Brazil: Macropolicies in the early 2000s. Mimeo.

Fraga, A., I. Goldfajn, and A. Minella. 2003. Inflation targeting in emerging market economies. *NBER Macroeconomics.*

Loyo, E. 1999. Tight money paradox on the loose: A fiscalist hyperinflation. June 1999. Mimeo. JFK School of Government, Harvard University.

Pastore, A., and M. Pinotti. 2003. Fiscal policy, inflation, and the balance of payments. Mimeo.

Santiso, J. 2004. Wall Street and emerging democracies; Financial markets and the Brazilian presidential elections. Mimeo, BBVA.

Sargent, T., and N. Wallace. 1981. Some unpleasant monetarist arithmetic. *Federal Reserve Bank of Minneapolis Quarterly Review* 5: 1–17.

Woodford, M. 2003. *Interest and Prices.* Princeton: Princeton University Press.

Comment on Chapter 2

Eduardo Loyo

A notion dear to central bankers everywhere is that monetary contraction brings inflation down. Tight money paradoxes (e.g., the unpleasant monetarist arithmetic and the fiscal theory of the price level) are read as cautionary tales: do not take the conventional wisdom for granted, for it may be reversed unless fiscal policy is properly attended to. Prospective real life cases of such reversion are hard to come by and even harder to authenticate.

Blanchard models a new variant of tight money paradox, and also claims to present a live specimen of his find. As they worsen public debt dynamics, high interest rates may scare away instead of attracting capital flows; hence the domestic currency depreciates and inflation increases. Blanchard's model illustrates how the fear of default can trump the attraction of interest rate disparity, switching the sign of the exchange rate effect of monetary policy. The accompanying parameter estimates indicate that it may have happened in a recent episode in Brazil.

An obvious pitfall—duly acknowledged by Blanchard—is that the empirical case for the tight money paradox is helped by not allowing monetary policy to have any impact on inflation through domestic aggregate demand. Restricting attention to exchange rate pass-through is defended on the ground that domestic demand should not be very responsive to monetary policy because the Brazilian economy works with chronically low levels of private credit. Skepticism toward the aggregate demand channel in Brazil, widespread as it may have been, ebbed in light of the country's disinflation experiment of 2003. In particular, sectors known to be more sensitive to credit conditions, such as capital and durable consumer goods, displayed the sharpest cyclical downturn as interest rates went up in the first half of 2003, and then led the recovery in response to monetary easing in the second half of the year. The *Inflation Report* published by the Central Bank of Brazil in September 2003 records rather unequivocal comovements between interbank market rates and final lending rates for closely matched maturities, and between those and the level of activity, over a longer time span.[1]

The gathering of more systematic econometric evidence on the monetary transmission mechanism in Brazil is held back by still recent regime instability. Nevertheless, judging from the dynamic responses of output and inflation to monetary shocks in reputable small-scale forecasting models of the Brazilian economy, their aggregate demand channel is no more negligible than that captured by standard VARs for the United States.[2]

Even if the aggregate demand channel were of no consequence, there would still be a distinct possibility of the empirical exercise being biased toward finding unconventional effects of monetary policy. Blanchard runs the regression:

$$\log \varepsilon = a - b(r - r^*) + cp\theta^* + u_\varepsilon, \tag{1}$$

where ε is the exchange rate, r and r^* are the domestic and the foreign riskless interest rates, and the product $p\theta^*$ is the default risk premium. Monetary policy is more prone to unconventional effects on the exchange rate the smaller is b (the exchange rate is insensitive to the interest rate differential) and the larger is c (it is sensitive to the risk premium).

A bias may arise if the Selic rate, used in estimation as a measure of the riskless domestic rate r, is actually Brazil's *risky* domestic rate r^R. The estimated regression would in reality be

$$\log \varepsilon = \tilde{a} - \tilde{b}(r^R - r^*) + \tilde{c}p\theta^* + \tilde{u}_\varepsilon. \tag{2}$$

Unlike (1), (2) is misspecified according to the theoretical model. The correctly specified relation between ε and r^R takes instead the form

$$\log \varepsilon = \hat{a} - \hat{b}(r^R - r^*) + \hat{c}p\theta^* + \hat{d}p + \hat{u}_\varepsilon, \tag{3}$$

showing that a variable (the probability of default) is omitted in (2). Reasonable assumptions about the partial correlations among the regressors in (3) imply that $\tilde{b}$ is biased downward as an estimate of $\hat{b}$, which in turn coincides with the model's true b, and that $\tilde{c}$ is biased upward as an estimate of $\hat{c}$, which is already larger than the true c. Inasmuch as b is underestimated and c is overestimated, stronger support is lent to unconventional results than is warranted.

The sole reason to think that the Selic is the domestic riskless rate, despite referring to repos backed by presumably risky government bonds, is the fact that it is an overnight rate. Overnight is usually too short a period for default to be seriously contemplated, so the risk premium in the Selic should be insignificant. But what matters here is not the absolute size of the one-day default risk premium but how small it is relatively to an interest rate for one day, itself a quite small number.[3] It is by no means a foregone conclusion that, as maturity shortens, the default risk premium will fall not only in absolute terms but also with respect to the riskless yield to maturity. A familiar example where the proportion between risk premium and riskless rate is invariant to maturity is a Poisson process for the arrival of defaults and CRRA utility.

Indeed, casual commentary on Brazilian monetary policy often revolves around the notion that the Selic contains some premium for risk. For example, monetary policy stance is sometimes gauged by the gap between the Selic and sovereign spreads on Brazil's external debt. Regardless of whether those particular spreads provide an entirely appropriate measure of the risks involved in Selic transactions and a fair indicator of policy stance, the fact remains that the Selic is seen as carrying a risk component.

Blanchard's tight money paradox driven by default risk and exchange rate pass-through is a plausible and very instructive conjecture. Less compelling is the verdict that Brazil was in that mode in 2002 and 2003, if it relies on the Selic as a measure of the domestic riskless rate and, above all, if it overlooks the aggregate demand channel of monetary transmission. Carneiro and Wu (2003), assessing the same tight money paradox in a full model of monetary transmission, find that it would only have happened if the debt/GDP ratio had been about one-third higher than the peak it reached in Brazil.

Notes

Deputy governor, Central Bank of Brazil, and assistant professor of economics, PUC-Rio.

1. The report is available at *www.bcb.gov.br*. See the box entitled "The interest rate, the cost of credit, and economic activity" on pp. 120–23.

2. In the VAR of Giannoni and Woodford (2004), for instance, the interest rate goes up by 1 percent in quarter 0, remains 0.5 percent above steady state in quarter 1, and gets back close to steady state thereafter. Output and inflation reach lows of −0.38 percent

(quarter 2) and −0.17 percent (quarter 5), respectively. Feeding the same interest rate trajectory into the model of Carneiro and Wu (2003), output and inflation reach lows of −0.09 percent (quarter 1) and −0.16 percent (quarter 4), respectively. The maximum response of output in Brazil is just about $\frac{1}{4}$ of its size in the US—still not negligible—while for inflation it is roughly comparable in the two economies. The results change very little if one turns off the exchange rate channel in Carneiro and Wu's Phillips curve.

3. I thank my colleague Márcio Garcia for drawing my attention to this fine point.

References

Carneiro, D. D., and T. Wu. 2003. Endividamento interno e eficácia da política monetária. *Carta Econômica Galanto.*

Giannoni, M. P., and M. Woodford. 2004. Optimal inflation targeting rules. In B. S. Bernanke and M. Woodford, *Inflation Targeting*. Chicago: University of Chicago Press, forthcoming.

3   Inflation Targeting and Debt: Lessons from Brazil

Carlo A. Favero and Francesco Giavazzi

3.1   Introduction

A single variable describes, day by day, what investors think about the state Brazil's economy: the Brazilian component of the Emerging Market Bond Index, the EMBI spread.[1] This spread is the difference between the yield on a dollar-denominated bond issued by the Brazilian government and a corresponding one issued by the US Treasury: it is thus a measure of the markets' assessment of the probability that Brazil might default on its debt obligations. The Brazilian EMBI spread was 700 basis points (bp) in February 2002 and reached a peak of 2,400 bp in July; after the October 2002 elections the spread has gradually fallen: it was 450 bp in December 2003, after Brazil's rating was raised from B to B+. (For a comparison, throughout this period the Mexican spread hovered around 300 to 400 bp.[2])

All financial variables in Brazil fluctuate in parallel with the EMBI spread, most notably the exchange rate. The channel through which fluctuations in the EMBI spread are transmitted to the exchange rate are capital flows: an increase in the country risk premium leads to a sudden stop of capital flows and to a *real* depreciation that is needed to generate the trade surplus required to offset the decrease in net capital inflows. In turn, fluctuations in the exchange rate induce corresponding fluctuations in the ratio of public debt to gdp, since one half of Brazil's debt (see table 3.1) is either denominated in dollars or indexed to the dollar, though payable in the domestic currency: the net public debt, as a share of GDP, was 0.54 January 2002, reached 0.62 in July and was back to 0.55 in October.

Domestic interest rates at all maturities are also affected by fluctuations in the EMBI spread. In the case of the policy rate, the Selic, the mechanism works via the exchange rate: exchange rate fluctuations

Table 3.1
Composition of the Brazilian public debt, December 2002

	Percent of total
US$ denominated bonds issued abroad	25.8
Domestic bills indexed to the dollar	23.9
Inflation indexed bonds	8.5
Fixed-rate bonds	3.0
Domestic floaters linked to the Selic	31.1
Other	7.7

move inflation expectations, and the central bank, as we will document in this chapter, looks at inflation expectations when deciding on the level of the Selic. An increase in the EMBI spread can also affect inflation expectations directly, if it is accompanied by concerns about the possibility of future monetization of part of the public debt.

Domestic interest rates at longer maturities (where "longer" in Brazil today means one to 18 months) are affected by the EMBI spread in two ways: indirectly through the Selic, because fluctuations in the Selic move the term structure, and directly, because long-term interest rates reflect term premia that are affected by default risk even at relatively short maturities.

The bottom line is that the cost of servicing the public debt fluctuates very closely with the EMBI spread. Understanding what determines this spread, how it responds to domestic monetary and fiscal policies and to international factors, how it interacts with the exchange rate and domestic interest rates, is thus the necessary first step in order to understand macroeconomic developments in Brazil.

In a number of papers Guillermo Calvo (Calvo et al., 1993; Calvo 2002) has observed that emerging market risk premia are correlated with international factors, in particular, with worldwide measures of investors' "appetite" for risk, such as the spread between the yield on US corporate bonds and that on US treasuries. In fact Calvo goes as far as suggesting that once one accounts for international financial shocks, domestic factors in emerging markets have a limited role in explaining variables such as EMBI spreads: "Volatility could partly be explained by financial vulnerability in the EMs themselves, but the global nature of the phenomenon raises the suspicion that there are systemic problems largely independent of each individual country.... Contagion

could stem from the way the capital market operates, e.g., crises generated by margin calls" (Calvo 2002, p. 1).[3]

The experience of Brazil supports Calvo's observation. The Brazilian
EMBI spread is indeed correlated with the US corporate spread, but
this correlation is not constant over time. Figure 3.1 shows the two
variables in the top panel, and in the lower panel, the time profile of
their correlation: the coefficients of recursive regressions of the EMBI
spread on the US corporate spread. One of the findings of this chapter
is that this nonlinearity depends on the state of domestic fiscal policy:
when the level of the primary budget surplus is large enough to keep
the debt-to-GDP ratio stable, the response of the EMBI spread to the
US corporate spread is muted; when instead fiscal fundamentals are
weaker the response is amplified.

The role of domestic fiscal policy in determining the response of the
EMBI spread to international shocks suggests that the effectiveness of
inflation targeting may depend on the fiscal policy regime.[4] Consider
the effects of a shock to the risk premium that depreciates the exchange
rate and raises inflation expectations. When the primary surplus is
constantly adjusted so that its level is always large enough to keep the
debt ratio stable, inflation targeting works: an increase in the Selic off-
sets the initial exchange rate depreciation, at least partially. With one-
half of the debt denominated in dollars, the partial stabilization of the
exchange rate limits the impact of higher short rates on the cost of debt
service: the increase in the primary surplus needed to stabilize the debt
is thus correspondingly small.

Instead, in a fiscal policy regime that keeps constant the level of
the primary surplus, an international financial shock may put the debt
ratio along an unstable path: in such a situation the economy may fall
in a "bad equilibrium" where monetary policy has perverse effects.

The dynamics in the bad equilibrium can be described as follows:
With a short duration of the public debt an increase in the Selic raises
the cost of debt service: if the primary surplus remains unchanged,
the debt level rises, and so does the EMBI spread. The increase in the
spread adds to the initial increase in debt, especially since it is accompanied by a depreciation of the exchange rate, which raises the value
of dollar-denominated bonds in terms of domestic gdp. The exchange
rate depreciation also affects inflation expectations and, eventually, inflation itself. This induces the central bank to increase the Selic further,
which further raises the cost of debt service, and so on.

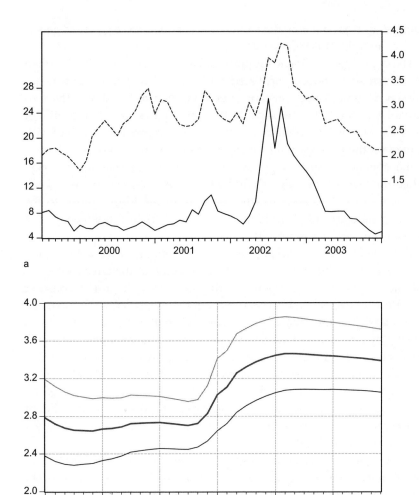

Figure 3.1
(a) EMBI spread (*left scale*, percentage points) and the spread between Baa corporate and the US government bonds (*right scale*, percentage points); (b) coefficients of recursive regressions of the EMBI spread on the US corporate bond spread (with two standard error confidence bands)

The difficulties of running monetary policy in an environment where financial markets judge fiscal policy as unsustainable—in the sense that it violates the conditions for the sustainability of the public debt— are well known. Sargent and Wallace (1981) were among the first to point out that a reduction in the growth rate of money can result in higher, rather than lower inflation if the government relies on seigniorage as a source of revenue and the budget surplus is not adjusted after the fall in seigniorage revenue. Sometimes, and often with specific reference to Latin America, this situation has been referred to as a regime of "fiscal dominance."[5] More recently, but in the same vein, the "fiscal theory" of the price level (as first discussed in Woodford 1994) has argued that if the primary budget surplus is exogenous, the price level is the only variable that can balance the government's intertemporal budget constraint: given an exogenous sequence of budget surpluses, there is only one price level that makes the stock of nominal bonds inherited from the past consistent with the present value of those primary surpluses. Thus, following a shock that raises the cost of debt service, if the sequence of primary surpluses does not change, the price level will have to rise for the government's intertemporal budget constraint to keep being balanced: this may result in an inconsistency between inflation targeting and fiscal policy (a point shown in Uribe 2003).[6]

While pointing in the right direction, the fiscal theory of the price level runs into a problem in countries, such as Brazil, where a significant fraction of the public debt is either denominated in a foreign currency or indexed to a foreign currency. In such a situation a jump in the price level may not be sufficient to balance the government's intertemporal budget constraint if the primary surplus is exogenous. When debt is dollar-denominated and risk premia are volatile, the channel through which—if the primary budget surplus is exogenous—international financial shocks can destabilize the economy is credit risk.[7] This is what we show in this chapter, with specific reference to the experience of Brazil in 2002 and 2003.

The discussion proceeds in three steps. We first document the nonlinearity in the response of the EMBI spread to international financial shocks. Then we study how the EMBI spread affects the cost of debt service and thus the dynamics of the public debt: we estimate risk premia on various financial instruments and on the exchange rate, and we show that they all move in parallel with the EMBI spread. Finally, we analyze a small short-run model of the Brazilian economy to show

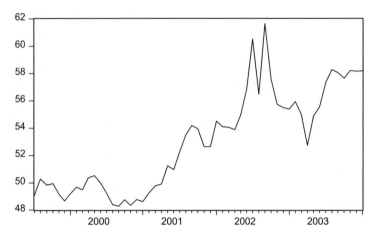

Figure 3.2
Brazil's net public debt, percentage of GDP

how the effectiveness of monetary policy depends on the fiscal policy regime.

3.2 Fiscal Fundamentals and Brazilian Risk

Since 1999 Brazilian public debt, as a fraction of GDP, steadily increased. This was in part because the primary surplus, though rising, had never been sufficient to stabilize the debt and in part because, over time, the government had recognized previously hidden liabilities— "skeletons" in Brazilian jargon, particularly in the balance sheets of state-owned banks (see figure 3.2).[8]

In looking for domestic factors that might explain Brazilian risk— beyond its correlation with international factors—it is thus natural to start from the level of the debt and of the primary surplus that would be required to keep the debt ratio stable. We can analyze the possibility that the response of the Brazilian EMBI spread to the US corporate bond spread is nonlinear, and depends on the state of fiscal policy, by estimating the following model which relates the EMBI spread to fiscal variables:[9]

$$\text{EMBI}_t = \gamma_0 + \gamma_1 \text{EMBI}_{t-1} + \gamma'_{2,t}\text{Spread}_t^{US} + \gamma_3 \Delta\text{Spread}_t^{US} + \varepsilon_{1,t}, \qquad (1)$$

where EMBI is the Brazil component of the EMBI spread, Spread^{US} is the spread between the yield on US corporate bonds rated Baa with

Table 3.2
Brazil's EMBI spread explained

	Sample 1999:08 to 2004:01 (TSLS)				
	γ_0	γ_1	γ_2	γ_3	σ
Using the deviation of the primary surplus from the debt-stabilizing level	—	0.85 (0.06)	0.88 (0.44)	4.50 (01.10)	2, 05

	Sample 1991:02 to 2003:06 (LS using an HP filter for b)					
	γ_0	γ_1	γ_2	γ_4	γ_3	σ
Using the debt level	1.38 (0.40)	0.81 (0.05)	0.44 (0.22)	53.3 (2.15)	4.17 (0.69)	1, 63

	Sample 1999:07 to 2003:06 (LS using an HP filter for b)					
	γ_0	γ_1	γ_2	γ_4	γ_3	σ
Using the debt level	1.12 (0.86)	0.74 (0.10)	0.71 (0.35)	54.4 (1.94)	4.85 (1.20)	2, 17

a maturity between 10 and 20 years, and a 10-year US Treasury bond, and ΔSpread^{US} denotes the first difference of the corporate bond spread. All spreads are measured in basis points. We also include ΔSpread^{US} to capture the effect of jumps in the EMBI spread, independently of the nonlinearity. The time-varying response of the EMBI spread to the US spread, $\gamma'_{2,t}$, is nonlinear and depends on the state of fiscal policy:[10]

$$\gamma'_{2,t} = \gamma_2(1 + e^{-(x_t^* - x_t)})^{-1}.$$

Here x_t is the primary budget surplus, and x_t^* is the level of the primary surplus that keeps the debt-to-GDP ratio constant.[11] For $x_t = x_t^*$, $\gamma'_{2,t} = \gamma_2/2$; $\gamma'_{2,t}$ rises as x_t falls below x_t^*.

We estimate (1) using lagged variables as instruments to take care of the endogeneity of x_t^*: the debt-stabilizing primary surplus is influenced by the exchange rate, which in turn, as we discussed in the introduction, is correlated with the EMBI spread. The results are reported in table 3.2.

We have also considered an alternative measure of fiscal fundamentals, the deviation of the debt-GDP ratio from an endogenously estimated threshold γ_4: that is, $\gamma'_{2,t} = \gamma_2(1 + e^{-(b_t - \gamma_4)})^{-1}$. For debt levels above γ_4 the response of EMBI to Spread^{US} increases (nonlinearly)

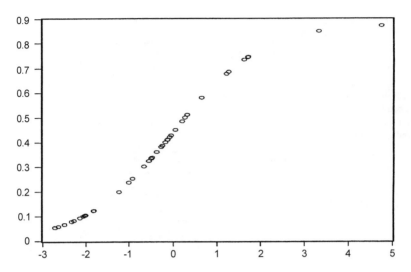

Figure 3.3
Elasticity of the EMBI spread with respect to the US corporate bond spread, as a function of $(x - x^*)$

above γ_2. Since the debt ratio is also correlated with the exchange rate, we instrument b with its trend, estimated using a Hodrick-Prescott filter: the filtered variable is no longer correlated with fluctuations in the exchange rate. The value of γ_4 we estimate is about 54 percent, the level of the net public debt, as a percent of GDP, in April 2002 (see table 3.2). The estimate is rather stable: when we restrict the sample and only use data from August 1999, it remains virtually unchanged; in the shorter sample, however, the elasticity of the EMBI spread with respect to the US corporate spread is significantly higher. Figure 3.3 shows the estimated values of γ_2', for the specification that makes this coefficient a function of $x_t - x_t^*$.[12]

In the econometric model of the Central Bank of Brazil[13] the equation for the EMBI spread includes foreign reserves, the current account and debt, all as a fraction of GDP, but not the US corporate spread. The debt variable is significant at the 10 percent level. When we add to our specification foreign exchange reserves and the current account, we find that they are not significant. We also tried including in this regression the Selic rate, to test whether monetary policy affects the risk premium directly: it is not significant. This finding suggests that monetary policy affects the risk premium only indirectly, through its effects on the debt level.

We have investigated the robustness of our specification by replacing the US corporate spread with alternative measures of international factors used in the empirical literature: the level of US long-term interest rates and the Fed funds rate. The main result, which is the non-linearity, is preserved.

3.3   EMBI Spread and Other Risk Premia

In economies like that of the United States, expected future interest rates account for the bulk of the spread between long-term rates and policy rates: this is because the volatility of future expected policy rates is low and credit risk is not an issue. In emerging markets, on the contrary, the volatility of policy rates is much higher and default risk generates sizable risk premia. The technique we show in this section allows to identify the role of credit risk in determining the slope of the yield curve.

We start by estimating a monetary policy rule, which we then use to predict the path of future Selic rates: comparing these forecasts with observed long-term yields (from swap contracts), and assuming no expetational errors, we can build an estimate of the credit risk component of the slope of the yield curve. We will close the section showing that our estimates of credit risk premia at various maturities are highly correlated with the EMBI spread.

3.3.1   The Monetary Policy Rule

The best way to describe Brazilian monetary policy since the adoption of a floating exchange rate regime, in February 1999, is through a simple monetary policy rule where the Selic rate responds to one-year-ahead inflation expectations:

$$\text{Selic}_t = \rho \text{Selic}_{t-1} + (1 - \rho)(\beta_0 + \beta_1(E_t \pi_{t,t+12} - \pi_t^*)) + \varepsilon_{2,t}. \tag{2}$$

$E_t \pi_{t,t+12}$ is the one-year-ahead expected inflation rate, measured from the daily survey conducted by the central bank and π_t^* is the central bank inflation target. We estimate this rule over a sample that starts in January 2000.[14] The results are given in table 3.3.

β_1, the response of the Selic rate to a deviation of inflation expectations from the target, is greater than unity: this indicates that monetary policy does not accommodate inflation, and that real interest rates are raised when inflation expectations increase. The Selic rate also appear to be rather persistent, with an autocorrelation coefficient of 0.92.[15]

Table 3.3
Parameters of the estimated monetary policy rule

Sample 2000:01 to 2004:01			
ρ	β_0	β_1	σ
0.92	15.5	4.03	0.59
(0.02)	(1.66)	(1.36)	

3.3.2 Term Premia on "Long-term" Interest Rates

Since the market for long-dated bonds is very thin, we study domestic long term interest rates using data on swap contracts. These are contracts where one party receives the Selic and pays a fixed rate for maturities up to 18 months. What gets exchanged in a swap contract are two flows of interest payments on a notional principal: the principal itself is never exchanged. "Default," in a swap contract, happens when one of the two parties stops paying: if this happens, the other side will do the same, with no loss of principal. There is a loss, but this is limited to the present discounted value of the contract which was interrupted. In other words, there is a loss, but only because investors lose the protection they thought they had bought by entering the swap contract. The default risk on swaps is therefore much smaller than that on bonds, as measured by the EMBI spread, though both may be affected by the same factors.

To construct a measure of term premia on swaps we start from a no-arbitrage condition. Consider, for simplicity, zero-coupon bonds and define a term premium per period, rather than over the entire life of the bond: then the difference between the one-period expected return of a multi-period bond and the risk-free rate can be written as

$$E_t(p_{t+1,T} - p_{t,T}) = i_{t,t+1} + \phi_{t,T},$$

where $p_{t,T}$ is the (log of) the price at time t of a bond maturing at T; $i_{t,t+1}$ is the one-period return on the safe asset, the Selic;[16] $\phi_{t,T}$ is the term premium, defined over a one-period horizon, on the bond maturing at T. As the relation between $p_{t,T}$ and the continuously compounded yield to maturity of a bond with maturity $T, i_{t,T}$, is

$$p_{t,T} = -(T - t)i_{t,T},$$

we have

$$i_{t,T} - (T - t - 1)E_t(i_{t+1,T} - i_{t,T}) = i_{t,t+1} + \phi_{t,T}.$$

By recursive substitution, we can write

$$i_{t,T} = \frac{1}{T-t} \sum_{j=1}^{T} E_t i_{t+j-1,t+j} + TP_{t,T},$$

$$TP_{t,T} = \frac{1}{T-t} \sum_{j=1}^{T-1} E_t \phi_{t+j-1,T}.$$

We apply this decomposition to fixed interest rates on swaps. The term premium on a T-month Brazilian fixed rate swap reflects, as discussed above, two components: the risk associated with the volatility of policy rates over the life of the swap and some credit risk. We will proceed as follows: We assume that the central bank inflation target remains unchanged, and we use the survey-based expectations to construct a path for expected one-year-ahead inflation. Simulating the estimated monetary policy rule forward, we construct future Selic rates, i^F_{t+h}, as

$$i^F_{t+h} = \hat{\rho} i^F_{t+h-1} + (1-\hat{\rho})(\hat{\beta}_o + \hat{\beta}_1(\pi^e_{t+h+12} - \pi^*_t)),$$

where the parameters are those estimated in (2) and h can extend up to 12 months, the longest horizon over which we observe 12-month-ahead inflation expectations.

The difference between the yield on a T-period swap, $i^{SW}_{t,T}$, and the appropriate average of future Selic rates thus includes two components: the pure term premium and a term which measures how the stream of our interest rate forecasts compares with market expectations, i^E_{t+j}:

$$i^{SW}_{t,T} - \frac{1}{T-t} \sum_{i=1}^{T} i^F_{t+j} = TP^{SW}_{t,T} + \frac{1}{T-t} \left(\sum_{i=1}^{T} i^E_{t+j} - \sum_{i=1}^{T} i^F_{t+j} \right). \qquad (3)$$

Assuming no expectational errors, we can use (3) to build an observable proxy of the term premium on T-period swaps.

To consider a concrete example of how swap rates decompose between expected future Selic rates and term premia, we compare the data for two dates: October 15, 2002, at the peak of the latest Brazilian crisis, and May 19, 2003, after the resolution of political uncertainty and a remarkable tightening of monetary policy. On October 15 the Selic rate was 20.90 percent, while the yield on a 12-month fixed interest rate swap was 32.69 percent. The total spread, 1.179 bp, decomposed in a decreasing pattern of expected policy rates coupled with a

risk premium as high as 1.315 points. On May the Selic was 26.32 while
the yield on a 12-month fixed interest rate swap was 23.19 percent. The
inverted yield curve is explained by a decreasing pattern of expected
Selic rates coupled with a value of the risk premium, which had fallen
to 275 bp.

Having constructed a measure of the term premium on swaps, we
can now study how it correlates with the EMBI spread. Before doing
that, however, we complete the analysis of term premia studying the
exchange rate risk premium.

3.3.3 Exchange Rate Risk Premium

Using the uncovered interest rate parity condition and survey data on
exchange rate expectations, we construct a measure of the exchange
rate risk premium. For both Brazilian and US interest rates we use
swap rates since, as discussed above, the market for Brazilian bonds is
too thin to be significant:

$$i_{t,T}^{SW} - i_{t,T}^{SW,US} = (E_t s_{t+T} - s_t) + \text{exchange rate risk premium} \tag{4}$$

where $i_{t,T}^{SW}$ and $i_{t,T}^{SW,US}$ are, respectively, the interest rates on Brazilian
swaps of maturity T and on similar dollar-denominated swaps, and
$(E_t s_{t+T} - s_t)$ denotes the survey-based expectations of the percent
change in the exchange rate over the life of these swaps. The Brazilian
central bank collects, as for inflation expectations, a daily survey of
one-year-ahead exchange rate expectations: using such surveys, and
12-month US and Brazilian swaps, we are able to measure the exchange rate risk premium.

3.3.4 Term Premia and the EMBI Spread

Table 3.4 shows the correlation between the EMBI spread, the one-year
ahead exchange rate risk premium and the term premia on domestic
swaps at three different maturities: 3, 6, and 12 months. For comparison we report an alternative measure of Brazilian default risk derived
from credit default swaps. A credit default swap (CDS) is a derivative
contract in which a bondholder buys a guarantee that covers him in
the event of default: if the underlying bond defaults the buyer of the
insurance receives an amount equal to the difference between the face
value of the defaulted bond and a conventional recovery rate.[17] From
such contracts it is possible to compute the risk premium. The main
advantage of CDS's over EMBI spreads is that CDSs also exist for rela-

Table 3.4
Correlations of default risk, term premia, and exchange rate risk premia

| | Sample: 1999:2–2003:1 | | | | | | | | |
	EMBI	e.r. r.p. 12-m	TP 3-m	TP 6-m	TP 12-m	CDS 3-m	CDS 6-m	CDS 12-m	CDS 36-m
EMBI	1	0.84	0.31	0.56	0.82	0.88	0.92	0.96	0.98
e.r. r.p. 12-m		1	0.63	0.79	0.89	0.73	0.76	0.80	0.83
TP 3-m			1	0.91	0.66	0.26	0.27	0.29	0.29
TP 6-m				1	0.88	0.51	0.54	0.56	0.55
TP 12-m					1	0.75	0.78	0.82	0.82
CDS 3-m						1	0.97	0.95	0.94
CDS 6-m							1	0.98	0.96
CDS 12-m								1	0.99
CDS 36-m									1

tively short maturities and are thus more directly comparable with swaps.

There is a remarkable degree of correlation among the four series (see table 3.4). Risk premia measured by CDSs and the EMBI spread are larger than the term premium implicit in 12-month fixed interest rates swap, consistently with the smaller exposure of swaps to default risk discussed above. The correlation between the risk premium on swaps and the EMBI spread rises as the maturity of the swaps increases: this is because the longer the life of a swap, the higher the probability that a default event might hit it. On 12-month swaps the correlation is surprisingly high (0.70), especially since the EMBI spread is computed on 10-year bonds, while swaps have a maturity of just 12 months. The correlation is high also with the one-year-ahead exchange rate risk premium indicating that default risk is an important determinant of exchange rate fluctuations.

3.4 Inflation Targeting, Country Risk, and Fiscal Policy

The analysis carried out so far helps us understand the way in which domestic fiscal policy and international financial shocks contribute to determine the EMBI spread and thus the cost of servicing the debt. The next step consists in analyzing the channel through which country risk determines the interaction between monetary and fiscal policy, and how it may prevent the central bank from effectively targeting inflation.

We do this by means of a small short-run model of the Brazilian economy that focuses on risk, debt, the exchange rate and two policy rules, one for the central bank and the other for the fiscal authorities. Because our focus is on the short run, we take output as given. This is not an innocuous assumption—output growth is obviously a critical factor in determining debt dynamics—but unavoidable to keep the analysis simple.[18]

3.4.1   Exchange Rate, Risk Premium, and Monetary Policy Rule

We start by showing the effects of the interaction between the exchange rate, the risk premium and the monetary policy rule, assuming for the moment that the risk premium is exogenous. The result—a negative correlation between the change in the exchange rate and the interest rate differential—has been shown by McCallum (1994) and discussed in the context of inflation targeting by Alexius (2002). The model consists of three equations:

$$i_t = \rho i_{t-1} + (1 - \rho)(\beta_o + \beta_1(E_t \pi_{t+12} - \pi^*)), \tag{5}$$

$$E_t s_{t+1} - s_t = (i_t - i_t^*) + \xi_t, \tag{6}$$

$$E_t \pi_{t+12} - \pi^* = \delta_1 (E_{t-1} \pi_{t+11} - \pi^*) + (1 - \delta_1)[\delta_2(s_t - s_{t-1}) - \pi^*] + \varepsilon_{3,t}. \tag{7}$$

• Equation (5) is the monetary policy rule estimated in section 3.3.1.

• Equation (6) is the uncovered interest rate parity condition (UIRP), where ξ_t represents the exchange rate risk premium.

• Equation (7) describes the inflation expectations that enter (5). In the case of Brazil these expectations are observed: we can thus analyze their statistical properties. When we do this, we find that they are autocorrelated and respond to the observed deviation of the rate of exchange rate depreciation from π^*. This motivates (7).

Assume, to save notation, that $\beta_o = \delta_1 = \varepsilon_{3,t} = i_t^* = \pi^* = 0$, and substitute (5) and (7) in the UIRP condition to get

$$E_t s_{t+1} - s_t = \rho i_{t-1} + (1 - \rho)\beta_1\delta_2(s_t - s_{t-1}) + \xi_t. \tag{8}$$

Defining $\Delta s_t \equiv s_t - s_{t-1}$, re-write (8) as

$$E_t \Delta s_{t+1} = \lambda \Delta s_t + \rho i_{t-1} + \xi_t$$

where $\lambda \equiv (1 - \rho)\beta_1\delta_2$. If we assume rational expectations, the reduced form solution of this equation is

$$\Delta s_t = -\frac{\rho}{\lambda} i_{t-1} + \frac{1}{\lambda + \rho} \xi_t. \tag{9}$$

Note, as discussed in McCallum (1994), that the co-movement between changes in the exchange rate and the interest rate differential described in (9), which is the result of the central bank following a rule such as (5), is one of the ways to explain the UIRP puzzle.

3.4.2 Inflation Targets, Country Risk, and Fiscal Policy

We now extend the model of the previous section by adding the determinants of the exchange rate risk premium, ξ_t, which, based on our analysis, we assume to coincide with the EMBI spread and thus to be determined as in (1). We also add a fiscal policy rule, which is needed to determine $(x_t - x_t^*)$ and thus the response of the EMBI spread to international shocks:

$$x_t = \varphi x_{t-1} + (1 - \varphi) x_t^* + \varepsilon_{4,t} \tag{10}$$

for $\varphi = 0$ the primary budget surplus keeps the debt ratio constant at all times; for $\varphi = 1$ the primary surplus is exogenous.[19]

When we add to the model of equations (5) through (7) equation (1), the nonlinear equation for the EMBI spread, we are no longer able to derive analytically a reduced form solution such as (9): we have thus estimated (9) using the EMBI spread as an explanatory variable and allowing for an error term reflecting deviations from UIRP other than the risk premium.[20] Using lagged variables as instruments, we obtain the estimates shown in table 3.5.

The coefficient on the interest rate differantial is negative: for a given US Fed Fund rate, a 1 percent increase in the Selic appreciates the exchange rate by 0.16 percent. The EMBI spread enters with a positive coefficient: a higher risk premium induces a depreciation. Note, however, that these are partial equilibrium effects. Both the Selic and the

Table 3.5
Exchange rate equation in reduced form

$\Delta s_t = \alpha_1 (\text{Selic}_{t-1} - i_{t-1}^{\text{US}}) + \alpha_2 \text{EMBI}_{t-1} + \alpha_3 \Delta(\text{EMBI})_t + \varepsilon_{5,t}$

Sample 1999:02 to 2003:12 (TSLS)

α_1	α_2	α_3	σ
−0.16	0.38	2.64	3.74
(0.06)	(0.11)	(0.42)	

EMBI spread are endogenous: it is impossible, from this equation, to conclude what is the overall effect of monetary policy on the exchange rate. In the bad equilibrium, following an increase in the Selic, the additional cost of debt service could induce a large increase in the default risk—large enough so that the net effect is a depreciation of the exchange rate. This effect is crucial for determining how monetary policy works.

Consider now the effect of an increase in Spread^{US}. The direct effect of the shock is an exchange rate is a depreciation: $(\gamma'_2 + \gamma_3)(\alpha_2 + \alpha_3)$. The extent to which monetary policy responds to the shock depends on its effect on expectations. The increase in the EMBI spread, and the accompanying exchange rate depreciation, raise inflation expectations: the reaction of the central bank dampens the initial depreciation so that the overall effect on the exchange rate remains ambiguous. It is $(\alpha_2 + \alpha_3)[1 - \alpha_1 \delta_2 (1 - \delta_1)\beta_1 (1 - \rho)]^{-1}$ with $\alpha_1 < 0$.

This, however, is not the end of the story. The shock raises x_t^*, both because the exchange rate depreciation raises the debt stock, measured in units of domestic goods, and because domestic interest rates also increase. If $\varphi = 0$, x_t will adjust one to one to match the increase in x_t^*: the burden of adjusting to the financial shock falls entirely on the fiscal authorities, while the central bank maintains the control of inflation. For $\varphi = 1$, x_t remains constant and $(x_t^* - x_t)$ increases. This raises γ'_2 and amplifies the effect of the financial shock on the risk premium. The result is further exchange rate depreciation, a further rise in the debt ratio, a further increase in x_t^*, and so on. The economy settles along an unstable path, where debt increases and the central bank is unable to control inflation.

3.4.3 Experience of Brazil

In this section we use the model just described to understand the interaction between country risk and monetary and fiscal policies in Brazil. We do this by simulating the model under two alternative fiscal rules: one that keeps the primary surplus constant,[21] and an "almost Ricardian" rule, such as (10) for $\varphi = 0.75$.[22] We take as starting conditions those prevailing in June 2002. We choose this date because this is when the EMBI spread jumps above 1,000 bp—a level the spread had never reached after the 1999 devaluation—the exchange rate starts depreciating and, most important, inflation expectations start rising. Since, as we have seen, monetary policy reacts to inflation expectations, this is when the action starts.

The model is composed of four equations: (5), (7), and (11) plus the fiscal policy rule. To run the simulation under the "Ricardian" rule we also need estimates of $x_t^* \equiv [(\bar{\imath}_t - n_t - \pi_t)/(1 + n_t + \pi_t)]b_{t-1}$. This requires that we specify the dynamics of inflation and output growth. One way would be to calibrate these two equations using, for example, the demand and supply equations estimated in the small econometric model of the Central Bank of Brazil. We choose the alternative route of fitting a very simple autoregressive process for real GDP growth,[23] and for inflation a model that is consistent with (7), the statistical properties of the observed inflation expectations.

We run the two dynamic simulations proceeding as follows:

• As already mentioned, we take as initial conditions those prevailing in June 2002: $b = 0.55$, $x = 0.035$, $\pi^e = 0.0049$, $\pi^* = 0.055$, $i = 0.184$, $i_{\text{FedFund}}^{\text{US}} = 0.018$, $\text{Spread}^{\text{US}} = 350$ bp.
• In the simulation we keep all exogenous variables constant, except for π^*, which we allow to follow the path announced, in January 2003, by the central bank: 0.085 in 2003 and 0.05 in 2004.[24]

The results of the dynamic simulations under the two fiscal rules are shown in figure 3.4.

In June 2003, 12-months ahead inflation expectations rise above the target and the central bank raises interest rates. Under the "Non-Ricardian" fiscal rule (the dotted line in each of the six panels) the Selic eventually rises above 30 percent, and the EMBI spread increases: the sharp monetary tightening cannot prevent the depreciation of the exchange rate and inflation expectations stabilize around 12 percent. The debt ratio explodes.[25]

When fiscal policy reacts (with $\varphi = 0.75 < 1$) to fluctuations in x^*, monetary policy is effective at stabilizing inflation expectations: this happens because the EMBI spread, after the initial shock stabilizes. The fiscal rule tightens the primary surplus, but eventually, as the economy stabilizes, the budget can be gradually relaxed. The fiscal tightening is particularly severe because the rule is not fully Ricardian: for $\varphi = 0.0$ the primary surplus would not need to increase so much.[26]

3.5 Conclusions

In studying the recent experience of Brazil, we have learned how default risk is at the center of the mechanism through which a central

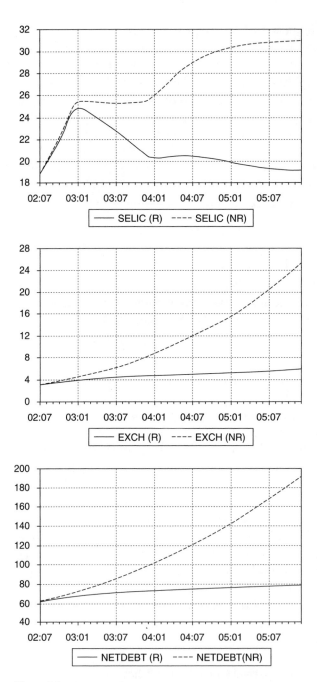

Figure 3.4
Targeting inflation with "Ricardian" and "non-Ricardian" fiscal policy rules ($\varphi = 0.75$ and $\varphi = 1.0$, respectively)

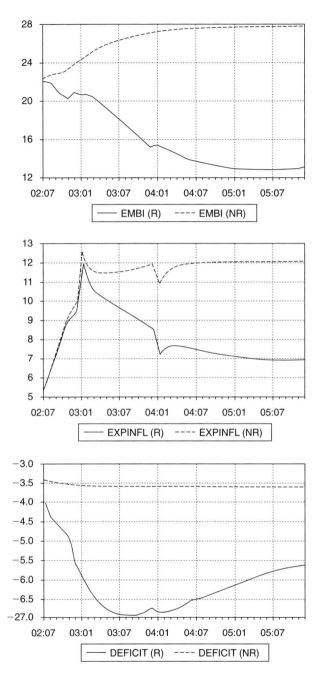

Figure 3.4
(continued)

bank that targets inflation can lose control of inflation. This is the mechanism through which the economy can move from a regime of "monetary dominance" to one of "fiscal dominance." The literature, from Sargent and Wallace (1981) to the modern fiscal theory of the price level has discussed how an unsustainable fiscal policy can hinder the effectiveness of monetary policy, to the point that an increase in interest rates will have a perverse effect on inflation. We have shown (consistently with the findings of Blanchard in this volume) that the presence of default risk reinforces the possibility that a vicious circle will arise, making the fiscal constraint on monetary policy more stringent.

In the experience of Brazil we believe that we have identified an interesting episode where this could have happened, at least for a short period during 2002. But the episode also shows how critical the behavior of fiscal policy is. Brazil, during 2002, had probably fallen into a bad equilibrium, where fiscal policy was hindering the effectiveness of monetary policy. But the economy was just over the edge: a small change in the fiscal rule, such as that announced by the Lula government upon taking office in January 2003, was enough to bring the economy back to normal conditions, and rapidly reduce the EMBI spread, stabilize the exchange rate, and, through these two variables, inflation expectations, inflation and the dynamics of the public debt.

Notes

We thank Olivier Blanchard, Ilan Goldfajn, Arminio Fraga, Eduardo Loyo, Afonso Bevilacqua, Santiago Herrera, Eustaquio Reis, and Fernando Blanco for their comments. We have benefited from discussions in Brazil, both at the Ministry of Finance and at the Banco Central do Brasil. Charles Goodhart and seminar participants at Princeton, the IMF and the LSE also made useful comments. We thank Andrea Civelli and Francesco Bianchi for excellent research assistance. Francesco Giavazzi thanks the Houblon-Norman Fund at the Bank of England for its hospitality while this chapter was written.

1. The Embi index is computed by J. P. Morgan.

2. For a persepctive on economic developments in Brazil from 1999 to 2003, the period studied in this chapter, see Pastore and Pinotti (chapter 1 of this volume).

3. While the empirical evidence consistently shows that one of the main determinants of emerging market spreads are international factors, there are different views as to what such factors might be. Kamin and von Kleist (1999) and Eichengreen and Mody (2000) report a negative relationship between the level of long-term US interest rates and spreads. Arora and Cerisola (2001) find that the stance and predictability of US monetary policy are also significant in determining capital market conditions in emerging markets. Herrera and Perry (2002) consider jointly the importance of US monetary policy and of US

corporate bond spreads and allow for different long- and short-run effects: their results strengthen the evidence on the importance of international factors.

4. Sims (2003) argues that unsustainable fiscal policy may render an inflation-trageting regime ineffective.

5. See Tanner and Ramos (2002) for a discussion of fiscal dominance in the context of Brazil.

6. In the context of Brazil a model with these features is analyzed by Loyo (1999). In Loyo's model higher interest rates cause the outside financial wealth of private agents to grow faster in nominal terms: this raises inflation. If the central bank responds by raising nominal rates, so that real interest rates increase as well, then a vicious circle might arise. In Loyo's model there are only one-period bonds. As we show in this chapter, term premia and credit risk reinforce the possibility that such a vicious circle might arise, making the fiscal constraint on monetary policy more stringent. (Niepelt 2004 shows, however, that in a rational expectations equilibrium the fiscal theory of the price level does not introduce fiscal effects beyond those suggested by Sargent and Wallace.)

7. Extensions of the fiscal theory to allow for the presence of credit risk are studied in Uribe (2003).

8. For an analysis of the recent dynamics of the public debt in Brazil, see Favero and Gia-vazzi (2002).

9. The idea of a nonlinear response builds on the intuition of Kamin and von Kleist (1999) who find that spreads respond to the interaction between the US term spread and the country's rating.

10. The nonlinearity makes our estimated equation a specific case of the LSTAR (logistic smooth transition autoregressive) model discussed for instance in Tong (1983). The LSTAR specification is more flexible than a simple interaction term: in our case it allows for the response of term premia to international factors to vary, depending on the level of the debt ratio relative to an estimated threshold.

11. $x_t^* \equiv [(\bar{i}_t - n_t - \pi_t)/(1 + n_t + \pi_t)]b_{t-1}$, where b is the debt-GDP ratio, π the infaltion rate, n real GDP growth, and $\bar{i}$ is the average interest cost of the debt. $\bar{i}_t = (1 - \mu)((1 + i_t)^{1/12} - 1) + \mu((1 + i_t^{US} + \text{EMBI}_t)^{1/12} - 1)(S_t/S_{t-1})$, where μ is the share of public debt denominated in dollars, or indexed to the dollar, $(1 - \mu)$ the share that is linked to the Selic rate, i_t, and S_t is the level of the exchange rate. We thus include in the cost of debt service the amortization of dollar-denominated bonds.

12. In building figure 3.3, we computed x_t^* by assuming that the nominal growth rate of the economy and the average nominal cost of debt service remain costant over time.

13. See Kfoury and Lago Alves (2003).

14. Both the monetary and the fiscal policy regimes changed sharply after the 1999 de-valuation: monetary policy shifted from an exchange rate peg to an inflation target, and the primary budget moved in a few years from balance to a sizable surplus. These policy shifts make the data up to 1999 of limited use for our purposes.

15. In Favero and Giavazzi (2002) we experimented adding to this monetary policy rule more arguments, such as the output gap and the realized change in the exchange rate. The coeffcients on such variables were not significant and the dynamic simulations of the extended version of the rule did not provide any substantial improvement on the

baseline with expectations only. We also experimented estimating the rule with daily data: even at this very high frequency the results are virtually identical. The following table shows the results using daily data and also adding the survey-based measure of exchange rate expectations and the EMBI spread on the right-hand side of the monetary policy rule.

Estimation of a monetary policy rule on daily data (January 3, 2000, to February 11, 2004)

	ρ	β_o	β_1	β_2	σ
—	0.994	16.6	3.10	—	0.20
	(0.002)	(1.40)	(1.05)		
$EMBI_t$	0.994	16.2	3.00	3.17E-06	0.21
	(0.002)	(2.67)	(1.12)	(1.72E-05)	
Δs^e_{t+260}	0.994	16.84	3.2	−0.011	0.21
	(0.003)	(1.72)	(1.47)	(0.034)	

16. We assume that the policy rate is a safe asset: the period-return of such an asset thus coincides with its yield to maturity.

17. After a default most bonds continue to be traded at positive prices that reflect the expectation of a settlement in which the entity that has defaulted will pay a fraction of the bond's face value. CDS are priced on the basis of conventional postdefault trading prices, based on past experience.

18. The evidence on the effect of interest rates on output is weak in Brazil. The central bank model finds a (negative) effect of real 12-month swap rates, but the significance of this variable is rather weak. This does not mean that one is allowed to assume the effect away. Rather, the evidence suggests a weak impact, at least in the short run.

19. Following the terminology used by Woodford (1994), the two rules can be labeled Ricardian and non-Ricardian, respectively.

20. An alternative consists in estimating (8) directly. This is the route followed by Blanchard (chapter 2 of this volume): he also finds a violation of UIRP.

A simple example helps understanding why we may observe a negative correlation between the expected depreciation and the interest rate differential. Assume $E_t s_{t+1} - s_t = i_t + \xi_t$, and $i_t = -\alpha\xi_t$, which means that monetary policy is responding directly to the exchange rate risk premium such that an increase in ξ_t leads to lower domestic interest rates. Then $E_t s_{t+1} - s_t = -[(1 - \alpha)/\alpha]i_t$: in words, the reason for the negative correlation is the deviation from UIRP (ξ_t), coupled with a monetary policy rule that responds to ξ_t.

21. This is essentially the fiscal rule followed by the Brazilian authorities since the 1999 devaluation and up to the 2002 election. When we estimate such a rule, we find that $x_t = 3.86(1 - 0.75) + 0.75x_{t-1}$. There is no evidence of a reaction of x_t to x_t^*: the primary surplus is very persistent and the estimated long-run level (3.86 percent of GDP) is below the sample average for x_t^*.

22. This exercize clearly defies the Lucas critique.

23. The evidence on the effect of interest rates on output is weak in Brazil. The central bank model finds a (negative) effect of real 12-month interest rates, but the significance of this variable is weak. This does not mean that one is allowed to assume the effect away in the short run. The output growth equation we estimate is $n_t = \gamma_1 + \gamma_2 n_{t-1} + u_t$.

24. We keep the target constant at 0.085 throughout 2003; in 2004 we allow it to fall gradually, reaching 0.05 in December.

25. In this exercise inflation does not display the explosive behavior described in Loyo (1999) and Sims (2003) in the case of a non-Ricardian fiscal regime. This is because the nonlinearity in the response of the Embi spread to the corporate bond spread eventually dies out in our specification.

26. We also computed the impulse responses to a shock to the corporate bond spread, starting from the same initial conditions. This exercise, however, is not very informative, since it is the nonlinearity of the model (which impulse responses fail to capture) that is responsible for the sharp difference in results between the Ricardian and non-Ricardian case.

References

Alexius, A. 2002. Can endogenous monetary policy explain the deviation from UIRP. University of Uppsala, Working Paper 2002–17.

Arora, V., and M. Cerisola. 2001. How does U.S. monetary policy influence sovereign spreads in emerging markets? *IMF Staff Papers* 48(3): 474–98.

Calvo, G., L. Leiderman, and C. Reinhart. 1993. Capital inflows and real exchange rate appreciation in Latin America: The role of external factors. *IMF Staff Papers* 40(1): 108–51.

Calvo, G. 2002. Globalization hazard and delayed reform in emerging markets. *Economía* 2(2): 1–29.

Eichengreen, B., and A. Mody. 2000. What explains changing spreads on emerging market debt? In S. Edwards, ed., *Capital Flows and the Emerging Economies: Theory, Evidence, and Controversies*. Chicago: University of Chicago Press, pp. 107–34.

Favero, C. A., and F. Giavazzi. 2002. Why are Brazilian interest rates so high? Mimeo. IGIER-Bocconi, Milan.

Herrera, S., and G. Perry. 2002. Determinants of Latin spreads in the new economy era: The role of U.S. interest rates and other external variables. Mimeo. World Bank.

Kamin, S. B., and K. von Kleist. 1999. The Evolution and determinants of emerging market credit spreads in the 1990s. International Finance Discussion Paper 653. Board of Governors of the Federal Reserve System.

Kfoury, M., and S. A. Lago Alves. 2003. Medium-size macroeconometric model for the Brazilian economy. Working Paper 64. Banco Central do Brasil.

Loyo, E. 1999. Tight money paradox on the loose: A fiscalist hyperinflation. Mimeo. J. F. Kennedy School of Government, Harvard University.

McCallum, B. T. 1994. A reconsideration of the UIRP relationship. *Journal of Monetary Economics* 33: 105–32.

Niepelt, D. 2004. The fiscal myth of the price level. *Quarterly Journal of Economics* 476 (February): 277–300.

Sargent, T., and N. Wallace. 1981. Some unpleasant monetary arithmetic. *Federal Reserve Bank of Minneapolis Quarterly Review*.

Sims, C. 2003. Limits to inflation targeting. Mimeo. Princeton University.

Tanner, E., and A. M. Ramos. 2002. Fiscal sustainability and monetary versus fiscal dominance: Evidence from Brazil, 1991–2000. IMF Working Paper 02/05.

Uribe, M. 2003. A fiscal thoery of sovereign risk. Mimeo. Duke University.

Tong, H. 1983. *Threshold Models in Non-linear Time Series Analysis.* Berlin: Springer.

Woodford, M. 1994. Monetary policy and price level determinacy in a cash-in-advance economy. *Economic Theory* 4: 345–80.

Comment on Chapter 3

Eliana Cardoso

Favero and Giavazzi, as much as Blanchard (in chapter 2), caution policy makers about inflation targeting as this can do more harm than good when there is a chance that the central bank cannot in fact control inflation. The discussion is persuasive in showing how credit risk is the channel through which international financial shocks can push an emerging economy into a regime of fiscal dominance—particularly in the case where dollar-denominated public debt interacts with external financial volatility and creates one more channel of instability.

Favero and Giavazzi start by examining what drives country risk in Brazil. They consider in part international factors such as the level of the US interest rates, the slope of the US yield curve, and the US corporate bond spread and in part the domestic factor affecting the response of the EMBI spread to international factors, which is the distance of the primary budget surplus from a level that is debt stabilizing.

One could question whether other variables, which investors see as important when evaluating country risk (e.g., the expected inflation rate or the ratio between external debt service and exports of goods and services), should also be part of the nonlinearity in the response of the Embi spread to international financial shocks. If these variables also count for the decisions of investors, they should also affect the EMBI spread beyond the effect of the budget surplus. But Favero and Giavazzi want to keep their model simple because their objective is to show that the effectiveness of monetary policy depends on the fiscal policy regime.

In the chapter monetary policy rule is modeled as consisting of a response of the Selic rate to the one-year-ahead inflation expectation measured by the surveys of the central bank. In the simulations the initial conditions are those prevailing in July 2002—when the Central Bank of Brazil started to increase the interest rate in response to the increase in expected inflation observed after the jump in country risk—and all exogenous variables are constant (except for expected inflation). The simulations are run under two fiscal regimes. In one simulation, the government uses an exogenous, constant primary surplus rule. In the other, the government uses a so called "Ricardian rule": an increase in the primary surplus responds to a rise in the debt-to-GDP ratio.

The simulations reinforce a very important insight from the model: this is to show that credit risk and its interaction with the fiscal policy regime can drive a country into a regime of fiscal dominance. Monetary policy may fail with a constant primary deficit rule. If a shock drives inflation expectations or the risk premium up and the central bank targets inflation expectations, the increase in real interest rates will increase the cost of debt service. At unchanged fiscal stance, the debt level rises, the country risk mounts, and the exchange rate further depreciates and further increases the debt level. The exchange rate depreciation raises inflation and inflation expectations and the Selic rises further. This is the vicious circle also described in Blanchard's model (in chapter 2) and depicted in the left arm of figure 3.5.

Brazil was close to this trap in 2002. If real interest rates had increased in 2002, perhaps its combination with high debt and risk aversion would have been responsible for a disaster that did not materialize. The reason for an increased probability of default in 2002 was not an increase in real interest rates but political uncertainty, coupled with the tightening of liquidity that followed the Enron scandal in the United States.

The combination of a domestic monetary policy that was not too tight and did not pursue the central point of the old target avoided the vicious circle in figure 3.5. The real exchange rate depreciated, and the share of dollar-denominated public debt in GDP increased. The net public debt–GDP ratio peaked at 63 percent in midyear. The decline in real Selic rate brought this ratio down to 56 percent at the end of 2002.

Finding it difficult to roll over the domestic debt, the central bank redeemed a fraction of debt falling due by money printing. Part of that money went back into the overnight market buying very short term government debt and thus shortening the average maturity of the debt. Part went into dollars and left the country fueling the depreciation of the exchange rate. Another fraction remained in the country as cash or demand deposit and the central bank seigniorage increased with the increase in required reserves over deposits after mid-2002.

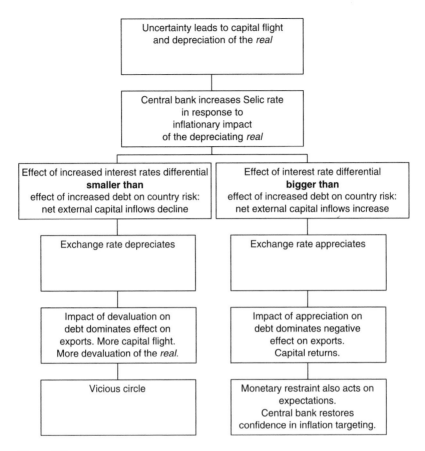

Figure 3.5
Exchange rate and interest rate dynamics: Two stories

Between May and October 2002 the central bank delayed an increase in interest rates. Part of the financial market feared that because more than half of the public debt was indexed to the interest rate, the central bank could partially default on its debt by keeping the Selic rate low and letting inflation go up. The fear of default through inflation in part explains the flight from debt indexed to the Selic rate into very short run dollar-denominated debt and into foreign assets. The one-year-ahead interest rates implied in the 360 days swaps between indexed and not-indexed public debt did run sharply ahead of the Selic rate and reflected both fear of default and the expectation of rising inflation rates.

At the time the central bank really tightened monetary policy, from the end of 2002 until June 2003, the situation was turning around. After the presidential election, the announcement of tight fiscal policy and coincided with an expansion of international liquidity. The country risk declined and the exchange rate started to appreciate. At the same time, as inflation came down, real interest turned sharply up. The central bank kept the nominal interest rates high until it felt more confident that inflation was converging to inflation targets. One consequence of the combined policy of higher real interest rates and tighter fiscal policy was the decline in GDP during 2003.

In their chapter Favero and Giavazzi take output as given. They recognize that output growth is a critical factor in determining debt dynamics but argue that the effect of interest rates on output is weak in Brazil. Yet the combination of higher real interest rates with an increase in the budget surplus can have a strong effect—as it did have in 2003.

If the multiplier effect of the surplus on income is one, the increase in the budget surplus would reduce both income and debt by the same amount. The so-called Ricardian rule would not offer a solution to the increase in debt from the rise in real interest rates. Debt dynamics would only be favorable if the multiplier is less than one or if the increase in the surplus induces confidence and thus a decline in real interest rates.

Favero and Giavazzi stop short of recommending a cut in interest rates as logic would suggest. Perhaps this is because they fear that interest rates have an important signaling effect (which is left out of the model for simplicity): a cut in interest rates could signal that the central bank is not actually committed to bringing inflation down and would scare investors away.

The analysis of 2002 and 2003 macroeconomic variables can lead to very different interpretations that are consistent with the data. One could argue that tightening of monetary policy in the fourth quarter of 2002 and in the first quarter of 2003 produced stabilization of the exchange rate and inflation in mid-2003—or that the exchange rate and inflation responded to confidence gains from the fiscal tightening, or that the combination of a fiscal–monetary policy mix that led to recession was essential to achieve stability. Finally, one could argue that the stabilization of the exchange rate was only possible because of an increase in international liquidity and renewed capital flows to emerging markets including Brazil. Probably all these elements played a role.

The central bank took too long to react to the rising inflation rate in 2002 because factors outside the control of the central bank imposed serious constraints on monetary policy. Perhaps, the combined shocks of the electoral uncertainty and Enron scandals were too big not to surprise the central bank. On the other hand, even if the central bank had predicted inflation with accuracy, it would have been difficult for a government coming to the end of its administration to convince investors that the opposition (that in the past had spoken in favor of a debt moratorium) would not present a threat to their capital. Thus, being difficult to convince investors on the run to leave their money behind by raising interest rates, the only choice was to accept partial monetization of debt, more inflation and then wait until a new government was in place to restore credibility. The central bank was wise in not trying to achieve the impossible.

In 2003 the central bank was too slow in responding to the fast declining inflation rates. It was cautious because a radical cut of the basic interest rate could have been perceived as signaling a weaker central bank with all kinds of bad expectation effects. Even if in hindsight I judge that the central bank did lose a good opportunity by letting interest rates down too slowly during 2003, this is a marginal critique. In 2002 inflation targeting in Brazil did survive the stress test imposed by the combination of electoral uncertainty and tight international liquidity. This is more than sufficient reason to recommend inflation targeting to other developing countries.

III

Debt Management and
Fiscal Institutions

4   Public Debt Management in Brazil

Alessandro Missale and
Francesco Giavazzi

4.1   Introduction

There are many different views as to the objectives of debt management but in the case of Brazil the paramount objective of debt management should be that of reducing the country's fiscal vulnerability.[1] This calls for funding at low cost but also for minimizing the risk of large interest payments due to unexpected changes in interest rates and/or in the exchange rate.[2] Risk minimization is accomplished, as shown by Goldfajn (1998), by choosing debt instruments that both ensure a low volatility of returns and provide a hedge against fluctuations in the primary budget, in the interest payments and in the value of the other liabilities.

In this chapter we present a simple model where debt management helps to stabilize the debt ratio and thus reduces the probability of a debt crisis. Reducing the uncertainty of the debt ratio, for any expected cost of debt service, is valuable in that it lowers the probability that the fiscal adjustment may fail because of a bad shock to the budget.

The optimal debt composition is derived by looking at the relative impact of the risk and cost of alternative debt instruments on the probability of missing the stabilization target. This allows one to price risk against the expected cost of debt service and find the optimal combination along the trade-off between cost and risk minimization.

The optimal debt structure is thus a function of the expected return differentials among debt instruments, of the conditional variance of debt returns and of their covariances with output growth, inflation, exchange rate depreciation, and the Selic rate. We estimate the relevant covariances with three alternative methods. The first approach exploits the daily survey of expectations on GDP growth, inflation, the exchange rate and the Selic rate. The second method relies on a small structural model of the Brazilian economy estimated on monthly data for the period 1999:03 to 2003:07. The one-year-ahead unanticipated components of the Selic rate, exchange rate depreciation, inflation, and output growth are estimated as the 12-month cumulated impulse responses of these variables to shocks to inflation, the output gap and the EMBI spread. The third approach approximates the one-year-ahead unanticipated components of the relevant variables using the residuals of forecasting regressions run on quarterly data for the period 1995:3 to 2003:1.

The empirical evidence suggests that a large share of the Brazilian debt should be indexed to the price level. Price indexation should be preferred to Selic rate indexation while the share of dollar denominated (and indexed) bonds should be further reduced from the current high level.[3] These policy prescriptions appear robust to alternative methods of estimating the optimal debt structure. The share of fixed-rate bonds should also be increased. Fixed-rate debt avoids large interest payments when the Selic rate rises during a crisis or reacts to negative supply shocks and thus when debt stabilization is endangered by slow output growth. Because of their short maturity, below two years, fixed-rate bonds ensure a sufficiently fast reduction of debt servicing costs in the event of a rapid fall in interest rates. If the term premium required on fixed-rate bonds is not too high, issuing such bonds in exchange for Selic-indexed bonds increases the probability of debt stabilization. We provide evidence on the term premium, which suggests that such a strategy is indeed optimal.

The empirical evidence strongly supports the funding strategy of Brazilian Treasury in 2003 of relying heavily on fixed-rate LTN bonds. It also supports its recent decision to revitalize the market for price-indexed bonds with the new NTN-B program of IPCA indexation. Although the exposure to exchange rate risk has been reduced in 2003, it is still large suggesting that more efforts should be made to reduce issuance of bonds denominated in foreign currencies.

4.2   The Government Problem

In this section we present a simple model where debt management helps to stabilize the debt ratio and thus reduces the probability of a debt crisis. Debt stabilization calls for funding at low cost but also for minimizing the risk of large payments due to unexpected changes in interest rates and the exchange rate. Hence the choice of debt instruments trades off the risk and the expected cost of debt service.

Risk minimization is accomplished by choosing debt instruments which both ensure a low return variability and provide a hedge against variations in the primary budget, and in the returns of the other liabilities (e.g., see Goldfajn 1998). Reducing the uncertainty of the debt ratio, for any expected cost of debt service, is valuable in that it lowers the probability that debt stabilization may fail because of bad shocks to the budget. This strategy is consistent with the asset-and-liability management approach adopted by the Brazilian Treasury (see Tesouro Nacional 2003a).

To provide insurance against variations in the primary surplus and the debt-ratio, public bonds should be indexed to nominal GDP. However, this would be a costly innovation. Indeed, a high premium will be paid for insurance, for the illiquidity of the market, and for the delay in the release of GDP data and their revisions. Therefore we focus on the main funding instruments that are currently available to the Brazilian Treasury: bonds indexed to the Selic rate (LFT), fixed-rate bonds (LTN), bonds indexed to the IPG-M price index (NTN-C) or to the IPCA index (NTN-B), domestic bonds indexed to the US dollar, and external debt denominated in foreign currency. (We refer to the latter two instruments as dollar-denominated bonds in what follows.)

The aim of the government is to stabilize the debt ratio, B_t. To this end, the government decides a fiscal correction taking into account the realization of debt returns, output, inflation and the exchange rate.[4] However, since the outcome of the government's efforts is uncertain (and the fiscal adjustment is costly), a crisis cannot be prevented with certainty. Denoting the outcome of the fiscal adjustment (in terms of GDP) with $A_{t+1} - X$, a debt crisis arises if the debt ratio increases:

$$B_{t+1}^T - A_{t+1} + X > B_t, \tag{1}$$

where A_{t+1} is the expected adjustment, X, denotes the uncertain component of the fiscal adjustment, B_t is the debt-to-GDP ratio, and B_{t+1}^T is the trend debt-ratio. The trend debt-ratio would prevail in period $t+1$ in the absence of the fiscal correction.[5] Alternatively, X can be viewed as a shock to the budget that occurs after the fiscal adjustment has been carried out or as a debt increase due to the discovery of hidden liabilities—"skeletons in the closet."

Absent government intervention the debt ratio increases because of the interest payments on the outstanding debt minus the trend primary surplus and the growth of nominal GDP. The debt also increases because of the revaluation of the dollar-denominated debt due to the depreciation of the domestic currency. Hence debt accumulation $\Delta B_{t+1}^T = B_{t+1}^T - B_t$ is equal to

$$\Delta B_{t+1}^T = I_{t+1}B_t + \Delta e_{t+1}qB_t - S_{t+1}^T - (\Delta y_{t+1} + \pi_{t+1})B_t, \tag{2}$$

where $I_{t+1}B_t$ are the nominal interest payments, e_t is the log of the nominal exchange rate, q is the share dollar-denominated debt, S_{t+1}^T is the trend primary surplus, y_{t+1} is the log of output, and π_{t+1} is the rate of inflation.

The interest payments depend on the composition of public debt chosen at the end of period t. The government can choose among bonds indexed to the Selic rate, dollar-denominated bonds, price-indexed bonds, and fixed-rate bonds. We take the time period as corresponding to one year and assume that all bonds have a one-year maturity, since the relevant decision for the Brazilian Treasury is whether one-year fixed-rate bonds should be issued. Focusing on a one-year horizon is a reasonable approximation even if LFT, NTN, and dollar-denominated bonds have much longer maturities because the stochastic component of their returns is dominated by movements in the Selic rate, the rate of inflation, and the exchange rate. Within a one-year horizon the nominal rate of return on fixed-rate one-year bonds is equal to the long-term interest rate, R_t, at which such bonds are issued. The nominal return on fixed-rate bonds is thus known at the time of issuance. The return in *reais* on dollar-denominated bonds depends on the US interest rate, R_t^{US}, the risk premium RP_t, and exchange rate depreciation. The nominal return on price-linked bonds is equal to the sum of the real interest rate, R_t^I, known at the time of issuance, and the rate of inflation, π_{t+1}. Finally, the return on Selic-indexed bonds is determined by the path of the Selic rate over the life of the bond and thus between periods t and $t+1$. The (average) Selic rate over this period, i_{t+1}, is not known at time t when the composition of the debt is chosen.

The interest payments are equal to

$$I_{t+1}B_t = i_{t+1}sB_t + (R_t^{US} + RP_t)qB_t + (R_t^I + \pi_{t+1})hB_t$$

$$+ R_t(1 - s - q - h)B_t, \tag{3}$$

where s is the share of Selic-indexed debt, q is the share of dollar-denominated debt, and h is the share of price-indexed debt at the beginning of period t and where the return on dollar-denominated bonds $(R_t^{US} + RP_t)(1 + \Delta e_{t+1})$ has been approximated by $R_t^{US} + RP_t$.

Finally, the ratio of the trend primary surplus to GDP, S_{t+1}^T, is uncertain, since it depends on cyclical conditions and on the rate of inflation as follows:

$$S_{t+1}^T = E_t S_{t+1}^T + \eta_y(y_{t+1} - E_t y_{t+1}) + \eta_\pi(\pi_{t+1} - E_t \pi_{t+1}), \tag{4}$$

where η_y is the semi-elasticity of the government budget (relative to GDP) with respect to output, η_π is the semi-elasticity of the budget with respect to the price level, and E_t denotes expectations conditional on the information at time t.

Hence the surplus-to-GDP ratio may be higher than expected because of unanticipated output, $y_{t+1} - E_t y_{t+1}$, and inflation, $\pi_{t+1} - E_t \pi_{t+1}$. While the impact of economic activity on the budget is well known from a number of studies, inflation also reduces the deficit if tax systems and spending programs are not fully indexed.[6]

4.3   Choice of Debt Denomination and Indexation

The objective of the Treasury is to minimize the probability that debt stabilization fails because the adjustment effort is unsuccessful, because revenues fall short of expected and/or spending programs cannot be cut. The government chooses s, q, and h to find

$$\min E_t \Pr[X > A_{t+1} - \Delta B_{t+1}^T] = \min E_t \int_{A_{t+1} - \Delta B_{t+1}^T}^{\infty} \phi(X)\, dx \tag{5}$$

subject to (2), (3), and (4). Here $\phi(X)$ denotes the probability density function of X.

Deriving (5) with respect to s, q, and h yields

$$E_t \phi(A_{t+1} - \Delta B_{t+1}^T)[i_{t+1} - R_t] = 0, \tag{6}$$

$$E_t \phi(A_{t+1} - \Delta B_{t+1}^T)[R_t^{US} + RP_t + e_{t+1} - e_t - R_t] = 0, \tag{7}$$

$$E_t \phi(A_{t+1} - \Delta B_{t+1}^T)[R_t^I + \pi_{t+1} - R_t] = 0, \tag{8}$$

where $A_{t+1} - \Delta B_{t+1}^T$ is the planned reduction in the debt-to-GDP ratio and $\phi(A_{t+1} - \Delta B_{t+1}^T)$ is a function of s, q, and h.

The first-order conditions (6) through (8) have a simple interpretation: they show that the debt structure is optimal only if the increase in the probability that stabilization fails, which is associated with the interest cost of additional funding in a particular type of debt, is equalized across debt instruments. If this were not the case, the government could reduce the probability of failure by modifying the debt structure; for example, it could substitute fixed-rate bonds for Selic-indexed bonds, and vice versa.[7]

To gain further intuition, we observe that the difference between the interest cost of Selic-indexed bonds and fixed-rate bonds is equal to the (average) Selic rate between time t and $t + 1$ minus its value as expected at the time t, and the term premium on fixed-rate bonds:

$$i_{t+1} - R_t = i_{t+1} - E_t i_{t+1} - TP_t, \tag{9}$$

where TP_t is the term premium on fixed-rate bonds and $E_t i_{t+1}$ is the expected average Selic rate between time t and $t + 1$.

Equation (9) shows that the expected cost of funding with Selic-indexed bonds is lower than fixed-rate bonds because of the term premium but, ex post, the cost may be greater if the Selic rate turns out to be higher than expected. It is also worth noting that equation (9) implicitly assumes that investors' expectations coincide with the expectations of the government. If this were not the case, the expected cost differential relevant for the government, TP_t, would include an informational spread:

$$TP_t = TP_t^I + (E_t^I i_{t+1} - E_t i_{t+1}), \tag{10}$$

where E_t^I denotes investors' expectations and TP_t^I is the true term premium.

The difference between the cost of funding with dollar-denominated bonds and fixed-rate bonds depends on the realization of the exchange rate. Between time t and $t + 1$ the return on dollar-denominated bonds (evaluated in domestic currency) differs from the return on fixed-rate bonds as follows:

$$R_t^{US} + RP_t + e_{t+1} - e_t - R_t = e_{t+1} - E_t e_{t+1} - FP_t, \tag{11}$$

where FP_t is the one-year exchange rate risk premium that is relevant for the government. Although the true exchange rate risk premium is likely to be small, dollar-denominated bonds may enjoy a liquidity premium due to the greater liquidity and efficiency of international bond markets. FP_t may also reflect the different views of the investors and the government regarding the exchange rate. If we consider this "credibility spread," FP_t, is equal to

$$FP_t = FP_t^I + E_t^I e_{t+1} - E_t e_{t+1}, \tag{12}$$

where E_t^I denotes investors' expectations and FP_t^I is the true foreign exchange risk premium.

Finally, the difference between the interest payments on price-indexed bonds and fixed-rate bonds is equal to

$$R_t^I + \pi_{t+1} - R_t = \pi_{t+1} - E_t \pi_{t+1} - IP_t, \tag{13}$$

where IP_t is the inflation risk premium that is relevant to the government. It may include, in addition to the true premium, a spread reflecting the lack of credibility of the announced inflation target:

$$IP_t = IP_t^I + E_t^I \pi_{t+1} - E_t \pi_{t+1}. \tag{14}$$

The return differentials (9)–(11)–(13) allow us to write the first-order conditions (6) through (8) as follows:

$$E_t \phi(A_{t+1} - \Delta B_{t+1}^T)(i_{t+1} - E_t i_{t+1}) = TP_t E_t \phi(A_{t+1} - \Delta B_{t+1}^T), \tag{15}$$

$$E_t \phi(A_{t+1} - \Delta B_{t+1}^T)(e_{t+1} - E_t e_{t+1}) = FP_t E_t \phi(A_{t+1} - \Delta B_{t+1}^T), \tag{16}$$

$$E_t \phi(A_{t+1} - \Delta B_{t+1}^T)(\pi_{t+1} - E_t \pi_{t+1}) = IP_t E_t \phi(A_{t+1} - \Delta B_{t+1}^T). \tag{17}$$

Equations (15) through (17) show the trade-off between the risk and expected cost of debt service that characterizes the choice of debt instruments.

At the margin the impact on the probability of debt stabilization of assuming more risk must be equal to the impact of reducing the expected cost of debt servicing. Hence the marginal increase in probability can be used to price risk against the expected cost of debt service and thus find the optimal combination along the trade-off between cost and risk minimization. For example, equation (15) shows that issuing bonds indexed to the Selic rate is optimal until the uncertainty of the Selic rate raises the probability of failure as much as paying the term premium on fixed-rate bonds.

Therefore the objective of debt stabilization offers a solution to the identification of the optimal debt structure that is independent of the government's preferences toward risk. This is because both the risk and the expected cost of debt service affect the probability of debt stabilization.

To derive an explicit solution for the optimal shares of the various types of debt, we must specify the probability density function, $\phi(X)$. Since this function cannot be estimated, we take a linear approximation of $\phi(X)$ over the range of bad realizations, $X > 0$, of the fiscal adjustment.[8] This implies a triangular probability density function equal to

$$\phi(X) = \frac{\bar{X} - X}{\bar{X}^2}, \tag{18}$$

where $X > 0$ and $\bar{X}$ is the worst possible realization of the fiscal adjustment.

In fact the triangular density is the linear approximation of any density function decreasing with X (for $X > 0$); it implies that bad realizations of the fiscal adjustment are less likely to occur the greater is their size.

Substituting equations (18) and (2) through (4) in the first-order conditions (15) through (17) yields the optimal shares of Selic-indexed debt, s^*, dollar-denominated debt, q^*, and price-indexed debt, h^*:

$$s^* = \frac{(\eta_y + B_t)}{B_t} \frac{\operatorname{cov}(y_{t+1} i_{t+1})}{\operatorname{var}(i_{t+1})} + \frac{(\eta_\pi + B_t)}{B_t} \frac{\operatorname{cov}(\pi_{t+1} i_{t+1})}{\operatorname{var}(i_{t+1})} - q^* \frac{\operatorname{cov}(e_{t+1} i_{t+1})}{\operatorname{var}(i_{t+1})}$$

$$- h^* \frac{\operatorname{cov}(\pi_{t+1} i_{t+1})}{\operatorname{var}(i_{t+1})} + TP_t \frac{\sqrt{2\operatorname{Pr}}}{1 - \sqrt{2\operatorname{Pr}}} \frac{E_t(A_{t+1} - \Delta B_{t+1}^T)}{B_t \operatorname{var}(i_{t+1})}, \tag{19}$$

$$q^* = \frac{(\eta_y + B_t)}{B_t} \frac{\operatorname{cov}(y_{t+1} e_{t+1})}{\operatorname{var}(e_{t+1})} + \frac{(\eta_\pi + B_t)}{B_t} \frac{\operatorname{cov}(\pi_{t+1} e_{t+1})}{\operatorname{var}(e_{t+1})} - s^* \frac{\operatorname{cov}(e_{t+1} i_{t+1})}{\operatorname{var}(e_{t+1})}$$

$$- h^* \frac{\operatorname{cov}(\pi_{t+1} e_{t+1})}{\operatorname{var}(e_{t+1})} + FP_t \frac{\sqrt{2\operatorname{Pr}}}{1 - \sqrt{2\operatorname{Pr}}} \frac{E_t(A_{t+1} - \Delta B_{t+1}^T)}{B_t \operatorname{var}(e_{t+1})}, \tag{20}$$

$$h^* = \frac{(\eta_y + B_t)}{B_t} \frac{\operatorname{cov}(y_{t+1} \pi_{t+1})}{\operatorname{var}(\pi_{t+1})} + \frac{(\eta_\pi + B_t)}{B_t} - q^* \frac{\operatorname{cov}(e_{t+1} \pi_{t+1})}{\operatorname{var}(\pi_{t+1})}$$

$$- s^* \frac{\operatorname{cov}(\pi_{t+1} i_{t+1})}{\operatorname{var}(\pi_{t+1})} + IP_t \frac{\sqrt{2\operatorname{Pr}}}{1 - \sqrt{2\operatorname{Pr}}} \frac{E_t(A_{t+1} - \Delta B_{t+1}^T)}{B_t \operatorname{var}(\pi_{t+1})}, \tag{21}$$

where var(.) and cov(.) denote variances and covariances conditional on the information available at time t and Pr is the probability of a debt crisis as perceived by the government.

The optimal debt shares depend on both risk and cost considerations. Risk is minimized if a debt instrument provides insurance against variations in the primary budget and the debt ratio due to output and inflation uncertainty and if the conditional variance of its returns is relatively low. This is captured by the first two terms in equations (19) through (21).

Equation (19) shows that floating-rate debt is optimal for risk minimization when the Selic rate, so the interest payments are positively correlated with unanticipated output and inflation. This allows the government to pay less interest when output and inflation, and thus the primary surplus, are unexpectedly low. More important, since lower output growth tends to increase the debt ratio, instruments with returns correlated to nominal output growth help stabilize the debt ratio, thus reducing the risk of a debt crisis. The case for indexation weakens as the conditional variance of the Selic rate increases, producing unnecessary fluctuations in interest payments.

Equation (20) shows that the optimal share of dollar-denominated debt increases as the exchange rate co-varies positively with output and inflation. If the exchange rate appreciated at times of unexpectedly low output—an unlikely event—cyclical variations in the government budget can be hedged by dollar-denominated debt. To the extent that exchange rate depreciation is associated with inflation, foreign currency debt helps stabilize the debt ratio. Clearly, exposure to exchange rate risk becomes less attractive as the volatility of the exchange rate increases.

Equation (21) shows that the optimal share of price-indexed debt increases with the covariance between output and inflation. If this covariance is positive, lower interest payments on price-indexed debt provide an insurance against the cyclical deficit due to unexpected slowdowns in economic activity. However, price-indexed debt can be optimal even if the covariance between output and inflation is zero. The reason is that price-indexed debt provides the perfect hedge against an increase in the debt ratio due to lower than expected nominal output growth.

Risk minimization also depends on the conditional covariances between the returns on the various debt instruments. For instance, a positive covariance between the returns on two types of debt makes the two instruments substitutes in the government portfolio. This is captured by the third and fourth terms in equations (19) through (21).

Leaving aside cost considerations, the government should choose the debt composition that offers the best insurance against the risk of deflation and low growth. But insurance is costly; higher expected returns are generally required on hedging instruments, and this leads on average to greater debt accumulation. Debt stabilization thus implies a trade-off between cost and risk minimization. The effect of expected return differentials (or risk premia) on the optimal debt composition is captured by the last term in the right-hand side of equations (19) through (21). This term increases with the risk premia, TP_t, FP_t, and IP_t, more precisely, with the excess return (as perceived by the government) of fixed-rate bonds relative to the instrument considered. As shown in equations (15) through (17), the impact of the excess return on the optimal share depends on the marginal increase in the probability of a debt crisis. The latter has been written as a function of the expected debt reduction $E_t(A_{t+1} - \Delta B_{t+1}^T)$ and the probability of a debt crisis, Pr, as perceived by the government. (It is worth noting, that the probability Pr also depends on the expected debt reduction, so the overall effect of a larger debt reduction is to reduce the impact of the expected cost differential.) Finally, a greater variance of the return on a given debt instrument reduces the importance and the impact of interest cost differentials on its optimal share as much as it reduces the relevance of its hedging characteristics. For example, equation (20) points out that the share of bonds denominated or indexed to foreign currencies should increase with the excess return, FP_t. However, as the variance of the exchange rate increases, cost considerations become less important for the choice of dollar-denominated bonds.

4.4   Estimating the Optimal Debt Structure

The optimal debt composition depends on the sensitivity of the primary surplus to unexpected variations in output and inflation, η_y and η_π, on the reduction in the debt ratio, and on the probability of debt stabilization as perceived by the government. At the end of October 2003, mainly because of lower nominal GDP growth, the net public debt was 57.2 percent of GDP, one percentage point higher than in 2002. Although the debt ratio is currently above the "optimistic" scenario presented in "Politica Economica e Reformas Estruturais" (Ministerio da Fazenda, April 2003), the debt should stabilize next year at around 56 percent of GDP. Therefore the expected debt reduction is assumed to be 1 percent. The probability that the stabilization plan may fail is tentatively set at 2 percent, which corresponds to a maximum negative shock to the budget, $\bar{X}$, equal to 1.5 percent of GDP. This scenario reflects the lower interest rates associated with restored market confidence as well as the high primary surplus targeted by the government.

For the increase of the primary surplus (as a percentage of GDP) due to a 1 percent growth in real GDP we rely on the estimate by Blanco and Herrera (2002) who suggest a 0.2 semi-elasticity of the primary surplus with respect to GDP (see also Bevilaqua and Werneck 1997). Evaluating the effect of unexpected inflation on the primary surplus (as a percentage of GDP) is a more difficult task. Although the effect should be substantial, as witnessed by the remarkable budget improvement in the first quarter of 2003, coming down to a single number is difficult.[9] As indirect taxation is the main source of revenues, these should remain roughly constant in terms of GDP. Public spending should instead fall relative to GDP because many categories of spending remains constant in nominal terms as set in the budget.[10]

Primary public spending is equal to 32 percent of GDP, but social security benefits and other components are linked to the inflation rate. This suggests a tentative estimate of the price elasticity of the primary surplus equal to 0.2, that is, lower than the ratio of primary public spending to GDP.

4.4.1 Expected Return Differentials

The expected return differential between fixed-rate bonds and Selic-indexed bonds over one-year horizon, TP_t, is the difference between the yield at auction of fixed-rate LTN bonds and the expected return on Selic-indexed LFT bonds. The latter can be estimated as the sum of expected Selic rate from the daily survey of expectations and the discount at which one-year LFT bonds are issued. At the end of October 2003 the average auction yield on one-year LTN bonds was 17.7 percent, the Selic rate expected for the end of October 2004 was 14.8 percent and LFT bonds were issued at a 0.4 percent discount. The expected return differential, TP_t, can thus be set at 2.5 percent.

To estimate the expected return differential between one-year fixed-rate bonds and dollar denominated bonds, FP_t, the one-year yield on LTN bonds must be compared to the expected return in *reais* on US$ global bonds. At the end of October global bonds with a five-year maturity have been issued at a rate of 9.45 percent, but the yield on bonds with a one-year maturity appears much lower; the yield curve shown on the Treasury website points to a 4 percent one-year yield (see Tesouro Nacional, December 2003b). In the same period the expected depreciation from the daily survey was 9.4 percent. With an interest rate of 17.7 percent on LTNs, the expected return differential, FP_t, can thus be estimated at around 4.3 percent.

The premium on price-linked bonds (NTN-C and NTN-B) over one-year fixed-rate bonds, IP_t, is the sum of an inflation-risk premium and, eventually, a "credibility spread" due to the higher inflation expected by the market than by the government. The inflation-risk premium can be estimated as the difference between the interest rate on LTN bonds and the (real) yield at issue of one-year price-linked NTN-C bonds augmented by the expected IPG-M inflation. At the end of October NTN-C bonds with a three-year maturity were issued at 9.32 percent while, according to the daily survey, the expected 12-month-ahead IPG-M inflation was around 6.5 percent. This implies an inflation-risk premium of 1.9 percent in October. As the real yield on one-year bonds might be lower than the yield on three-year bonds, the cost advantage of one-year NTN-C bonds could even be greater than 1.9 percent. We do not add to this estimate the difference between the inflation expected by the market and by the government (i.e., the "credibility spread") because there is no official target for IPG-M inflation. It is worth noting, however, that expected IPCA inflation from the daily survey was 6.2 percent, only slightly higher than the inflation rate implicit in the projection of the ninetieth COPOM meeting of November.

4.4.2 Uncertainty of Debt Returns

The conditional variance of debt returns and their covariances with output growth and inflation can be estimated from one-year-ahead forecast errors of the Selic rate, the exchange rate, inflation, and output growth. Ideally one would like to run forecasting regressions on yearly data for such variables. Then the residuals of the regressions could be taken as the estimates of the one-year-ahead unanticipated components of the Selic rate, the exchange rate, inflation, and output growth. Unfortunately, this procedure is precluded in the case of Brazil because time series at yearly frequency are not sufficiently long but, more important, because of the frequent regime shifts experienced over the last two decades.

To circumvent this problem, we consider the following three alternatives. The first exploits the daily survey of expectations of GDP growth, inflation, the exchange rate, and the Selic rate. The unexpected components of these variables can be obtained as the difference between the realization of the relevant variables and their expectations one year earlier. The conditional covariances can then be computed as the mean of their cross products.

The second method focuses on the most recent period of inflation targeting, starting in mid-1999, and relies on a structural backward-looking model of the Brazilian economy estimated with monthly data. The model, which is presented in appendix A, is consistent with that proposed by Favero and Giavazzi (2003) under the hypothesis of "Ricardian fiscal policy." Because we use monthly data, the one-year-ahead unanticipated components of the Selic rate, the exchange rate, inflation, and output growth are estimated as the 12-month cumulated impulse responses of these variables to shocks of inflation, the output gap, and the Embi spread.

The third approximates the one-year-ahead unanticipated components of the relevant variables using the residuals of forecasting equations estimated on quarterly data for the period 1995:3 to 2003:1. This method requires the extension of the sample period to include the fixed exchange rate period and the currency crisis of 1999. On the other hand, the estimated stochastic structure is independent of the modeling strategy.

4.4.3 Estimating the Debt Composition from the Daily Survey of Expectations

Table 4.1 decomposes GDP growth, IPCA inflation, exchange rate depreciation (relative to the US dollar), and the Selic rate between its expected and unexpected components in 2000, 2001, and 2002 for which expectations can be obtained from the daily survey.

Except for the first year, when output growth was higher than expected, the Brazilian economy performed much worse than expected. Output growth was substantially lower in 2001, while inflation and exchange rate depreciation exceeded expectations in both 2001 and 2002. The Selic rate also turned out much higher than expected. Had the government issued fixed-rate conventional bonds instead of Selic-indexed bonds and dollar-denominated bonds, debt sustainability would not be a problem for Brazil. Hence prima facie evidence appears to make a strong case for fixed-rate long-term debt. This depends, however, on the specific (short) period considered. If times of unexpected deflation, falling short-term interest rates and unexpected appreciation, as those

Table 4.1
Economic indicators

	π	Δy	Δe	Selic
Realized				
2000	5.97	4.4	9.3	15.84
2001	7.67	1.4	18.7	19.05
2002	12.53	1.5	52.3	24.90
Unanticipated				
2000	−1.03	1.4	0.3	−0.81
2001	3.37	−2.6	16.4	5.05
2002	7.73	−0.9	26.0	7.90

Note: IPCA inflation, US dollar exchange rate depreciation, and end-of-period Selic rate.

experienced in 2003, are as likely as the events of the period 2000 to 2002, then issuing fixed-rate bonds paying a high term premium will be a poor strategy.

To correctly address the issue of the optimal debt composition, we must look at the covariances of debt returns with output and inflation. Table 4.1 clearly points to a negative correlation between all types of indexation and unexpected output growth but also shows that unexpected inflation has been positively associated with higher returns on dollar-denominated bonds and Selic-indexed bonds. Unexpected inflation has also led to higher returns on price-indexed bonds. This suggests a role for price indexation (and, to a lesser extent, for the other types of indexation) in hedging against unexpected deflation. This would require, however, that the observed comovements between inflation and debt returns were a systematic feature of the Brazilian economy and not just an episode confined to the period under consideration. The qualification makes it clear that policy indications are not robust when the available evidence is limited to a short period of time as in the present case.

The conditional covariances of debt returns with output and inflation (relative to the conditional variance of returns) are presented in table 4.2. The covariances of output growth with all types of indexed debt are negative but small, while inflation displays a strong positive covariance with the Selic rate and a mild covariance with the exchange rate. Hence all types of indexation are useful hedges against inflation, although they introduce additional risk when negative output shocks already impair debt sustainability.

Table 4.2
Covariances from survey of expectations

$\mathrm{cov}(yi)/\mathrm{var}(i)$	-0.24	$\mathrm{cov}(i\pi)/\mathrm{var}(i)$	0.89
$\mathrm{cov}(ye)/\mathrm{var}(e)$	-0.07	$\mathrm{cov}(e\pi)/\mathrm{var}(e)$	0.27
$\mathrm{cov}(y\pi)/\mathrm{var}(\pi)$	-0.24	$\mathrm{cov}(e\pi)/\mathrm{var}(\pi)$	3.55
$\mathrm{var}(i)$	0.30	$\mathrm{cov}(ie)/\mathrm{var}(i)$	3.25
$\mathrm{var}(e)$	3.15	$\mathrm{cov}(ie)/\mathrm{var}(e)$	0.30
$\mathrm{var}(\pi)$	0.24	$\mathrm{cov}(i\pi)/\mathrm{var}(\pi)$	1.09

Note: Variances are multiplied by 100.

Importantly the magnitude of these effects is in sharp contrast with evidence from OECD economies shown in Missale (2001). In the OECD countries a strong negative covariance between short-term interest rates and output growth is observed over the period 1970 to 1998 while the covariance between short-term rates and inflation is small and not significant. Only Greece, Portugal, and Sweden display a correlation between short-term rates and inflation as strong as in Brazil. This fact can be explained by the specific shocks experienced by the Brazilian economy during the short period considered. However, these correlations could also reflect structural features of the economy and/or the need for a more flexible approach to inflation targeting in emerging economies exposed to large shocks. In particular, the low correlation of output with the policy rate may reflect a lower elasticity of the output gap to such rate or the case for a smoother convergence of the inflation rate to the target. Quoting the Open Letter sent by the Central Bank of Brazil's governor to the Minister of Finance (BCB January 2003): "It is a standard practice among central banks when facing supply shocks of great magnitude to postpone the convergence of current inflation toward the targets over a longer period, avoiding unnecessary costs to the economy. This was the case faced by Brazil in the last year."

As the positive correlation of the Selic rate and the exchange rate with inflation dominates their negative but small correlation with output growth, bonds indexed to the Selic rate, inflation, and the exchange rate all provide some insurance against variations in the primary surplus and the debt ratio due to unexpected changes in nominal output growth. This is shown in the first column of table 4.3, which reports for each type of debt the optimal share for risk minimization in the case where we abstract from hedging against variations in the returns

Table 4.3
Debt composition from survey of expectations

	Risk (no hedge)	Risk	Risk + cost	Risk + cost (fixed = Selic = 0)
Selic rate	0.88	−4.14	−1.80	0
Foreign exchange	0.27	0.73	−0.12	0.01
Price index	1.03	2.98	2.61	0.99
Fixed rate	−1.18	1.43	0.08	0

Note: The debt composition is derived from equations (19) through (21).

of the other instruments. All shares are positive, reflecting the fact that variable-rate instruments have the same distribution of returns.

Column 2 shows the debt composition that allows one to minimize both the risk of variations in the primary surplus and in the returns of the other instruments. As Selic-indexed, price-indexed, and dollar-denominated bonds are close substitutes in the government portfolio, variations in their returns should be hedged by holding a long position in Selic-indexed bonds (e.g., by means of foreign currency swaps).

When cost considerations are introduced into the analysis, the composition of the debt clearly moves in favor of price-indexed bonds. Column 3 shows that the government should issue price-indexed bonds in an amount far exceeding the total debt and hedge this position by holding assets denominated in dollars, along with Selic-indexed bonds. This result may look surprising given the cost advantage, 2.3 percent, of dollar-denominated bonds over price-indexed bonds, but it is worth recalling that expected return differentials must be normalized by the conditional variance of returns and the standard deviation of exchange rate depreciation has been 3.6 times that of inflation. Since for practical reasons a structure of assets and liabilities as shown in column 3 is clearly unfeasible, in column 4 the share of price-indexed bonds is estimated in the case the government cannot hold Selic-indexed bonds. The case for price-indexed bonds is again strong.

Evidence from the daily survey of expectations thus suggests price indexation as the optimal strategy for debt management, thus supporting the policy indications by Bevilaqua and Garcia (2002). As bonds indexed to the price level currently represent less than 15 percent of the domestic marketable federal debt (in the hands of the public), this implies that funding in the next few years will have to rely on price indexation. It is, however, important to realize the risk of a strategy

Table 4.4
Covariances from structural model, for demand shock

cov(yi)/var(i)	12.9	cov($i\pi$)/var(i)	0.76
cov(ye)/var(e)	−10.7	cov($e\pi$)/var(e)	−0.63
cov($y\pi$)/var(π)	11.3	cov($e\pi$)/var(π)	−0.70
var(i)	0.038	cov(ie)/var(i)	−0.80
var(e)	0.054	cov(ie)/var(e)	−0.56
var(π)	0.049	cov($i\pi$)/var(π)	0.58

Note: Variances are multiplied by 100^2.

that increases the exposure of the government budget to unexpected output fluctuations. In fact fixed-rate bonds appear to be the only available instruments to ensure against the impact of unanticipated output slowdowns on debt sustainability. As highlighted in the discussion above, the fact that such shocks have played a minor role compared to variations in the exchange rate and inflation over the period considered does not mean that they will continue to do so in the future. A debt structure that comprises fixed-rate conventional bonds along with price-indexed bonds would better balance the risks that the Brazilian economy may face in the years ahead. In the next section we present results for different shocks identified with a structural model of the Brazilian economy, and we examine whether and how the optimal debt composition depends on the types of shocks hitting the economy.

4.4.4 Estimating the Debt Composition with a Structural Model

The structural model used to estimate the optimal debt composition is made of five equations for (1) the inflation rate, (2) the output gap, (3) the Selic rate, (4) the exchange rate, and (5) the EMBI spread. The model is estimated on monthly data for the period 1999:3 to 2003:7 and is presented in appendix A.

We consider three types of shocks: a supply shock (in the inflation equation), a demand shock (in the output-gap equation), and a shock to the EMBI spread. We want to compute the 12-months cumulated impulse responses of the Selic rate, the exchange rate, inflation, and output for 1,000 extractions from the distribution of each type of shock.[11] The cumulated responses are then used to estimate the ratios of conditional covariances relative to conditional variances, which are shown in tables 4.4, 4.6, and 4.8 for the demand shock, the supply

Table 4.5
Debt composition for demand shock

	Risk (no hedge)	Risk	Risk (fixed = foreign = 0)	Risk + cost	Risk + cost (fixed = foreign = 0)
Selic rate	18.4	7.5	−3.3	8.3	−3.2
Foreign exchange	−15.3	−6.2	0	−5.1	0
Price index	16.6	7.9	4.3	8.3	4.2
Fixed rate	−18.6	−8.1	0	−10.5	0

Note: The debt composition is derived from equations (19) through (21).

shock, and the EMBI shock, respectively. The optimal debt composition is reported in tables 4.5, 4.7, and 4.9 for each type of shock.

Demand Shocks Table 4.5 shows the debt composition that stabilizes the debt ratio against demand shocks—that is, against shocks to the output-gap equation. The first column of table 4.5 reports the shares of each type of debt that are optimal for minimizing the risk of variations in the primary surplus and the debt ratio, namely when we abstract from hedging against variations in the returns of the other instruments. The shares of Selic- and price-indexed bonds are positive and exceed several times the total debt; such bonds offer a valuable insurance against variations in the primary surplus and the debt-ratio. As demand shocks induce a positive covariance of output and inflation and a strong reaction of the policy rate, the returns on both Selic- and price-indexed bonds are strongly correlated with output and inflation. As the monetary reaction leads to an appreciation of the exchange rate, the return on dollar-denominated bonds is negatively correlated with both output and inflation. This explains the large negative share of dollar-denominated debt; the government should rather hold foreign assets to hedge against output shocks.

Column 2 shows the debt composition that minimizes risk when we consider, along with budget and debt-ratio uncertainty, the role of each instrument in hedging against the returns of the other instruments. Since Selic- and price-indexed bonds are close substitutes in the government portfolio (they returns covary positively), their optimal shares decrease. The long position in foreign assets also decreases as Selic- and price-indexed bonds are hedged by dollar-denominated bonds.

The risk-minimizing debt structure calls for issuing large amounts of indexed instruments to fund unlimited holdings of foreign assets. Since

Table 4.6
Covariances from structural model for supply shock

$\mathrm{cov}(yi)/\mathrm{var}(i)$	−0.42	$\mathrm{cov}(i\pi)/\mathrm{var}(i)$	0.64
$\mathrm{cov}(ye)/\mathrm{var}(e)$	0.33	$\mathrm{cov}(e\pi)/\mathrm{var}(e)$	−0.57
$\mathrm{cov}(y\pi)/\mathrm{var}(\pi)$	−0.53	$\mathrm{cov}(e\pi)/\mathrm{var}(\pi)$	−1.23
$\mathrm{var}(i)$	0.109	$\mathrm{cov}(ie)/\mathrm{var}(i)$	−0.96
$\mathrm{var}(e)$	0.172	$\mathrm{cov}(ie)/\mathrm{var}(e)$	−0.61
$\mathrm{var}(\pi)$	0.079	$\mathrm{cov}(i\pi)/\mathrm{var}(\pi)$	0.89

Note: Variances are multiplied by 100^2.

taking such position is clearly unfeasible, in column 3 we restrict the shares of dollar-denominated debt and fixed rate debt to be nonnegative. In this case risk minimization clearly favors price indexation over Selic rate indexation.

The optimal debt composition does not change when cost minimization is considered along with risk insurance. Column 4 shows that both Selic- and price-indexed bonds should be issued if large holdings of foreign assets were feasible. However, when the debt shares are constrained to be nonnegative, price indexation clearly emerges as the optimal choice: column 5 shows that all the debt should be indexed to the price level.

Supply Shocks Table 4.7 shows the optimal debt composition that stabilizes the debt ratio against supply shocks, namely against shocks to the inflation equation. Column 1 shows that fixed-rate bonds, Selic rate, and price-indexed bonds, all provide insurance against variations in the primary surplus and in the debt ratio due to lower than expected inflation and output growth. In particular, more than one-third of the debt should be at fixed rate while the other two-thirds should be indexed to the Selic rate and the price level. Although Selic-indexed and price-indexed bonds are good hedges against lower than expected inflation, they provide limited insurance against budget risk, since their returns are now negatively correlated with output (see table 4.6). Since supply shocks lead to a negative covariance of output with both inflation and the Selic rate, fixed-rate debt helps to stabilize the debt ratio.

Column 2 shows that when we consider the risk of variations in debt returns along with budget risk and debt-ratio uncertainty, a role emerges for dollar-denominated bonds. The optimal composition for risk minimization comprises a small share of dollar-denominated

Table 4.7
Debt composition for supply shock

	Risk (no hedge)	Risk	Risk + cost	Risk + cost (fixed = Selic = 0)	Risk + cost (no other)
Selic rate	0.30	−0.26	0.03	0	0.37
Foreign exchange	−0.32	0.06	0.54	0.18	−0.24
Price index	0.63	0.89	1.35	0.82	0.71
Fixed rate	0.38	0.26	−0.92	0	0.16

Note: The debt composition is derived from equations (19) through (21).

bonds and a negative share of Selic-indexed bonds. The reason is that, even if dollar-denominated bonds are poor hedges against variations in the primary surplus, they are good complements of price-indexed bonds. This is because the exchange rate covaries negatively with inflation; it appreciates when the Selic rate is raised to counter (negative) supply shocks. By contrast, the share of Selic-indexed bonds becomes negative, since such bonds are close substitutes for price-indexed bonds while they offer a limited insurance against inflation uncertainty. Finally, fixed-rate bonds still appear to play an important role in risk minimization; about one-fourth of the debt should be at fixed rate.

Although fixed-rate debt helps stabilize the debt ratio by insulating the budget from supply shocks, the higher expected cost of such debt has a negative impact on the probability of stabilization. Column 3 shows the debt composition that maximizes the probability of stabilizing the debt ratio when cost considerations are taken into account. Since variable-rate bonds have lower expected returns than fixed-rate bonds, their shares increase substantially, leaving no role for fixed-rate bonds; it would even be optimal to hold fixed-rate assets and fund this position with the other instruments. Finally, column 4 shows that, when the optimal shares are constrained to be nonnegative, there is a strong case for price indexation; more than 80 percent of the debt should be indexed to the price level with the remaining part denominated in dollars.

The absence of fixed-rate bonds in the optimal debt structure is partly explained by the strong complementarity between price-indexed and dollar-denominated bonds that arises because of the exchange rate appreciation that follows an inflation shock. If we abstract from the insurance provided by dollar-denominated debt against the returns of

Table 4.8
Covariances from structural model for EMBI shock

$\mathrm{cov}(yi)/\mathrm{var}(i)$	−2.14	$\mathrm{cov}(i\pi)/\mathrm{var}(i)$	1.50
$\mathrm{cov}(ye)/\mathrm{var}(e)$	−0.38	$\mathrm{cov}(e\pi)/\mathrm{var}(e)$	0.27
$\mathrm{cov}(y\pi)/\mathrm{var}(\pi)$	−0.95	$\mathrm{cov}(e\pi)/\mathrm{var}(\pi)$	1.65
$\mathrm{var}(i)$	0.038	$\mathrm{cov}(ie)/\mathrm{var}(i)$	3.71
$\mathrm{var}(e)$	1.187	$\mathrm{cov}(ie)/\mathrm{var}(e)$	0.12
$\mathrm{var}(\pi)$	0.194	$\mathrm{cov}(i\pi)/\mathrm{var}(\pi)$	0.30

Note: Variances are multiplied by 100^2.

the other instruments, then some fixed-rate debt is optimal. Column 5 shows that, in this case, fixed-rate bonds still account for 16 percent of the debt despite their higher expected return. This would be the relevant case if negative supply shocks, by inducing a deterioration of the fiscal position (which our model fails to capture), led to a wider EMBI spread and a depreciation of the exchange rate. The effects of shocks to the country risk premium are discussed in the next section.

EMBI Shocks Table 4.9 shows the debt composition that stabilizes the debt ratio against shocks to the EMBI spread. Changes in the country risk premium may capture changes in international risk factors or in the perception of risk as well as domestic fiscal shocks, for example, negative shocks to the budget that increase country risk.

The first column of table 4.9 reports the debt composition that stabilizes the debt ratio against variations in output and inflation, that is, in the case where we abstract from hedging against variations in debt returns. The shares of Selic-indexed bonds and dollar-denominated bonds are negative, reflecting the strong negative covariances of their returns with output growth that are shown in table 4.8. In fact EMBI shocks also lead to both unexpected inflation and exchange rate depreciation, but the negative covariances of the Selic rate and the exchange rate with output dominate their positive covariances with inflation. It follows that fixed-rate bonds should be issued in amounts exceeding the total debt so as to insulate the budget from unexpected output contractions.

Column 2 shows that issuing fixed-rate debt is still optimal for risk minimization when we consider the role of each instrument in hedging against the returns of the other instruments. The government should issue an amount of fixed-rate bonds larger than the total debt and hold both foreign assets and Selic-indexed bonds. When, as in column 3, the

Table 4.9
Debt composition for EMBI shock

	Risk (no hedge)	Risk	Risk (Selic = foreign = 0)	Risk + cost	Risk + cost (Selic = foreign = 0)
Selic rate	−0.86	−1.24	0	−0.79	0
Foreign exchange	−0.15	−0.22	0	−0.25	0
Price index	0.07	0.80	0.07	0.76	0.11
Fixed rate	1.95	1.66	0.93	1.28	0.89

Note: The debt composition is derived from equations (19) through (21).

debt shares are constrained to be nonnegative, the share of fixed-rate debt reaches 93 percent.

When cost considerations are introduced into the analysis, as in columns 4 and 5, the optimal debt composition moves toward price indexation, but the share of fixed-rate bonds remains substantial despite the higher expected return. Column 5 shows that when debt shares are constrained to be nonnegative, the optimal share of fixed-rate bonds is as high as 89 percent.

Conclusions from the Structural Model   Results from the structural model suggest that a large share of the Brazilian debt should be indexed to the price level. Price-indexed bonds appear to consistently provide a good hedge against all types of shocks, although their role is limited in the case of EMBI shocks. Indexation to the Selic rate should be avoided if supply shocks and EMBI shocks prevail, while Selic-indexed bonds are a worse alternative to price indexation in the case of demand shocks. Importantly there appears to be little role for dollar-denominated bonds. Exposure to exchange rate risk should be avoided in the case of demand shocks and EMBI shocks and limited in the case of supply shocks. In particular, the greater volatility of the exchange rate implies that for dollar-denominated bonds to be preferred to price-indexed bonds, their expected return differential should be much higher than that currently observed.

Whether one-year fixed-rate bonds should be issued depends on the type of shocks hitting the economy. While fixed-rate LTN bonds have no role in the case of demand shocks, they are the best instruments to cope with shocks to the country risk premium. If EMBI shocks prevail, a share of such bonds substantially higher than that currently observed would be optimal even after considering their greater expected cost. LTN bonds may also provide insurance against variations in the primary budget and the debt ratio induced by supply shocks, but their optimal share is small because of their higher expected return. A stronger argument for fixed-rate bonds (in exchange for dollar-denominated bonds) can be made if negative supply shocks increase fiscal vulnerability, thus leading to a depreciation of the exchange rate.

These policy implications obviously depend on the correct specification of the structural model. So it is important to check whether they continue to hold under different estimation methods.

4.4.5   Estimating the Debt Composition with Forecasting Regressions

In this section the conditional covariances of debt returns, output, and inflation are estimated using the residuals of forecasting equations run on quarterly data for the period 1995:3 to 2003:1. We proceed in two steps. We first run regressions of output, inflation, the exchange rate, and the Selic rate separately on one lag of each variable and take the residuals as an estimate of the unanticipated component of the dependent variable. Then we estimate the ratio of the conditional covariance between, say, output and inflation to the variance of inflation as the coefficients of the regression of the residuals of output on the residuals of inflation obtained in the first stage.

Table 4.10 shows that these ratios are small and not statistically significant except for the negative covariance of the Selic rate with output. This finding is consistent with the results from the structural model in the case of supply shocks and shocks to the EMBI spread: unexpected increases of the Selic rate appear to be associated with significant reductions in output growth. On the other hand, the Selic rate does not bear any systematic relation with unexpected inflation. The conditional covariance between inflation and output (and thus between the returns on price-indexed bonds and output) is negative but small and not significant. The exchange rate also appears to be uncorrelated with both output and inflation over the period considered.

Table 4.11 presents the optimal debt composition. Column 1 reports the shares of the various types of debt that are optimal for risk minimization, that is, in the case where all bonds have the same expected return. Column 2 does the same when the debt composition is computed using only the covariance–variance ratios that are statistically significant. Columns 1 and 2 show that for the purpose of minimizing

Table 4.10
Covariances from forecasting regressions

cov(yi)/var(i)	−0.536	cov($i\pi$)/var(i)	−0.016
	(0.002)		(0.93)
cov(ye)/var(e)	0.018	cov($e\pi$)/var(e)	−0.017
	(0.38)		(0.45)
cov($y\pi$)/var(π)	−0.042	cov($e\pi$)/var(π)	−1.170
	(0.81)		(0.45)
var(i)	0.012	cov(ie)/var(i)	−2.166
			(0.19)
var(e)	0.899	cov(ie)/var(e)	−0.027
			(0.19)
var(π)	0.013	cov($i\pi$)/var(π)	−0.014
			(0.93)

Note: Quarterly data with P-values in parenthesis. Variances are multiplied by 100.

Table 4.11
Debt composition from forecasting regressions

	Risk	Risk (significant)	Risk (Selic = 0)	Risk + cost (significant)	Risk + cost (fixed = Selic = 0)
Selic rate	−0.72	−0.73	0	−0.42	0
Foreign exchange	0.00	0.00	0.00	0.01	0.01
Price index	1.30	1.36	1.35	1.56	0.99
Fixed rate	0.42	0.37	−0.35	−0.15	0

Note: The debt composition is derived by assuming that the one-year-ahead conditional variances are four times the three-month-ahead conditional variances.

risk, all the debt should be indexed to the price level. While dollar-denominated bonds play no role, the government should hold assets indexed to the Selic rate and fund this position with fixed-rate bonds. This is probably the result of including the 1999 currency crisis into the sample. Indeed, the negative and large share of Selic-indexed bonds reflects the negative covariance between output and the policy rate that characterizes crisis events. This evidence suggests that a large exposure to floating rates makes the budget vulnerable to high interest rates when this is less desirable, namely at times of output contractions and when credit availability is a problem.

Although the share of fixed-rate debt in columns 1 and 2 is substantial, such debt is used to fund the long position in Selic-indexed bonds. If the share of Selic debt is constrained to be nonnegative as in column

3, then fixed-rate bonds should not be issued. Hence price-indexed bonds appear the optimal choice for risk minimization. This is because their returns are unrelated to output fluctuations and provide a natural hedge against lower than expected inflation.[12]

Then the interesting issue is whether differences in expected returns imply a role for Selic-indexed bonds and dollar-denominated bonds in debt stabilization. The optimal debt shares are shown in column 4. Cost differentials make it optimal to issue larger amounts of indexed and dollar-denominated bonds in exchange for fixed-rate debt. However, the share of Selic-indexed debt remains negative while that of dollar-denominated debt is positive but small. Since price-indexed bonds should be issued in amounts exceeding the total debt, column 4 also shows a long, though small, position in fixed-rate bonds. Since these large asset holdings are clearly unfeasible, column 5 shows the optimal debt composition when the shares of Selic-indexed bonds and fixed-rate bonds are constrained to be nonnegative. The case for price indexation is again strong; almost the whole debt should be indexed to the price level.

Therefore results from forecasting equations strengthen our previous conclusions: price indexation should be preferred to Selic rate indexation while the share of dollar-denominated (and indexed) bonds should be drastically reduced from the current high level. Indeed, the lack of correlation of the Selic rate with inflation and its negative covariance with economic activity provide strong evidence against Selic rate indexation. These risk-return characteristics may have changed with the monetary regime and/or reflect the particular events covered by the sample period. However, if the observed negative correlation between the Selic rate and economic activity were due to the 1999 currency crisis, policy indications against floating-rate debt would even be stronger.

The results of forecasting regressions strongly support the decision of the Brazilian Treasury to revitalize the market for price-indexed bonds. It is, however, worth recalling that the simulations of the structural model presented in the previous section suggest that fixed-rate bonds are better instruments than price-indexed bonds to cope with shocks to the EMBI spread.

Even if we restrict the attention to the results of forecasting regressions there are several reasons why indexing a large share of debt to the price level may not be optimal or feasible. For instance, while we focus on one-year bonds, NTN-C and NTN-B bonds are issued at longer maturities, probably reflecting the preferred holding periods of institutional investors. Issuing five- to twenty-year bonds at a real 10 percent interest rate may not be advisable if the fiscal authorities are determined to carry out the fiscal stabilization. In this case issuing fixed-rate bonds with a one-year maturity would be a more effective strategy for cost minimization (at the cost of increasing the exposure to rollover risk).

Second, it is likely that the amount of price-indexed bonds that the market is willing to absorb at current interest rates is limited. If the government placed increasing amounts of such bonds, their interest rate would rise. The extent of indexation may also be limited by reason of political opportunity: inflation indexation of interest income may give rise to pressures for extending indexation to other types of income. Moreover it is often argued that indexation reduces the cost of inflation and thus the incentives for anti-inflationary fiscal and monetary policy. Fixed-rate debt may also enhance the effectiveness of monetary policy in controlling aggregate demand (see Falcetti and Missale 2002). Finally, issuance of fixed-rate conventional bonds can be motivated by the objective of developing a domestic market for fixed-rate bonds.

It is worth examining under which conditions substituting fixed-rate one-year bonds for dollar-denominated bonds and for Selic-indexed bonds is optimal, while taking the shares of the other types of debt constant at the current level. Table 4.12 shows (for various pairs of the expected debt reduction and the probability that debt stabilization fails) the interest rate differential between one-year fixed-rate bonds and dollar-denominated bonds, *FP*, below which it is optimal to issue fixed-rate bonds in exchange for dollar-denominated bonds. Note that the exposure to exchange rate risk (after swaps), in terms of the net external debt, is at the end of 2003 as high as 40 percent. Therefore sub-

Table 4.12
Cutoff of exchange rate risk premium for substituting fixed rate for foreign exchange

Probability of failure	Expected reduction of debt ratio			
	2.5%	2.0%	1.5%	1.0%
20%	18.9	23.7	31.6	47.4
25%	13.5	16.8	22.5	33.7
30%	9.4	11.8	15.8	23.7
35%	6.3	7.9	10.6	15.9
40%	3.8	4.8	6.4	9.6

Note: Risk premium in percent.

stituting fixed-rate bonds for foreign currency debt is optimal even for a very high perceived probability that debt stabilization will fail. For instance, for the 4.3 percent expected return differential recorded in October 2003, the exposure to exchange rate risk is optimal only if the perceived probability that debt stabilization will fail is as high as 40 percent.

Table 4.13 shows the interest rate differential between one-year fixed-rate bonds and Selic-indexed bonds, TP, below which issuing fixed-rate bonds in exchange for Selic-indexed bonds is optimal. With an expected debt reduction equal to 2 percent of GDP, and 6 percent probability that the debt ratio will not stabilize, fixed-rate bonds should replace Selic-indexed bonds as soon as the term premium falls below 2.8 percent. However, if the probability of failure is lower, say 3 percent, then fixed-rate bonds should be issued even if the term premium is as high as 4.6 percent. Although these numbers can be regarded as merely indicative, they show the large scope for improvement in the composition of the Brazilian debt.

4.5 Conclusions

In this chapter we presented a framework for the choice of debt instruments in countries where fiscal vulnerability makes debt stabilization the main goal of debt management. The optimal debt composition was estimated by looking at the relative impact of the risk and cost of various debt instruments on the probability that the government might miss the stabilization target, which we have defined as a pre-assigned level of the debt-to-GDP ratio.

The empirical evidence suggests that a large share of the Brazilian debt should be indexed to the price level. Price-indexed bonds appear

Table 4.13
Cutoff of term premium for substituting fixed rate for Selic rate

Probability of failure	Expected reduction of debt ratio			
	2.5%	2.0%	1.5%	1.0%
2%	4.80	6.00	8.01	12.0
3%	3.70	4.63	6.17	9.25
4%	3.04	3.81	5.07	7.61
5%	2.60	3.25	4.33	6.49
6%	2.27	2.83	3.78	5.66

Note: Risk premium in percent.

to consistently provide a good hedge against all types of shocks, although their role is limited in the case of EMBI shocks. Price indexation should be preferred to Selic rate indexation, and the share of dollar-denominated (and indexed) bonds should be drastically reduced. These policy prescriptions are robust to alternative methods of estimating the optimal debt structure.

Fixed-rate LTN bonds also help stabilize the debt ratio. Although such bonds have no role in the case of demand shocks, they are the best instruments to cope with shocks to the country risk premium. If EMBI shocks prevail, a share of fixed-rate bonds substantially higher than currently observed would be optimal even after considering their greater expected cost. Fixed-rate bonds can further provide insurance against fluctuations in the primary budget and in the debt-ratio induced by supply shocks, but their optimal share should be smaller than that of price-indexed bonds because of their higher expected return.

The scope for improving on the current structure of the Brazilian debt is substantial. In October 2003 the composition of the net public debt in Brazil was still strongly biased toward foreign-currency-denominated and dollar-indexed debt. Once we account for net external debt and for the foreign currency swaps of the central bank, the exposure to the exchange rate reached 40 percent. The share of debt indexed to the Selic rate was also as high as 40 percent. By contrast the share of debt indexed to the price level was slightly above 10 percent and the fixed-rate component was about 8 percent.

These facts suggest simple policy prescriptions. First of all, the exposure to exchange rate risk should be reduced. The cost advantage of bonds denominated or indexed to foreign currency is not sufficient to compensate for the high risk of variations in the exchange rate. The exposure to the exchange rate is so high that betting in the direction of a further appreciation of the exchange rate is rather risky. One of the reasons such a large share of the domestic debt is indexed to the dollar is the demand for hedge by the private sector. In Brazil the only entities that bear exchange rate risk are the government and the central bank: the private sector fully hedges its dollar exposure by entering into swap contracts with the central bank. Such a large amount of outstanding hedge cannot be rapidly reduced: the currency falls sharply whenever the central bank announces that it will not fully roll over the outstanding stock of hedge. The current account surplus that Brazil is now running offers an opportunity to reduce the demand for hedge by the private sector. This constraint, however, does not apply to Treasury funding in foreign currencies, which should be avoided, thus reducing exchange rate exposure at least on this front. Since vulnerability to exchange rate risk is valued by investors, a smaller share of dollar-denominated debt could lower the risk premium on the Brazilian debt.

The second advice is to increase issuance of price-indexed bonds. Price indexation, especially the new IPCA indexation program, provides a natural hedge against the impact of inflation on both the primary surplus and the debt ratio. In the perspective of the asset-and-liability management approach of the Brazilian Treasury, NTN-C and NTN-B bonds do not only match future revenues but also the risks of price-indexed assets in the government portfolio (see Tesouro Nacional 2003a). Since NTN-C bonds have a long maturity, they also insulate the government budget from rollover risk, thus representing an important factor of stability for public debt dynamics. Thus, the decision of the Brazilian Treasury to revitalize the market for price-indexed bonds finds a strong support in our analysis.

How large the share of price-indexed bonds should be is more difficult to say. Although our analysis suggests that such a share should be large, there are a number of reasons why this may not be optimal or feasible. The amount of price-indexed bonds that can be issued may be limited by reasons of political opportunity or by the likely increase in the expected return that investors require to hold such bonds when their share increases.

The main obstacle against a strategy of price indexation lies, however, in the long maturity of price-indexed bonds, which can lock in the cost of debt service at real interest rates as high as 10 percent for many years ahead. In fact this could be too high a cost for a government fully determined to carry out the fiscal stabilization.

A role for nominal debt instruments of short duration emerges if the stabilization program does not enjoy full credibility and long-term interests are too high relative to government expectations of future rates. The decision of the Treasury to rely on bonds indexed to the Selic rate clearly finds a strong motivation in this argument; floating-rate LFT debt ensures that a fall in interest rates would be immediately transmitted into a lower debt service cost. Although our analysis cannot capture such an effect, it points to fixed-rate bonds with a one-year maturity as an attractive alternative to Selic rate indexation.

Indeed, the third policy indication that emerges from this study is to substitute fixed-rate bonds for bonds indexed to the Selic rate. Fixed-rate debt avoids large interest payments when the Selic rate rises during a crisis or reacts to negative supply shocks, and thus when debt stabilization is endangered by slow output growth. We find evidence that issuing fixed-rate bonds in exchange for Selic-indexed bonds increases the probability of debt stabilization even if the 12-month term premium is as high as 4 percent. Since realistically the maturity of fixed-rate bonds will have to remain relatively short, within two years, a greater share of such bonds will not preclude the benefit of a fall in interest rates. The only objection against such policy is that short maturity debt may expose the Treasury to a rollover crisis, an event that we have not modeled.

Issuance of fixed-rate bonds can bring additional benefits as they play a key role in the creation of a domestic bond market. The resumption in 2003 of LTN auctions for maturities longer than one year goes in the right direction. The Treasury should commit to this strategy by announcing a regular program of fixed-rate bond auctions, since the success of this strategy hinges on the market perception that the program will not be changed or interrupted because of unfavorable market conditions.

Appendix A: The Monthly Model

The model used in the simulation exercises to obtain the impulse responses to supply, demand, and EMBI spread shocks is made of the following equations:

- EMBI spread equation

$$\text{EMBI}_t = \mu_0 + \mu_1 \text{EMBI}_{t-1} + \mu_2 B_{t-1} i_{t-1} + \mu_3 \text{SpBaa}_t + \mu_4 \text{DU} + v_{\text{Embit}}, \tag{22}$$

where EMBI_t is the EMBI spread, SpBaa_t is the US corporate bond spread and DU is a dummy variable taking the value of 1 for the crisis period 2002:06 to 2002:12.

- Exchange rate equation

$$e_t = \delta_0 + \delta_1 e_{t-1} + \delta_2 (i_{t-1} - i_{t-1}^{\text{US}}) + \delta_3 \text{EMBI}_t + \delta_4 \Delta \text{EMBI}_t + v_{et}, \tag{23}$$

where i^{US} is the US federal funds rate.

- Output-gap equation

$$y_t = \gamma_0 + \gamma_1 y_{t-1} + \gamma_2 y_{t-2} + \gamma_3 i_{t-6} + \gamma_4 \text{EMBI}_{t-1} + v_{yt}. \tag{24}$$

- Inflation equation

$$\pi_t = \alpha_0 + \alpha_1 \pi_{t-1} + \alpha_2 y_{t-1} + \alpha_3 (e_{t-6} - e_{t-12}) + \alpha_4 \sum_{i=1}^{4} \text{EMBI}_{t-i} + v_{\pi t}. \quad (25)$$

· Selic rate equation

$$i_t = \rho i_{t-1} + (1-\rho)[\beta_0 + \beta_1 (\pi_{t-1} - \pi^T) + \beta_2 \Delta e_{t-4}] + v_{it}, \quad (26)$$

where π^T is the inflation target.

The inflation rate, the interest rates, the spreads, and the output gap are in monthly terms and have not been multiplied by 100. The exchange rate e_t is the logarithm of the R\$/US\$ exchange rate. Since the inflation rate is obtained by computing the annual growth rate of

Table 4.14
Estimated model, 1999:03 to 2003:07 sample

	Coefficient	Standard error	t-ratio	Adj R^2	SE eq.	SE dep.va	DW
μ_0	−0.132	0.182	−0.72	0.85	0.156	0.406	2.01
μ_1	0.254	0.114	2.23				
μ_2	19.78	11.22	1.76				
μ_3	187.8	68.34	2.75				
μ_4	0.618	0.116	5.32				
δ_0	0.032	0.021	1.53	0.97	0.036	0.249	1.95
δ_1	0.977	0.032	30.2				
δ_2	−2.724	1.010	−2.69				
δ_3	0.044	0.019	2.23				
δ_4	0.215	0.028	7.47				
γ_0	0.037	0.013	2.79	0.40	0.020	0.026	1.77
γ_1	0.465	0.173	2.68				
γ_2	−0.244	0.162	−1.50				
γ_3	−1.452	0.680	−2.13				
γ_4	−0.020	0.007	−2.56				
α_0	−0.0005	0.0002	−2.04	0.98	0.0004	0.0028	1.44
α_1	0.9470	0.0370	25.0				
α_2	0.0077	0.0039	1.99				
α_3	0.0017	0.0005	3.42				
α_4	0.0002	0.00004	5.97				
ρ	0.866	0.034	24.9	0.94	0.0006	0.0025	1.04
β_0	0.012	0.001	10.1				
β_1	1.569	0.394	3.97				
β_2	0.025	0.013	1.97				

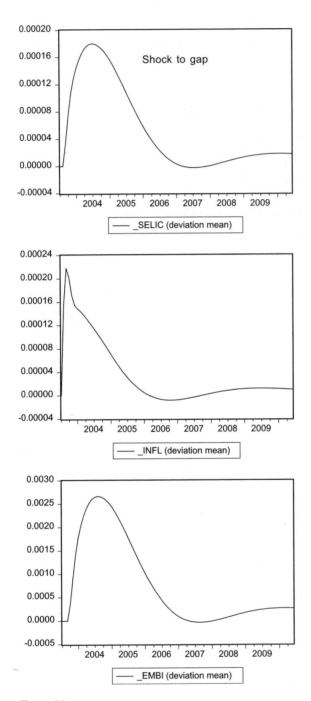

Figure 4.1
Demand shock: Impulse responses to output gap equation

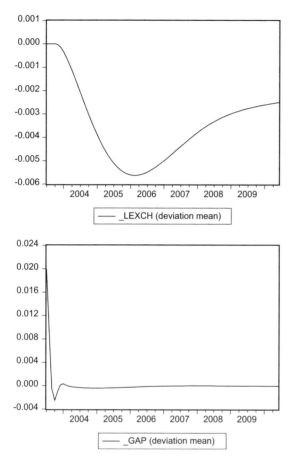

Figure 4.1
(continued)

IPCA (see appendix B) the impulse response at the twelfth month converted in annual terms (instead of the 12-month cumulated responses)
is taken as the estimate of the one-year-ahead unanticipated component of the inflation rate. The impulse response of the log of the
exchange rate at the twelfth month is taken as the estimate the one-
year-ahead unanticipated component of the percentage change of the
exchange rate.

An EMBI spread shock is a one standard deviation shock to equation
(1), a demand shock is a one standard deviation shock to equation (3),
and a supply shock is a one standard deviation shock to equation (4).
The model is estimated by iterative least squares. The results of the
estimation are reported in table 4.14. Figures 4.1, 4.2, and 4.3 show the

A. Missale and F. Giavazzi

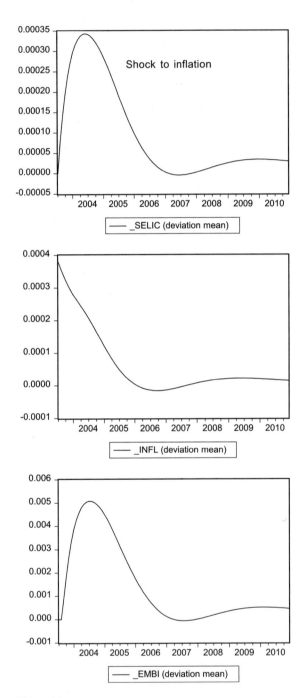

Figure 4.2
Supply shock: Impulse responses to inflation equation

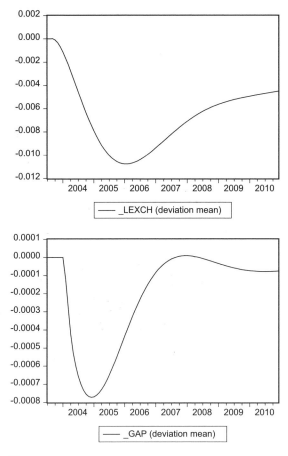

Figure 4.2
(continued)

impulse responses to a demand shock, to a supply shock, and to an EMBI shock, respectively.

Appendix B: Data Sources and Definitions

Monthly data for nominal GDP, the broad national consumer price index (IPCA), the *real* per US dollar exchange rate, the Selic rate, and the net public debt (in terms of GDP) are taken from the Central Bank of Brazil's Web site. The series are identified by the following codes: GDP monthly current prices (R$ million), Code 4380; IPCA monthly percentage change, Code 433; exchange rate R$/US$ (sale), end of period,

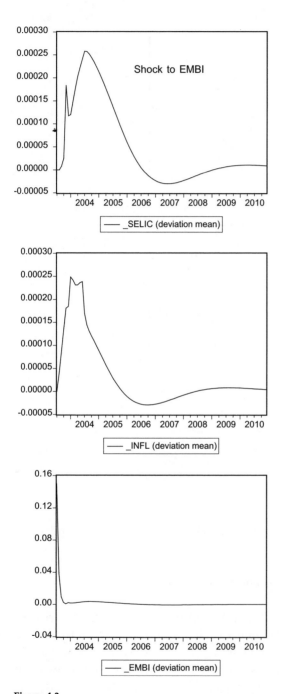

Figure 4.3
EMBI shock: Impulse responses to EMBI spread equation

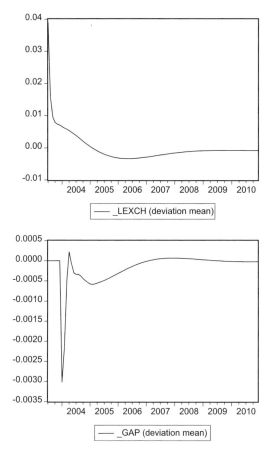

Figure 4.3
(continued)

Code 3696; Selic accumulated in the month in annual terms (percentage), Code 4189; net public debt (percentage of GDP), total, consolidated public sector, monthly, Code 4513.

The monthly inflation rate is obtained by first computing the annual growth rate of IPCA and then converting this growth rate into a monthly growth rate. The Selic is also converted into monthly terms.

The EMBI spread is computed as the difference between the yield on Brazilian government bonds in US dollars and the yield on US Treasury bonds. Both yields are taken from Bloomberg with code 9128273×8 GOVT for Brazilian bonds and code 105756AG5 GOVT for US bonds.

The corporate spread is computed as the difference between the yield on Lehman US corporate Baa long (red.yield) and the yield on US benchmark 10 year DS government index (red.yield). Both yields are taken from Datastream with codes LHIBAAL(RY) and BMUS10Y(RY), respectively.

All the financial variables series are constructed by using the last available observation in the month. Interest rates are converted into monthly terms.

Data on the composition of the public debt are taken from the Web site of the Tesouro Nacional, *http://www.tesouro.fazenda.gov.br*, and from Tesouro Nacional (2003c, 2003d).

Notes

We thank Fernando Blanco and Santiago Herrera for valuable information and data on the Brazilian economy. We are grateful to Afonso Bevilaqua and Paulo Levy for insightful discussions on the effect of GDP growth and inflation on the primary surplus. We thank Carlo Favero for many comments and suggestions. We also benefited from comments of participants in the seminars at the Brazilian Ministry of Finance, the Banco Central do Brazil, and IPEA. Marco Aiolfi and Andrea Civelli provided excellent research assistance. Financial support from the World Bank is gratefully acknowledged. The authors are associated with Università di Milano; IGIER-Università Bocconi, NBER and CEPR, respectively.

1. See Missale (1999) for a review of the literature on the objectives of debt management.

2. See Garcia (2002).

3. For a similar conclusion in favor of price indexation, see Bevilaqua and Garcia (2002). Goldfajn (1998) also hardly finds an explanation for the high share of foreign-denominated debt.

4. The choice of the government can be modeled by assuming that it weighs the cost of the adjustment against the probability of debt default. The formal analysis of the government problem is not carried out since it does not affect the results for debt management.

5. The analysis can be extended to the case where the debt ratio exceeds a given threshold for a crisis, by interpreting A_{t+1} as the sum of the expected adjustment and the difference between the current debt ratio and its threshold.

6. The effects on net lending of an increase in output by 1 percent are reported for OECD countries in the *OECD Economic Outlook* (1999) and by Van der Noord (2000). With the notable exceptions of Austria, Denmark, Ireland, the Netherlands, and Sweden, OECD countries have elasticities in the 0.4 to 0.7 range. The effects of inflation on government budgets have not been measured to the same extent, but they appear to be substantial. For Sweden, Persson, Persson, and Svensson (1998) estimate a budget improvement of 0.4 percent of GDP on a yearly basis for a 1 percent increase in the inflation rate.

7. The argument assumes that there are nonnegative constraints to the choice of debt instruments.

8. We assume that the fiscal adjustment is expected to stabilize the debt, so that $A_{t+1} > B_{t+1}^T - B_t$.

9. The positive effect of inflation is known as "Patinkin effect" (according to Eliana Cardoso); it is the opposite of the Olivera-Tanzi effect.

10. This information was provided by Paulo Levy at IPEA.

11. For the exchange rate the response at the twelfth month was used instead of the cumulated responses. See also appendix A.

12. Note that the debt composition that is optimal for risk minimization does not depend on the covariances between the returns on the various types of debt, that is, on complementarities and substitutabilities between debt instruments.

References

Bevilaqua, A. S., and M. G. P. Garcia. 2002. Debt management in brazil—Evaluation of the real plan and challenges ahead. *International Journal of Finance and Economics* 7(1): 15–35.

Bevilaqua, A. S., and R. L. F. Werneck. 1997. Fiscal impulse in the Brazilian economy, 1989–1996. Working Paper 379, Department of Economics, PUC-RIO.

Blanco Cosio, F. A., and S. Herrera. 2002. The quality of fiscal adjustment and pro-cyclical policies in Brazil. Background Paper for World Bank Country Economic Memorandum, Brazil. Washington, DC.

Falcetti, E., and A. Missale. 2002. Public debt indexation and denomination with an independent central bank. *European Economic Review* 46(10): 1825–50.

Garcia, M. G. P. 2002. Public debt management, monetary policy and financial institutions. PUC-Rio Working Paper.

Goldfajn, I. 1998. Public debt indexation and denomination: The case of Brazil. IMF Working Paper 98/18.

Banco Central do Brazil. 2003. Letter sent by Banco Central do Brasil's Governor to the Minister of Finance. January, at *http://www.bcb.gov.br*.

Ministerio da Fazenda. 2003. Politica Economica e Reformas Estruturais. April, at *http://www.fazenda.gov.br*.

Missale, A. 1999. *Public Debt Management*. Oxford: Oxford University Press.

Missale, A. 2001. Optimal debt management with a stability and growth pact. *Public Finance and Management* 1(1): 58–91.

Persson, M., T. Persson, and L. E. O. Svensson. 1998. Debt, cash flows and inflation incentives: A Swedish example. In G. Calvo and M. King, eds., *The Debt Burden and its Consequences for Monetary Policy*. London: Macmillan, pp. 28–62.

Tesouro Nacional. 2003a. Public debt: Annual borrowing plan 2003. Number 3, January, Brasilia, at *http://www.tesouro.fazenda.gov.br*.

Tesouro Nacional. 2003b. Divida Publica Federal, Eventos Recentes. December 2, 2003, at *http://www.stn.fazenda.gov.br*.

Tesouro Nacional. 2003c. Public debt report. Various issues, at *http://www.tesouro.fazenda.gov.br*.

Tesouro Nacional. 2003d. Informe divida. Various issues, at *http://www.tesouro.fazenda.gov.br*.

Van Den Noord, P. 2000. The size and the role of automatic fiscal stabilisers in the 1990s and beyond. OECD Economic Department Working Paper 230.

Comment on Chapter 4

Joaquim Levy

Missale and Giavazzi address one of the most debated issues on public debt management and yield interesting results. The careful modeling and conclusions appear to reflect the increasing understanding by the international community of key features of the Brazilian public debt, which has benefited from a rich supply of recent data and the open dialogue maintained by the Brazilian authorities with experts and investors. Their overall conclusions are in line with the guidelines adopted by leading public debt agencies in the world and the output of the toolbox used by the Brazilian Treasury in preparing its annual borrowing plan. On the other hand, the model does not deal with the trade-off between volatility of interest payments and refinancing risk, which is central to the issue of financial crises. Moreover it assumes that changes in the supply of instruments would not affect their prices, when in truth the actual structure of the public debt is owed both to supply considerations and to the appetite of investors for specific debt instruments. Drastic changes in the current debt composition could entail important adjustment costs.

Summary of the Missale and Giavazzi Model and Policy Recommendations

Missale and Giavazzi argue that reducing the country's fiscal vulnerability should be the main objective of public debt management in Brazil. In line with this assumption, they develop a two-period model of portfolio optimization in which the objective function is the probability of missing an arbitrary stabilization target for the debt-to-GDP ratio.

Four classes of debt instruments are considered (fixed rate, floating rate, exchange rate linked, and inflation linked), as well as macroeconomic shocks that can affect variables such as tax revenues and the primary surplus. First and second moments (including cross variances) of these variables, as well as those driving the returns of each class of instruments, are estimated using three different methods and data sets.

The optimal portfolio yielded by the three methodologies is found to be broadly the same. It implies that a large share of the debt should be indexed to prices, while instruments linked to the exchange rate should be avoided. Fixed-rate instruments are also favored, due to their hedging properties against negative supply shocks, although the authors reckon that large reliance on them can be costly in the case of Brazil. They also acknowledge that the model takes prices as given, and portfolio adjustments could entail important costs.

Is the Objective Function Chosen the Right One, and If So, Does the Model Capture the Key Aspects of the Problem?

The main policy conclusion of the chapter 4 does not depart from those in several studies, including on mature markets, as well as management practices in Sweden, France, the United States and the United Kingdom, where fixed-rate debt is prominent. On the other hand, one could ask whether debt management in Brazil should focus primarily on avoiding a crisis—meaning to simply reduce the probability of payments exceeding a certain threshold in the short term—and not, as it is usual in most countries, on minimizing long-term financing costs subject to prudent risk levels. The authors seem to fixate goals on arbitrary thresholds for the debt, which may not be justifiable.

Moreover, if the focus is to avoid a financial crisis, the model fails to consider a key trade-off, which is the refinancing risk.[1] The large share of three- to seven-year maturity Selic debt in Brazil is an evidence of this trade-off, where investors agree to hold long-term assets for reducing duration risk (until 2003, it was very difficult to sell fixed-rate debt of more than a year). To the extent to which financial turbulence is temporary, it is worthwhile for the government to pay a higher *temporary* interest cost while reducing refinancing risks. The model in chapter 4 cannot capture this trade-off because it has only two periods.

Some Data Considerations

There are two issues with the data. First, the return differentials used in the optimization are artificial, as actual fixed-rate instruments have shorter maturities and price-indexed bonds longer ones. Hence the stochastic properties of their returns should be taken with a grain of salt. Second, the period covered by the data is relatively short and includes 2002, to which no allowance was made. Relying too much on such results may distort any medium-term debt strategy.

Use of Stochastic Models by the Brazilian Treasury in Setting Its Strategy

It may be useful to compare the "crisis" model developed by Missale and Giavazzi with standard tools for debt management that have been in use by the Brazilian Treasury and inform the strategy supporting the annual borrowing plans (PAF) published since 2001. Among the most popular tools for debt management are stochastic risk indicators such as the cost-at-risk (CaR), cash-flow-at-risk (CfaR), and budget-at-risk (Bar) models, all of which are of current use by the Brazilian Treasury. All of these tools can be used to design an "optimal" portfolio by assigning a penalty to larger payments, rather than by simply focusing on an arbitrary threshold.

Asset and liability management (ALM) analysis has also proved to be useful. This approach is pertinent to a key issue in the chapter, as it helps gauge the impact of shocks on both sides of the government's balance sheet, including the correlation of taxes and IGP.

The debt structures suggested by these tools are not very different from those in the chapter, and are in line with a broad consensus among practitioners. Importantly, whenever market conditions have allowed, the Brazilian Treasury has vigorously geared its policy toward expanding the share of fixed interest and price-indexed instruments in total debt.

The strategy followed by the Treasury in 2003 was recently discussed in the *Annual Review of the Debt* (2004). As shown below, the Treasury took advantage of the more benign environment observed in the aftermath of the new government's adherence to strong fiscal policies to improve most debt indicators. These included issuing a four-year fixed-rate bond, which was a novelty in Brazil, as there was no medium-term nominal yield curve (see figure 4.4).

Refinancing risk was also addressed in 2003, with a substantial drop in the share of the debt maturing in up to 12 months. Also cash reserves, which proved instrumental to overcome the 2002 crisis, were rebuilt to levels that would allow the central government to stay away

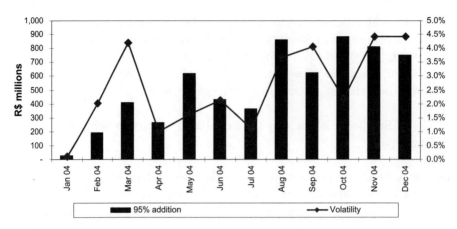

Figure 4.4
Cash-flow-at-risk of baseline portfolio in the 2004 PAF

Table 4.15
Targets and outcomes of the 2003 annual borrowing plan

Indicators	December 2002	December 2003	PAF-2003 Minimum	Maximum
Domestic outstanding debt (R$ bil)	623.2	731.4	690.0	750.0
Average life (months)	33.2	31.3	34.0	38.0
Maturing in 12 months (%)				
Former methodology	38.9	33.4	35.0	40.0
New methodology[a]	41.1	35.3	37.0	42.0
Composition of domestic outstanding debt				
Fixed rate (%)	2.2	12.5	5.0	15.0
Floating rate (%)	60.8	61.4	52.0	60.0
Exchange rate (%)	22.4	10.8	13.0	22.0
Price index (%)	12.5	13.6	12.0	18.0
Others (%)	2.1	1.8	2.0	4.0

a. The new methodology includes intermediate flows of interest payments.

from markets for four to six months, before drawing on the income from the primary surplus (table 4.15).

Note

1. Avoiding refinancing risk is not unique to emerging markets. Portugal, Denmark, Sweden, and many other countries set targets for the debt average maturity and the share of debt maturing in the short term.

References

Danmarks Nationalbank. 2001. *Danish Government Borrowing and Debt*. Copenhagen.

Holmlund, A., et al. 2001. *A Simulation Model Framework for Government Debt Analysis,* Stockholm.

IMF and World Bank. 2001. *Guidelines for Public Debt Management*. Washington, DC: GPO.

Matos, P. P. 2001. Portfolio benchmarking for public debt management: The case of Portugal. SpiE Annual Meeting. ISEG.

Secretaria do Tesouro Nacional. 2003. *Plano Anual de Financiamento—PAF 2003.*

Secretaria do Tesouro Nacional. 2004. *Relatório Anual da Dívida Pública.*

5

A Risk Management Approach to Emerging Market's Sovereign Debt Sustainability with an Application to Brazilian Data

Márcio Garcia and Roberto Rigobon

5.1 Introduction

There are several ways to assess debt sustainability. A widely used criterion is the gap between the actual primary budget deficit and the one required to keep the debt-to-GDP ratio stable (called the debt-stabilizing primary balance).[1] This measure has several drawbacks, however. If the purpose of incurring debt in the first place is to smooth consumption, why should a country keep the debt-to-GDP ratio constant? On the other hand, if the country is already heavily in debt, it would not be feasible to keep the debt-to-GDP ratio constant.

Other measures have been proposed. IMF (2003) uses estimates of the fiscal reaction function. The idea is similarly to estimate the coefficient of the expected inflation in a Taylor rule, and check whether it exceeds one, as required for the rule to provide a stationary inflation. In using the fiscal reaction function, the aim is to estimate how the primary balance reacts to increases in the debt-to-GDP ratio. Another measure is to compute a ratio between the actual debt level and a benchmark level and compare it to the present value of future primary surpluses computed under conservative assumptions. If the ratio exceeds one, the country is overborrowing (IMF 2003).

Risk-based measures of fiscal sustainability have been adapted from the financial literature. One of them is the well-known value at risk (V@R). Other sustainability measures include stress testing through Monte Carlo simulations.[2]

Here we introduce a related measure: the debt accumulation equation, which includes variables that in each country are stochastic and closely intertwined. We aim to show that the study of debt sustainability can be extended to include the stochastic properties of the debt dynamics. We will depend on the VAR (vector autoregression) function to estimate the correlation pattern of the macro variables and also on Monte Carlo simulations. These simulations allow us to compute risk probabilities, which are probabilities that the simulated debt-to-GDP ratio exceeds a given threshold deemed risky (e.g., 75 percent of GDP).[3] The time series of such probabilities can be used to investigate whether or not it is correlated with the market risk assessment, measured by the spread on sovereign dollar-denominated debt. The application of our methodology for Brazil shows that although the debt may be sustainable in the absence of risk, there are paths by which it is clearly unsustainable. Further we show that properties of the debt dynamics are closely related to the EMBI + Brazil spread.

In the next section, we describe the data used and perform a few debt decomposition exercises. In section 5.3, we present the core methodology and the application to Brazilian data. In section 5.4, we make some concluding observations.

5.2   Brazilian Sovereign Debt

5.2.1   Data Description

The simulation of the debt dynamics requires the compatibility of many statistics that are produced in different places. Bevilaqua and Garcia (2002) performed a decomposition exercise of the growth sources of the domestic bonded debt in Brazil. The domestic bonded debt is the component of the net public debt that grew the most in Brazil: from 11.81 percent of GDP in December 1994 to 48.95 percent of GDP in September 2003. We will use a similar framework to decompose the sources of growth of the Brazilian net debt.

Putting together the data was not a straightforward task. It took us several months and many communications with the Central Bank of Brazil's staff to sort and adapt the data to the format needed in the simulations.[4] These data are now available at the Central Bank of Brazil's Web page (*www.bcb.gov.br*).

We now briefly describe the data. We use debt stocks (domestic and foreign, both gross and net) monthly series. These stocks are converted to ratios of GDP using the "valorized" GDP,[5] which we used to compute all ratios. The public sector borrowing requirements (PSBR) were computed to include three different concepts: primary, operational, and nominal. We found that the operational and primary approaches could mitigate the effects of high inflation, since our sample was taken in the immediate aftermath of the *Real* Plan when inflation fell from almost 50 percent in one month. Massive distortions (see figure 5.2a) had crept into the nominal deficit figures right after the *Real* Plan started (July 1, 1994), so we used twelve-month moving averages to provide comparability and control for extreme fluctuations.[6] Even with moving averages, over the entire year the distortionary effects of the hyperinflation were still evident in the nominal deficit figures until mid-1995 (see figure 5.2).

Therefore two other adjustments had to be considered to make the debt statistics compatible with the PSBRs. First, there were the privatization revenues used to reduce the debt but not treated as fiscal revenues in calculating the PSBR. Second, there were the many expenditures incurred from previous contingent liabilities that eventually materialized. These "skeletons" have the (accounting) effect of increasing the debt, but are omitted as fiscal outlays in the PSBR calculations.[7]

The remaining data used were standard. Inflation was measured through the CPI (IPCA) and WPI (IGP-M) indexes. Domestic interest rates were measured by the Selic rate.[8] The country risk was measured through the EMBI and the EMBI + Brazil indexes produced by JP Morgan. Exchange rates are the month-end PTAX.

5.2.2 Decomposition of Debt Shocks

Figure 5.1 shows the rise of the net debt-to-GDP ratio since 1994. A few months after the start of the *Real* Plan, the net debt-to-GDP ratio started to increase almost monotonically from the 30 percent level, reaching levels above 60 percent during the 2002 financial and political crisis and, by September 2003, hovering around 58 percent. This very fast increase is a sign of the fragility of Brazilian macroeconomic indicators. Although some writers contend that the level of the net debt can be high because of investors' collective behavior,[9] the net debt-to-GDP ratio in Brazil was not especially high compared to that of other nations. The total (gross) debt averages 70 percent of GDP for emerging market economies (IMF 2003, p. 116). However, the speed with which it increased (doubled from 30 to 60 percent in eight years), or rather, its "debt velocity," was unambiguously very concerning.

The fiscal condition that generated such tremendous growth in the net debt-to-GDP ratio is displayed in figure 5.2a. The operational and primary deficit measures show the fiscal stance deterioring after the first quarter of 1995. However, no inference about the nominal deficit can be made in the first year of the *Real* Plan because it was still heavily

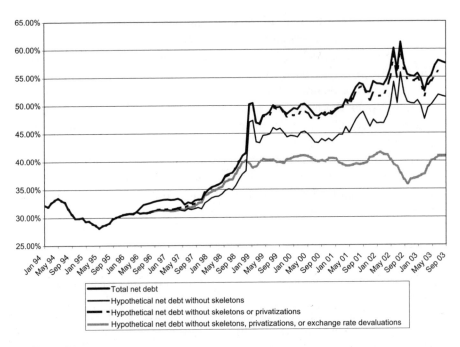

Figure 5.1
Brazilian public net debt as percentage of GDP

influenced by the earlier high inflation rates. It is only after October 1998[10] that the fiscal condition begins to improve.

However bad the period 1995 to 1998 was, the fiscal stance was not solely responsible for the doubling of the net debt-to-GDP ratio. Many other factors influenced the behavior of the debt. Bevilaqua and Garcia (2001), in analyzing the increase in the bonded public debt in the period 1995 to 2000, have pointed to the extremely high interest payments as the main cause of the debt explosion.[11] It has indeed been a matter of great discussion in Brazil how much of the high interest rates were caused by weak fiscal stance. At one corner, the central bank managers during the first term of President Fernando Henrique Cardoso argued that to keep inflation at bay they had to maintain a very high real interest rate given the weak fiscal stance. At the opposite corner, other economists argued that interest rates were kept that high only to maintain the (overvalued) exchange rate. This was based on the notion that during good times (between the Mexican crisis and the Asian crisis, and for a few months between the end of the Asian crisis and the start of the Russian crisis) interest rates were kept above what

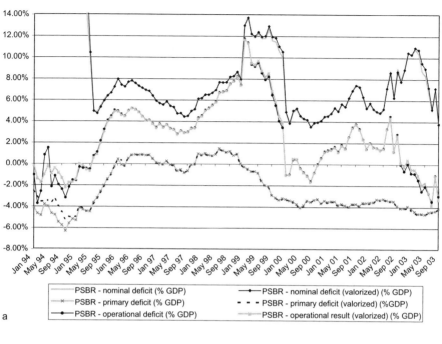

a

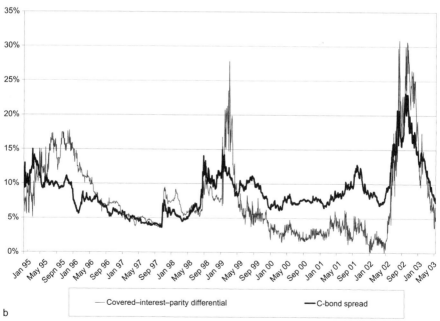

b

Figure 5.2
(a) PSBR nominal, primary, and operational deficits as percentage of GDP; (b) measures
of Brazil risk constructed from domestic and foreign debt

was required by covered interest parity to fight inflation. Figure 5.2b shows the behavior of two measures of country (Brazil) risk, one constructed with external debt yield (C-bond yield minus the yield of the T-bill of equivalent duration) and the other with the domestic one-year interest rate (the covered interest parity differential).[12] In the tranquil period before the floatation of the *real* (January 1999), to avoid the inconsistent trinity, controls on capital inflows were put in place so that the restrictive monetary policy could be undertaken.[13] In bad times, during periods of high risk aversion in international financial markets, interest rates were raised even higher to avoid capital outflows that would crush the exchange rate peg. It is only reasonable to assume that a tougher fiscal policy would have resulted in a smaller real interest rate. Indeed, had the peg ended before 1999, a lower real rate might have been paid in the intervening years. Therefore, in a debt decomposition exercises such as those presented below, one has to bear in mind the stochastic relations between the variables, and these are at the core of the simulation procedures presented in section 5.4.

Besides the high interest payments, the so-called skeletons (contingent liabilities that turned sour) significantly increased the debt. Figure 5.1 gives a hypothetical evolution of the debt-to-GDP ratio had the skeletons *not* existed. Note that the net debt-to-GDP ratio would have fallen by more than 6 percent of GDP. However, if the government had not privatized, the debt would have increased. The net effect of both privatizations and skeletons is negligible, as shown in figure 5.1 by the dashed line representing the "hypothetical net debt without skeletons and privatizations" series.[14]

The effect of the devaluations can be seen in the series "hypothetical net debt without skeletons, privatizations, and exchange-rate devaluations." Again, since this is not a counterfactual exercise, the series has a downward bias. This is because lower interest rates accrued on public bonds denominated or indexed in US dollars (vis-à-vis the nonindexed ones) due to the forecasted devaluation and the currency risk. A flexible exchange rate regime would probably have required higher dollar rates, leading to higher net debt-to-GDP ratios along the counterfactual path. Despite these flaws this series shows that the net debt-to-GDP ratio would hover around 37 percent by August 2003 if skeletons and privatizations were being out of the picture, and the nominal exchange rate remained (*à la chinoise*) at par with the US dollars.

A complete counterfactual exercise can be used to perform the simulation procedure of section 5.4. For example, by hypothesizing a different path for the primary deficit from the structures of correlations estimated by the VAR, one could change the (endogenously determined) interest rates, affecting the debt both directly (through the primary deficit) and indirectly (through the interest payments).[15]

5.3   Risk Management Approach

In this section we evaluate the debt sustainability question from a risk management perspective. Most of the debt sustainability literature concentrates on the debt accumulation equation

$$d_t = (1 + r_t - g_t)d_{t-1} + f_t,$$

where d_t is the debt-to-GDP ratio, r_t is the real interest rate paid, g_t is the growth rate of GDP, and f_t is the primary deficit. The idea behind this equation is to determine the primary deficit or growth rate of GDP that would maintain the debt at certain level. The literature offers insights on the importance and timing of stabilization programs as well as debt restructuring.[16]

We recognize that the variables entering this equation are stochastic, and perhaps, correlated. Furthermore we consider the possibility that there are other external variables (e.g., the exchange rate and inflation rate) that can generate co-movements in the variables entering the debt accumulation equation. In particular, we assume that

$$d_t = (1 + \tilde{r}_t - \tilde{g}_t)d_{t-1} + \tilde{f}_t + \tilde{\varepsilon}_t,$$

$$\{\tilde{r}_t, \tilde{g}_t, \tilde{f}_t, \tilde{\varepsilon}_t, \tilde{s}_t, \tilde{\pi}_t\} \sim N(\vec{\mu}_t, \Sigma_t),$$

where $\tilde{r}_t, \tilde{g}_t, \tilde{f}_t, \tilde{\varepsilon}_t, \tilde{s}_t,$ are $\tilde{\pi}_t$ the stochastic real interest rate, growth rate of GDP, primary deficit, debt shocks (including skeletons $(+)$ and privatizations $(-)$), the real exchange rate, and the inflation rate. We also assume that they are distributed multinomial[17] with conditional mean $\vec{\mu}_t$, and conditional covariance matrix Σ_t.

The risk management approach to debt sustainability is simply the characterization of the evolution of all the relevant stochastic variables and the calculation of the different debt paths. The idea is to estimate the conditional means and variances from the data and simulate the different paths of the debt—from these paths we can compute the probability that the debt will reach some level within some time and thus measure risk accordingly.

The properties of the covariance matrix are important to debt sustainability. For example, in developed economies recessions (lower growth) are usually accompanied by a decrease in the interest rate (expansionary monetary policy). As this occurs, the recession and the deterioration of the primary deficit—which impinge negatively on debt sustainability—come with a reduction in the interest rate—which aids debt sustainability. A *real* depreciation also helps debt sustainability by lowering the real value of the debt vis-à-vis the GDP. There is an automatic stabilizer in the equation. In emerging market economies, a recession can lead to a deterioration of the fiscal accounts, increasing the real interest rate, inducing inflation, and depreciating the exchange rate. If the sovereign debt is in dollars (which is usually the case), then all the variables contribute to making the debt dynamics worse. Therefore, for emerging economies, the risk (covariance) part of debt sustainability is important, and simulations that postulate independent paths for the relevant variables have badly missed this key feature.

5.3.1   Methodology

To compute the debt dynamics, we used the real growth of GDP, the real interest rate, the primary deficit measured as a share of GDP, the skeletons derived from the debt dynamics equation, the real exchange rate computed as the nominal depreciation minus inflation, and the inflation rate. All were monthly data.

To compute the debt shocks, or skeletons, we used actual debt data and realizations of the growth rate and interest rates as follows:

$$\tilde{\varepsilon}_t = d_t - (1 + \tilde{r}_t - \tilde{g}_t)d_{t-1} - \tilde{f}_t.$$

We then obtained a VAR using the macro variables. In general, if a problem arises in using a VAR when the variables are nonstationary but cointegrated, a error correction model is run. However, the data we used were extremely short term, and no standard tests are strong enough to produce definitive results. Since we know that even in near unit root setups VAR's produce consistent estimates (see Rothenberg and Stock 1997), we decided to pursue this alternative. Therefore we used the macrovariables

$$X_t = c + B(L)X_t + v_t,$$

$$X_t \equiv (\tilde{r}_t, \tilde{g}_t, \tilde{f}_t, \tilde{\varepsilon}_t, \tilde{s}_t, \tilde{\pi}_t),$$

$$v_t \sim N(0, \Omega),$$

where v_t are the reduced form residuals distributed multinomially with mean zero and covariance matrix Ω, and $B(L)$ are the coefficients of the lags. We used the Choleski decomposition of the reduced form residuals to generate several paths of the shocks, and we used the coefficients from the VAR to compute the path of the variables in X_t—which can be used to estimate the path of the debt.

With this simple procedure we could proceed to the Monte Carlo simulations to obtain the several paths of debt. This method has several advantages: First, since we are not interested in estimating the contemporaneous causality between the macrovariables, the VAR is used only to produce the best predictor for the joint dynamics of the macrovariables. Although most analyses of monetary policy are applied to computing impulse responses and identifying structural shocks from a reduced form, this was not our objective. We were interested in understanding the dynamics of the macrovariables, so to attempt this we had to consider only the contemporaneous correlation produced by a Choleski decomposition. In fact any Choleski decomposition (meaning any ordering of the variables in the VAR) will yield the same reduced form covariance matrix, and this explains why for risk management applications the ordering is irrelevant.[18]

Second, the procedure can be used to estimate rolling regressions—used to assess the predictive power of the model and perform out-of-sample tests. This way we could compute different debt dynamics for the more recent conditions. We then compared how different exchange rate regimes might affect the debt sustainability by focusing on the correlation structure.

Third, variables and shocks that are not part of the debt accumulation equation can nevertheless impinge on debt dynamics. For this reason, the exchange rate, the terms of trade, and inflation are included as variables in the VAR, and we analyze their impacts on the debt.

Finally, even without certain variables, it is possible to observe their effects by the VAR. For example, even if terms of trade is not included, its impact on the debt dynamic is going to show up as output, inflation, or a real exchange rate depreciation. So the effect of a variable that does not appear in the VAR does not mean that its effect is not felt in the variance-covariance matrix of the reduced form residuals.

5.3.2 Debt Sustainability
In this section we present the results obtained from applying the procedure described previously to the case of Brazil. Choosing the relevant

Table 5.1
Covariance and correlation matrix

	Real interest rate	Real growth rate	Primary deficit	Debt shocks	Real exchange rate deprecia-tion	Nominal inflation (WPI)
Real interest rate	1.9249	0.5218	0.4930	−0.8032	−0.1197	4.4742
Real growth rate	**35.2%**	1.1388	0.3883	−0.1694	2.6442	−2.2608
Primary deficit	**17.8%**	**18.2%**	3.9911	−3.5271	1.6101	−1.9419
Debt shocks	**−25.5%**	**−7.0%**	**−77.7%**	5.1605	−1.6374	−0.8513
Real exchange rate depreciation	**−1.0%**	**28.6%**	**9.3%**	**−8.3%**	74.8589	−14.2580
Nominal inflation (WPI)	**34.8%**	**−22.8%**	**−10.5%**	**−4.0%**	**−17.8%**	86.0028

interest rate is important in the estimation, as is shown later in detail. Further we considered the sensitivity of the results to changes in some of the assumptions.

The variables we included are (1) total net debt, (2) GDP growth computed from the 12-month "valorized" GDP, (3) the real interest rate computed as the Selic rate minus the inflation in the WPI, (4) the primary deficit is the "valorized" deficit divided by the "valorized" GDP, (5) the real exchange rate change computed as the change in the nominal *real*–US dollar exchange rate minus the inflation rate (WPI),[19] and (4) the inflation rate used is the monthly WPI.[20]

So first we computed the skeletons and estimated the VAR using these six variables. Because the point estimates of the VAR are of little interest, they are not shown here; the covariance of the reduced form residuals, on the other hand, deserved special attention.

In table 5.1 we show the covariance matrix of the reduced form residuals on the upper triangular, and in the lower triangular we show the correlations in boldface. Some patterns of correlation are worth noting. First, the primary deficit is positively associated with the real interest rate and the growth rate. These correlations are compatible with the standard Keynesian fiscal multiplier effect. Second, the inflation rate is positively correlated with the real interest rate, and negatively correlated with the growth rate. As we mentioned before, in emerging markets it is common for inflation scares to be recessionary and to increase real interest rates. Further note that the inflation rate is negatively correlated with the real exchange rate but the pass-through is less than one to one given that the correlation is quite small. Third, a real exchange rate depreciation is associated with an increase in the fiscal deficit (the correlation is small but positive) as well as with an increase in growth. Recall that these correlations reflect partial correlations, and therefore in this discussion the real exchange rate depreciation can be assumed to have happened without inflation. In other words, this is a true real exchange rate depreciation and therefore expansionary in terms of output. On the other hand, most of the depreciations we observed in Brazil are accompanied by both the change in the real exchange rate and an increase in the inflation rate. In this case the first movement increases output, while the second one reduces it. The final effect is computed by looking at impulse responses. See section 5.4.4 below.

Before focusing on impulse responses, which are sensitive to the ordering of the variables in the VAR, we study the implications of the correlation structure on the debt. To compute the debt path, we need to determine the initial conditions, meaning the initial primary deficit, interest rate, growth rate, and so on? To simplify the analysis, we used averages of these variables from the previous 9 months. We estimated the same path using only 6 months, and extending to 12 and 24 months. The results are almost unaltered by this assumption—hence we use 9 months to determine the initial conditions and all the data available up to that point to estimate the VAR and the covariance matrix.

In figure 5.3 we show the debt path reflecting the initial conditions computed at the end of September 2003. It was derived with the debt accumulation equation using the inflation rate, interest rate, primary deficit, growth rate of the previous 9 months, and the final debt; the path of future debt due to these variables, which are assumed to remain constant, is shown in figure 5.3. This is the path for the 30 months after September 2003.

Starting from a nearly 60 percent debt, we see the debt to gradually fall to just above 50 percent of GDP 30 months hence. It is possible to conclude from this exercise that the debt in Brazil, given the value of the current macroeconomic variables, is sustainable. However, this can be shown to be the wrong conclusion by the Monte Carlo simulation exercise. The results are projected in figure 5.4 for the paths of debt, maximum and minimum debt, the 95 and 5 percent bands, and the standard deviation of the debt-to-GDP ratio. In the figure the standard

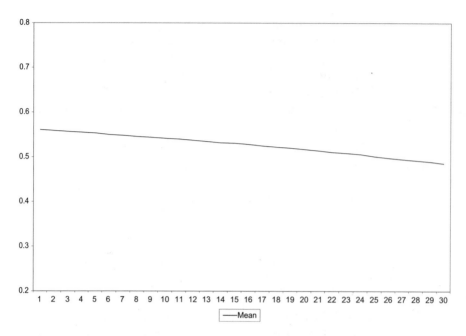

Figure 5.3
Debt sustainability in the absence of risk

deviation of the debt-to-GDP ratio is measured at the right-hand side scale; all other variables are measured at the left hand side.[21]

Several important results can be extracted from figures 5.3 and 5.4. First, it is clear that the debt, on average, is falling, as our standard debt sustainability exercise implied. Second, there is a nontrivial number of realizations in which the debt increases to more than 70 percent—a level of debt that is considered to be extremely large for emerging markets.[22] Recall that the horizon of study is only two and a half years. The debt-to-GDP ratio reaches 80 percent in that period, which represents a very fast accumulation rate, as it starts from less than 60 percent, whereas the means of the stochastic variables is pointing to a debt reduction. Third, the volatility of the debt-to-GDP ratio appears to be increasing through time. The debt-to-GDP ratio has also a variance that is increasing faster than any obtained from a random walk. That is to say, the variance T periods ahead is larger than T times the variance of one period ahead. The variance thus is increasing not only because simulation period is longer but because the covariance matrix is such that the opposite of a diversification effect arises. This is

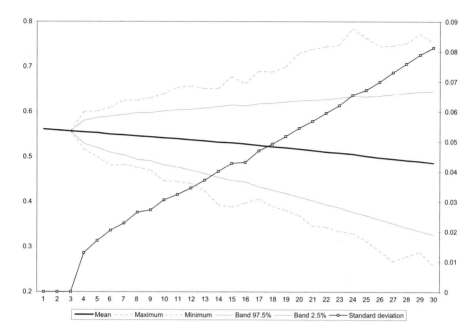

Figure 5.4
Debt sustainability with risk

the opposite of the automatic stabilizer effect that occurs in developed economies, as was mentioned earlier.

In figure 5.5 we present the standard deviation of the debt adjusted by the horizon. The simulations are for the next four years. As can be seen, after one year, the volatility increases more than proportionally to time. This is the result found in several of the simulations; the real interest rate in some of them is larger than the growth rate of output generating an exploding debt path.

5.3.3 Debt Sustainability and Sovereign Spreads

In this section we repeat the exercise of the preceding section for each month, starting in January 2001. The idea is to compute the VAR with the available data up to month t, and then the path of the debt for the next 10 years. Using these paths, we can compute a statistic on the debt: such as the probability that the debt-to-GDP ratio is larger than 75 percent. As we repeat the exercise for month $t + 1$, this rolling exercise will produces a path representing several statistics of the debt.

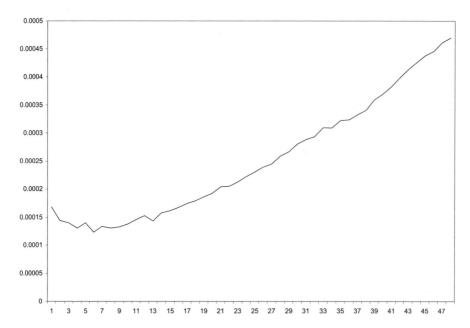

Figure 5.5
Adjusted variance by horizon

In figure 5.6 we give the results for the probabilities of a debt reaching more than 66, 75, 85, 95, and 100 percent of GDP over the next 10 years. Our interpretation is as follows: To obtain the probabilities for June 2002, we use all the data up to May 2002 and estimate the VAR and the covariance matrix of the shocks. We then generate the Monte Carlo simulations (500 replications of 120 months). For each simulated path we compute the debt by way of the debt accumulation equation and the estimates from the VAR. Next we compute the number of times the debt reaches some threshold (e.g., 75 percent of GDP) in any month of the next 10 years. Hence, for June 2002, from the initial conditions at that time and the real interest rate and the covariance matrix estimated until the previous month, we find that the probability of a debt-to-GDP ratio larger than 75 percent is 79 percent, but it has a 59 percent chance of being larger than 100 percent of GDP. So in this time frame it is clear that the debt situation in Brazil suggests a very risky rise in the path of debt, whereas in May or June 2003, the probabilities appear to be much smaller. The exercise performed here is something like a stress test (see figure 5.6).

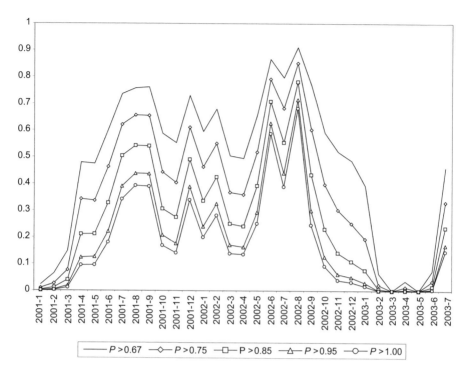

$$\boxed{\ \text{——} \ P>0.67 \quad \text{—◇—} \ P>0.75 \quad \text{—□—} \ P>0.85 \quad \text{—△—} \ P>0.95 \quad \text{—○—} \ P>1.00\ }$$

Figure 5.6
Probability of debt to GDP ratio reaching more than threshold in following ten years

It is worthwhile to mention here that to construct these paths, we used only information from the past. Hence this is an out-of-sample exercise. The objective is to compare one of the paths with the EMBI + Brazil spread, the preferred measure of country risk for Brazil. (The methodology of the Emerging Market Bond Index plus (EMBI+) can be found at the JP Morgan Web site at *http://wwz.jpmorgan.com/ MarketDataInd/EMBI/embi.html*.) Figure 5.7 shows the results.

As can be seen in figure 5.7, the probability and the spread on the EMBI + Brazil are closely related. First, our procedure is out-of-sample in the sense that to compute the probability in month t, we used only information until time $t - 1$, and we compared the probability with the average spread on the EMBI + Brazil on month t.

The correlation between these two series is 54 percent on levels and 33 percent in changes. A simple regression analysis shows that our variable has strong predictive power on the future EMBI + Brazil spreads. A simple AR(2) model produces

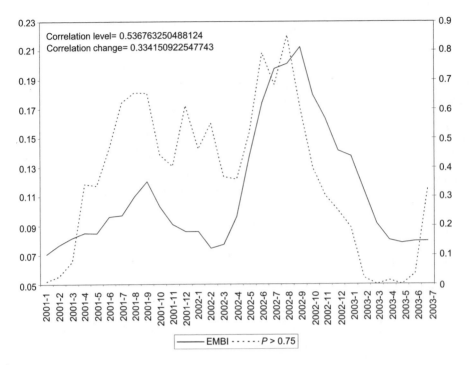

Figure 5.7
Probability of total debt to be larger than 75 percent of GDP at any time in the following
ten years, and the EMBI + Brazil spread

$$\Delta s_t = \underset{1.58}{0.3155}\Delta s_{t-1} + \underset{0.54}{0.0970}\Delta s_{t-2} + \underset{2.14}{0.0354}p_{t-1} + \underset{2.28}{0.0428}p_{t-2},$$

where Δs_t is the change in the EMBI + Brazil spread, and p_t is the probability that the debt reaches some threshold in our Monte Carlo exercises. As can be seen the probabilities are significant—though they
have been computed with data before the month when the change in
the EMBI + Brazil is taking place. The R^2 of the regression is economically important: 56 percent. In fact the AR(2) without the probability
measures has only one of coefficient significant (Δs_{t-1}) and an R^2 of 38
percent. Indeed, the simple F tests show that the p-value of the significance of the lagged changes in the EMBI + Brazil spread is 8.9 percent
(H_0: the coefficients on the two lagged changes in the EMBI + Brazil
spread are zero), and 2.2 percent for the probabilities lags (H_0: the coefficients on the two lagged probabilities are zero).

As these results suggest, our methodology captures the bulk of market perception of the default risk in the Brazilian sovereign debt, and

such risk measure is largely correlated with the Brazilian risk spread. We therefore believe that these probabilities constitute an alternative, and very effective, method for assessing debt sustainability.

5.3.4 Impulse Responses

One of the advantages of our procedure for evaluating the path of the debt is that we do not have to commit to a particular structural model or distribution of residuals. This is practical in countries such as Brazil where the standard triangular assumption imposed in a monetary economy is rarely satisfied. It is rarely the case when decisions of monetary policy in a certain month do not affect prices, output, and exchange rates contemporaneously.

We showed by the previous analysis how, by concentrating on the contemporaneous covariance of the residuals, we could study the path of debt for a *typical* mixture of shocks that have hit the Brazilian economy. The only property imposed was that they had to satisfy the covariance matrix computed in the sample.

However, looking at a mixture of shocks does not always provide the best description. For example, questions such as what is the impact of a depreciation of the exchange rate on the path of the debt cannot be answered. In this section we will introduce a triangular decomposition of the reduced form shocks, though we believe that it can be a poor description of what really takes place in the Brazilian economy. This exercise should provide some further intuition about the behavior of debt, though it remains subject to the critique that the outcome depends crucially on the identification assumptions. This is an important limitation, but unfortunately, it is the best we can do with the available data.

In particular, we assume that the ordering of the equations is as follows: real interest rate, GDP growth rate, primary fiscal deficit, skeletons, real exchange rate, and inflation. This order implies that inflation affects all the variables contemporaneously, while the real interest rate only acts with a lag.

In figures 5.8 to 5.13 we present the impulse responses of all the shocks plus the implied debt accumulation. The impulse response of each of the shocks is computed using the Choleski decomposition and the estimates from the VAR. The impulse response of the debt accumulation is calculated using the response of each of the shocks, the initial conditions at the end of the sample, and the debt accumulation equation.

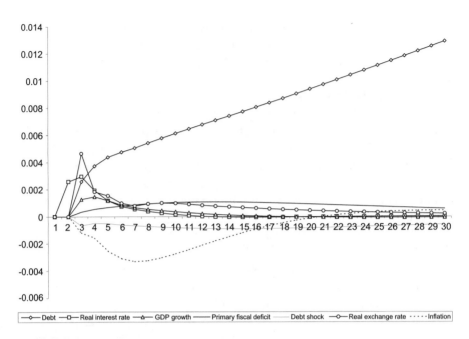

Figure 5.8
Impulse response to an increase in the interest rate

In figure 5.8 the impulse response to a one standard deviation increase in the real interest rate is depicted. As can be seen, the increase
in the real interest rate is persistent, and it lasts around 10 months.
Notice that the increase in the real interest rate depreciates the real exchange rate and reduces the inflation rate. It has a small impact on the
growth rate and the primary deficit. The net effect on the debt path is
that an increase in the real interest rate increases the debt-to-GDP ratio,
and according to our simulation and the given initial conditions, the
debt keeps on growing for a long period of time even after the variables have returned to steady state.

In figure 5.9 the impulse response to a one standard deviation
increase on the growth rate of output is depicted. As can be seen, the
increase in the growth rate is associated with a contemporaneous increase in the real interest rate but subsequent reductions—a reduction
in inflation rate and a small real exchange rate appreciation.

In the end the path of the debt reflects a permanent improvement.
Notice that when the variables are close to the steady state, the debt
is almost constant at a lower level. One surprising result, at least to us,

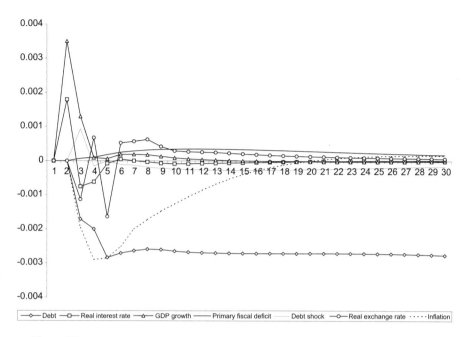

Figure 5.9
Impulse response to an increase in the growth rate of monthly output

is that the primary deficit is almost unaffected by the output increase. It is possible that this is the result of the bad identification, but also it could reflect that in the sample output increases are associated with expansionary fiscal policy.

Figure 5.10 shows the impulse response after an increase in the primary deficit. In this case the increase in the primary deficit is associated with a depreciation of the real exchange rate, an increase in the inflation rate, an increase in the interest rate, and a transitory increase in the growth rate. The shock and the first three reactions should cause the debt-to-GDP ratio to deteriorate, but the increase in growth should improve it. In the end our simulations show that the negative effects outweigh the positive effects as the debt-to-GDP ratio increases. In comparison to the previous two shocks, the innovations to the primary deficit have the largest impact.

These three impulse responses confirm our intuition about the impact of these shocks on the path of Brazilian debt. We can expect that increases in the real interest rate and deteriorations of the primary deficit will increase the debt, while increases in the growth rate will improve

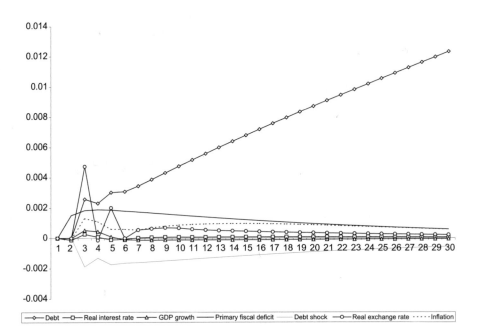

Figure 5.10
Impulse response to an increase in the primary deficit

it. It is not appropriate to judge the identification of shocks by their impulse responses, but at least the results are not contradicting it.

In figure 5.11 we study the impact of an increase in skeletons. Our simulations show that there is a transitory rise in the debt-to-GDP ratio followed by a decline. This impulse response is hard to reconcile by intuition, as among the responses this is the most inconsistent one.

In figure 5.12 we show the impulse response to a real exchange rate depreciation. Before we draw any conclusions, recall that from our identification assumption this is a very odd form of depreciation. This is an exchange rate depreciation that is not accompanied by an increase in the inflation rate. In other words, this is a true real exchange rate depreciation. Increases in inflation rate, which can also cause a depreciation of the real exchange rate, form the next shock. We can think of this shock as the good part of the depreciation, and the next shock as the bad part.

Notice that in accord with our "good" depreciation interpretation, an increase in the real exchange rate is accompanied by an increase in the growth rate, a moderate increase in the interest rate (smaller than

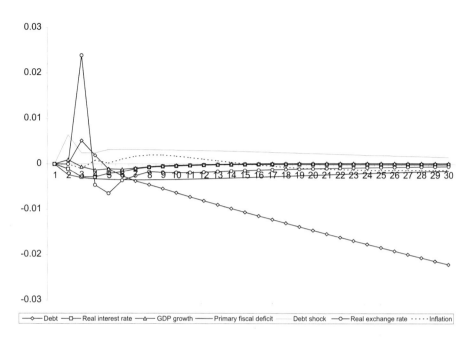

Figure 5.11
Impulse response to an increase in the skeletons

the growth rate), and a large improvement in the primary deficit. This is precisely the outcome of a real depreciation rate that is expansionary. Because the increase in the growth rate is higher than the increase in the real interest rate in the end the debt-to-GDP ratio improves permanently.

The final exercise is shown in figure 5.13. In it we study the impulse response to an increase in the inflation rate. From the identification assumption it is possible to interpret this shock as a nominal shock that depreciates the exchange rate and increases the inflation rate at the same time. Indeed, in the impulse response it can be seen that the increase in inflation depreciates the real exchange rate significantly. Further the real interest rate increases on impact while the growth rate declines, and the primary deficit deteriorates. The movements of all these variables point to a clear increase in the debt-to-GDP ratio, which is what takes place.

Comparing the previous impulse responses to the increase in the primary deficit and the increase in the inflation rate are the two most important exercises—quantitatively speaking. However, the results

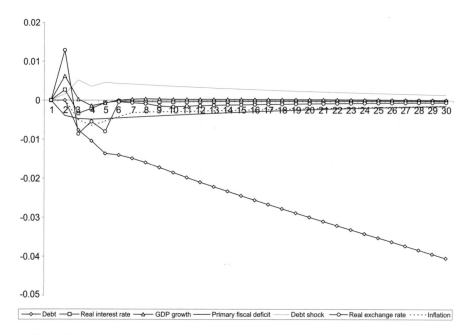

Figure 5.12
Impulse response to an increase in the real exchange rate (depreciation)

depend—crucially—on the identification assumptions, which are not
likely to be evident in the data. With this caveat in mind, we suggest
the value of these exercises to be as follows: First, the co-movements
observed in the variables of interest and the debt dynamics are close
to what we intuited,[23] which is reassuring. Second, the magnitudes
involved show that the debt-to-GDP ratio is most sensitive to innovations to the primary deficit and the inflation rate; here we interpreted
the innovations of the inflation rate to be nominal shocks or "bad"
exchange rate depreciations.

5.4   Conclusions

In this chapter we proposed a risk-based measure to assess debt sustainability. Our main insight, which led to this measure, was that debt
in emerging market economies is quite risky. An increasingly larger
number of models and body of empirical evidence show that emerging
market economies lack the natural stabilizing features that make countercyclical policies effective. For example, during a recession, real inter-

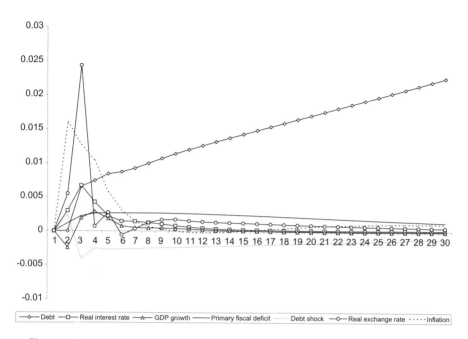

Figure 5.13
Impulse response to an increase in the inflation rate

est rates tend to fall in developed economies, which makes room for larger primary expenditures given the reduction in interest payments. In emerging market economies, often the reverse happens: real interest rate rises, government revenues fall, and government outlays increase, thereby negatively leveraging the debt impact.

The proposed measure was constructed from a framework that combines a statistical model to uncover the stochastic relations among the variables that directly or indirectly influence debt accumulation with a simulation engine that computes future paths for the debt-to-GDP ratios. The Monte Carlo simulations allowed us to compute "risk probabilities," namely probabilities that the simulated debt-to-GDP ratio exceeds a given threshold deemed risky (e.g., 75 percent of GDP). The time series of such probabilities was then used to investigate whether or not it is correlated with the market risk assessment, measured by the spread on sovereign dollar-denominated debt.

The application of our methodology to Brazil showed that although debt is sustainable in the absence of risk, there are many paths in which it is clearly unsustainable. Although, on average, the

Brazilian debt is sustainable, the correlation structure under which the Brazilian economy operates poses a huge question mark on its debt sustainability.

We also showed that properties of the debt dynamics are closely related to the EMBI + Brazil spread. This is a remarkable result, because our methodology used out-of-sample simulations, and not regressors related to the risk aversion of international investors, as the high-yield spread in the United States, which are deemed very important in the determination of the EMBI + spread. Thus our measures constitute an alternative, and very effective, method to assess debt sustainability.

Notes

1. See IMF (2003, p. 124) for references.

2. Garcia (2002) computes a VaR for the Brazilian debt and performs Monte Carlo simulations to implement a CFaR (cash-flow at risk).

3. For a financial institution, this probability would be analogous to the probability of wiping out the net worth.

4. Box 3.1 (Data on Public Debt in Emerging Market Economies) of the last *World Economic Outlook* (IMF 2003) describes the many difficulties involved in gathering such data.

5. Valorized GDP is a better measure than nominal GDP because, even under moderate inflation, the simple addition of the GDP flow within a 12-month period distorts the statistic. For example, for a 10 percent yearly inflation, each unit of domestic currency of the last month will be worth 1.1 units of domestic currency of the first month included in the sample. The valorization procedure mitigates this distortion. Under zero inflation, the valorization procedure reverts to usual addition of monthly GDP flows. Box 3.1 of the *World Economic Outlook* (IMF 2003) comments on the effects of such procedure, grossly exaggerating them.

6. Since the deficits are so important to determine debt sustainability, we opted to use 12-month-moving averages instead of monthly figures. This is because the latter series is very volatile, often changing signs. For example, if some expenses were concentrated in a given month, the monthly series would show a large deficit among many surpluses, while the moving average would better reflect the fiscal stance.

7. Other minor adjustments have to be performed in order to make the debts statistics compatible with the PSBR's, as explained in Bevilaqua and Garcia (2001).

8. The equivalent of the US Fed-fund rate.

9. For the "debt intolerance" phenomenon, see Reinhart, Rogoff, and Savastano (2003) and IMF (2003).

10. Although correlation does not imply causation, the change in the fiscal stance was simultaneous to the agreement with the IMF.

11. Here we use the primary deficit as a measure of the fiscal stance, according to the usual practice of successful stabilization programs (see Missale, Giavazzi, and Benigno

2000). This is because the nominal (and, in lesser measure, real) interest payments are determined by many factors and may hinder the actual changes in the fiscal stance.

12. There are many differences between the domestic and the external bond whose yields are used to compute the two-country risk measures, among them the much longer duration of the C-bond. Nevertheless, the regularity pointed out is valid. For an explanation, see Garcia and Didier (2003).

13. A description and an evaluation of the effectiveness of the capital controls on inflows is presented in Garcia and Valpassos (2000). See also Cardoso and Goldfajn (1998).

14. Here we perform an accounting exercise, not a counterfactual one. For a counterfactual exercise, see Goldfajn and Guardia (2003).

15. We plan to perform such a full counterfactual exercise in a future work.

16. For a review of the possible criteria to determine debt sustainability, see chapter 3 of the September 2003 *World Economic Outlook* (IMF 2003).

17. We can assume that the variables are normally distributed, though some cannot be negative. This is a simplification that can be easily corrected in the Monte Carlo simulations. Here it is made mainly for expositional purposes.

18. The intuition is that the covariance matrix of the reduced form can have several triangular factorizations, which in VAR language means they have different orderings. There are as many triangular factorizations as the factorial of the number of variables (or columns of the matrix) that correspond to the number of different permutations of the variables. Each factorization recovers, by definition, the original matrix but implies different Choleski decompositions.

19. Since the US inflation has very low variance in the sample, we exclude it from the real exchange rate calculation. In our framework the constant term in the regression takes care of the effect of the US inflation on the real exchange rate.

20. We also computed the model using the CPI, but no difference from the main message was found.

21. The shocks are zero in the first two periods because the VAR was estimated using two lags.

22. See Reinhart, Rogoff, and Savastano (2003).

23. We are excluding the skeletons here.

References

Bevilaqua, A., and M. Garcia. 2002. Debt management in Brazil: Evaluation of the real plan and challenges ahead. *International Journal of Finance and Economics* 7(1): 15–35.

Cardoso, E., and I. Goldfajn. 1988. Capital flows to Brazil: The endogeneity of capital controls. *IMF Staff Papers* 45(1): 161–202.

Garcia, M. 2002. Public debt management, monetary policy and financial institutions. PUC-Rio Working Paper.

Garcia, M., and T. Didier. 2003. Very high rates and the cousin risks: Brazil during the real plan. In J. González et al., eds., *Latin American Macroeconomic Reforms: The Second Stage*. Chicago: University of Chicago Press.

Garcia, M., and M. Valpassos. 2000. Capital flows, capital controls and currency crises: The case of Brazil in the nineties. In F. Larrain, ed., *Capital Flows, Capital Controls, and Currency Crises: Latin American in the 1990s*. Ann Arbor: University of Michigan Press.

Goldfajn, I., and E. Guardia. 2004. Fiscal rules and debt sustainability in Brazil. In G. Kopits, ed., *Rules-Based Fiscal Policy in Emerging Markets*. Palgrave Macmillan.

International Monetary Fund. 2003. *World Economic Outlook*. Washington: International Monetary Fund.

Missale, A., F. Giavazzi, and P. Benigno. 2002. How is debt managed: Learning from fiscal stabilization. *Scandinavian Journal of Economics* 104(3): 443–69.

Reinhart, C., K. Rogoff, and M. Savastano. 2003. Debt intolerance, *Brookings Papers on Economic Activity* 0(1): 1–62.

Rothemberg, T., and J. Stock. 1997. Inference in a nearly integrated autoregressive model with nonnormal innovations. *Journal of Econometrics* 80(2): 269–86.

Comment on Chapter 5

Ilan Goldfajn

Marcio Garcia and Roberto Rigobon's study goes beyond the usual debt sustainability analysis where one asks what are the conditions (primary surplus, real interest rate, and GDP growth) for debt to stabilize at current levels. They study the question of debt sustainability under risk. They use a VAR approach to gauge the correlations between the variables and then analyze the stochastic properties of the debt dynamics. For example, when a real exchange rate depreciation is associated with an increase in the fiscal deficit, and the debt is partially dollarized, the debt is viewed as more risky, since there is a lack of a stabilizing feature. This framework allows them to find that in Brazil where the debt appears to be sustainable in the absence of risk, there are paths at which the debt is not sustainable.

In the process of constructing this risky measure of debt sustainability, interesting correlations emerge. Let me point them out:

1. *Primary deficit is positively associated with the real interest rate and the growth rate.* This is compatible with the standard Keynesian fiscal multiplier effects.

2. *Inflation rate is positively correlated with the real interest rate, and negatively correlated with the growth rate.*

In Brazil lately inflation bouts have been often accompanied by recessions. Supply shocks have dominated, sometimes as a result of exchange rate depreciations from balance of payments problems (e.g., sudden stops), and wages and consumption have fallen as a result. The latter correlation is problematic because it introduces an unstable component to the debt dynamics.

3. *Inflation rate is negatively correlated with the real exchange rate.* The pass-through coefficient is less than one and the correlation is quite small.

4. *Real exchange rate depreciation is associated with an increase in the fiscal deficit and growth.*

The authors' finding that debt in Brazil is "mean-sustainable" is consistent with previous studies. Brazil has made an important swing in its fiscal accounts in the last few years. The primary fiscal surplus, which includes total revenues and expenditures but excludes interest payments, increased from around balance in the period 1995 to 1998 to 4.3 percent in 2003. The nominal deficit, or public sector borrowing requirement (PSBR), which includes all revenues and expenditures as well as interest rate payments, improved to 3 and 4 percent in 2004 from around 7 percent of GDP in 1995.

Notwithstanding this fiscal effort, public debt-to-GDP ratio has continued to increase. There are good and bad reasons for such outcome. On the good side, there are the increased transparency and debt recognition—the so-called skeletons. Also the required adjustment in the real exchange rate, in the last three years, to improve the external accounts, influenced significantly the rise in the debt ratio. Importantly these factors have been nonrecurrent because of the adjustment to the real exchange rate (the real exchange rate is no longer overvalued) and a large share of skeletons now recognized.

Of the less commendable reasons for the increase in the debt-to-GDP ratio is the following: It was only after 1998 that Brazil started producing significant and consistent primary surpluses. If the current policy had been applied in the period 1995 to 1998, and other factors maintained, the debt–GDP ratio would have shown a stabilizing path, reaching 31 percent of GDP in 2002. The favorable dynamics allows a considerable decline in the debt ratio over that period, and in such a virtuous context, one could expect lower interest rates. Under the same

Table 5.2
Primary surplus required to stabilize debt–GDP ratio

GDP growth	Real interest rates				
	6	8	9	10	12
1.5	2.5	3.2	3.6	4.0	4.8
2.5	2.0	2.7	3.0	3.4	4.2
3.5	1.4	2.1	2.4	2.8	3.6
4.5	0.9	1.6	1.8	2.3	3.1
5.5	0.4	1.1	1.3	1.8	2.5

fiscal policy and a reduction of 5 percent in the basic interest rates in the period 1995 to 1998, the outcome would have been a steeper decline of the debt ratio. The debt–GDP ratio would have reached 27 percent in December 2002, a reduction of 3 percent of GDP compared to the 1995 level.

What about the future? Has the current fiscal adjustment sufficient to stabilize the debt-to-GDP ratio? Table 5.2 provides a first-pass answer. Under reasonable assumptions the debt to GDP ratio should decline in the following years, provided that the current primary surplus of around 4.25 percent of GDP is sustained. Only it is in the case where both real interest rates are above 12 percent and growth below 1.5 percent in the long run that the debt is not sustainable. This means that the essential ingredient for debt sustainability is to maintain the primary surplus over the years.

The table also shows that if bad realizations of the main variables occur debt dynamics could be perverse. Garcia and Rigobon compute "risk probabilities," namely probabilities that the simulated debt-to-GDP ratio exceeds a given threshold deemed risky (75 percent of GDP) using Monte Carlo simulations. They show that this probability reached 80 percent in mid-2002.

They find that their risk probability is strongly correlated to the EMBI + Brazil spread and conclude that their method is "an alternative, and very effective, method to assess debt sustainability." I am less convinced by this correlation. The correlation is driven by the fact that both had peaks in 2002: their risk measure as a result of the jump in debt-to-GDP ratio in 2002 and the EMBI as a result of both a widening of international yields and an increase in risk perception regarding future policies in Brazil. I wonder what is the correlation once this "outlier" is removed.

Finally, in the simulations it is interesting to note that the volatility of the debt-to-GDP ratio is increasing through time, not only because simulation period is longer but because the covariance matrix is such that the outcome is unstable. This is, in my opinion, the main contribution of chapter 5. But why is it in Brazil that the dynamics can take a bad turn? One answer is certainly that the debt composition in Brazil is still composed by dollar-linked and short-term interest rate indexed debt. I believe that other answers can be found in several other chapters of this volume.

6

Institutions for Debt Sustainability in Brazil

Charles Wyplosz

6.1 Introduction

Even before President Lula da Silva was elected and took office, Brazil was in crisis. The prospect of his election had triggered a vicious cycle that ran a depressed currency and high interest rates to a burgeoning debt service that threatened to drain the budget, further increase debt, and lead to high-risk premia. Strangely, an assortment of commitments by the outgoing Cardoso administration, and encased in the Fiscal Responsibility Law, had delivered a budget surplus, and the candidate Lula had pledged to uphold these commitments. However, the pledge was not credible, and markets remained skeptical even after Lula assumed office, although he reiterated his commitment to a very conservative policy mix and to its monitoring by the IMF.

For most of its first year in office the Lula administration's main challenge was to bring down the real interest rate. This meant reassuring the financial markets, which required a tight fiscal policy and a high real interest rate. The real interest rate of 10 percent and more, coupled with the restrictive fiscal policy, had severely limited the economy's ability to grow.

One key lesson from the events in the early days of the Lula government is that a large primary surplus is not sufficient to reassure financial markets that fiscal discipline will be enforced regardless of political changes. This is a point forcefully made by Goldstein (2003). Despite a reassuring outlook based on reasonable assumptions presented by Goldfajn (2002) and Goldfajn and Refinetti (2003), the market's view had been that moderately pessimistic assumptions—within the horizon of a decade—can derail a safe-looking median scenario. The reason is that sizable slippages in the risk premium, always a distinct possibility, can quickly undermine debt sustainability and significantly worsen the policy trade-offs. If the authorities then waver, as markets presumed Lula would do, the dark scenario unfolds and the markets' skepticism is vindicated ex post, a classic example of multiple equilibria.[1] In the end, as we now know, the Lula administration and the Central Bank of Brazil stood firm and interest rates have now started to decline, but 2003 was a lost year of no growth. The price of this vicious circle was high, both economically and politically.

The only way to thwart this vicious circle is to provide an iron-clad guarantee that the public debt will remain under control in the medium to long run. Such a guarantee, if possible, would make shorter-term budgetary slippages acceptable. To that effect it must be possible to unambiguously relate any slippage to either a high interest rate or to a temporary growth shortfall, ruling out true indiscipline. In Brazil, fiscal discipline rests on the Fiscal Responsibility Law (FRL) and a public commitment to achieve a 4.25 percent primary surplus. In the next section, I review the main relevant features of the FRL. In section 6.3, I argue that the FRL is a major progress toward debt sustainability but that it lacks a number of features that the financial markets are likely to consider essential. In section 6.4, I go back to basics and propose five necessary conditions for establishing credible debts sustainability. In section 6.5, I examine how a fiscal policy rule might look, ask whether the OECD countries can be described as following such a rule, and consider what the rule would mean for Brazil. In section 6.6, I explore a new approach that would delegate the task of setting the primary surplus to an independent fiscal authority. In section 6.7, I provide some concluding observations.

6.2   The Fiscal Responsibility Law

Adopted in 2000, the FRL represents a major step toward debt sustainability as well as fiscal transparency. Building on contracts signed in 1997 and 2000 as part of a massive federal bailout of state and municipal debts, it brings all budgets, from the federal down to the municipality level, under common requirements. The FRL relies on five main measures:

• A limit on personnel expenditures set by the Senate as a percentage of tax revenues, shown in table 6.1. The law actually includes a breakdown for each authority at each level (judiciary, executive, legislative).

Table 6.1
Overall limits on personnel expenditures

Level	Percentage of revenues
Federal	50
State	60
Municipality	60

Table 6.2
State and municipal debt limits (2001)

Level	Percentage of revenues
Federal	NA
State	200
Municipality	120

• A limit on debts, also set as a percentage of tax revenues. The limits are set at the federal level by the Senate, following a budget proposal from the president. The limits can be changed by the Senate upon request by the federal government in times of economic instability. In 2001 the Senate also set limits for states and municipalities, as indicated in table 6.2. These limits were to be reached within 15 years, during which time any preexisting excess is to be eliminated by every January 15. For states and municipalities that start below the ceiling but breach through it, the Senate resolution called for a correction within one year. Due to the turmoil that occurred in 2002, the Senate has not yet adopted debt ceilings for the federal government, although the current proposal is 350 percent.

• A Budget Guidelines Law (*Lei de Diretrizes Orçamentárias*, LDO). Strengthening the LDO, the FRL mandates that fiscal goals regarding both expenditures and revenues be set for the next three years for all three levels of government, based on explicit macroeconomic projections and including some contrasted scenarios.

• Election year provisions. These provisions prevent borrowing that anticipate future revenues, they mandate that expenditures be carried on only if the corresponding revenues are available in the current year, and they forbid any new hiring during the 180 days preceding the election.

• New transfers among the different levels of governments are prohibited. This concerns both cash transfers and the refinancing of debts. Thus the only transfers that are legal are those planned in the normal budgetary procedures, and emergency support is prohibited. Given the history of recurrent bailouts, this was meant to eliminate the moral hazard of subnational debt accumulations.

The FRL also includes detailed specifications on bookkeeping, generally bringing to public accounts the transparency of international standards. It also includes a list of sanctions to be effected when the law is breached.

If fully applied, the FRL can meet a number of essential goals. It provides for integrity at all levels of public accounts, it limits the drift to overhiring, it prevents the use of budgets for electoral purposes, and it rules out the bailouts of one level of government by the other levels.

6.3 Fiscal Policy and Debt Sustainability

6.3.1 Limits of the Current Setup

While the FRL measures provide for the proper conduct of fiscal policy in a federal system, they stop short of a full guarantee of debt sustainability. The triennial planning of expenditures and revenues is not binding and therefore unlikely to carry much weight in the actual design of annual budgets. The FRL approach to debt sustainability rests on ceilings set by the Senate, but these ceilings are uniform across states and municipalities. They ignore both different initial conditions and possibly differing intertemporal needs, which is likely to eventually generate controversies. Last, but not least, there is no indication that the Senate will always consider debt sustainability as an overriding objective.

This is perhaps why, since 1998, the federal government undertook to commit itself to a pre-announced primary budget balance. The record so far has been good, and the Lula's administration early decision to increase the balance for 2003 indicates that this procedure is taken seriously. Since the authorities have no control on the interest rate and since the debt is largely indexed (18.4 percent to the exchange rate, 56.1 percent the Selic interest rate, 11.4 percent to price indexes), the debt service component of the budget primary budget is beyond control. Focusing on the primary budget therefore is the only logical possibility. Yet the overall budget, and hence the evolution of the public debt, remains vulnerable to changes in the interest and exchange rates that can significantly raise the debt local currency valuation.

In addition the mandated efforts at strengthening fiscal discipline have contributed to making the budget procyclical. This is clearly the case of the FRL rule that sets spending on personnel as a proportion of tax revenues. This is also the case of the primary budget commitment. By setting the budget ahead of time, the government risks boxing itself into an impossible situation in the event of a slowdown that erodes revenues: either the objective is upheld and the only solution is to raise taxes or cut spending, or a new lower target must be officially announced, which sends the wrong signal in terms of debt sustainability. One solution is, of course, to tighten fiscal policy while relaxing monetary policy, leaving it to the central bank to bear the credibility cost. The reason the central bank is better able to withstand such a policy change is that it has already accumulated credibility, and its credibility can be enhanced as it is granted operational independence. While this might be the least bad move under current institutions, trading off the credibility of one branch of government against the credibility of another branch is not an optimal solution.

6.3.2 How to Guarantee Debt Sustainability?

Debt sustainability is understood to be an intertemporal, forward-looking property. The simulations presented in Goldfajn (2002) illustrate how it can be assessed by making assumptions on a large set of plausible outcomes extending several years into the future. For reassurances that this logic provides a debt-to-GDP ratio that will decline over a long horizon, the debt path must be stress-tested, and corrective measures must be available in the event of a succession of adverse outcomes. But a fiscal rule cannot be comprehensive, there are just too many possible contingencies. The best efforts at planning for all sorts of adverse situations are bound to fall short of exhaustivity. In the end, credibility is compromised.

Today, with the FRL in place, the uncertainty regarding public spending or taxation at all levels of government is significantly reduced. The main remaining source of budgetary uncertainty is the economy's growth rate, which affects tax revenues and the nonprimary part of the budget (i.e., the size of the indexed debt and the rate of interest). Goldstein (2003) makes a strong case for the interest rate premium and debt valuation operating in a vicious cycle that can quickly enlarge the overall deficit even under the most conservative primary budget assumptions. The solution is to lengthen the debt maturity and to remove indexation.[2] However, such policy is only possible once credibility is achieved, which means until after debt sustainability is established.

Credible procedures that establish debt sustainability under adverse scenarios are in fact badly needed. Tightening up fiscal policy is definitely not the solution, for two related reasons. First, in the presence of adverse shocks, which both reduce growth and erode the budget, procyclical fiscal policy is not desirable. Second, tightening fiscal policy in a recession is politically expensive, hence a concern for markets. The theoretical literature has amply demonstrated the potential for self-fulfilling crises under such a scenario, and supports the result empirical examples from both developed and developing countries.

Although a procyclical fiscal policy is not the solution, counter-cyclical policies should not be allowed to become part of the problem either. Any worsening of the primary budget balance must be credibly seen as temporary. The authorities must be able to make the case that the worsening is entirely due to the prevailing economic conditions, namely that it is not a signal of a relaxation of budgetary discipline.

The point is that fiscal policy should combine some short-term flexibility with a long-term commitment to debt sustainability. This is a tall order but not necessarily an impossible one. Inflation-targeting central banks routinely face a similar challenge: they promise—and, nowadays, generally deliver—long-term price stability while attending to shorter term considerations such as employment and growth or asset price instability. As a result they can tolerate some temporary departure of inflation from its target level without incurring credibility losses.

Fiscal policy thus requires establishing a reputation. Reputations take time to establish—an option not open to Brazil at this critical junction. Recent improvements in market sentiments indicate some market responsiveness, but still a limited one in view of the prevailing interest rates. The opportunity exists to strengthen the debt sustainability institutions, as at this historic time they can quickly deliver deep relief.

6.4   Necessary Conditions for Credible Debt Sustainability

The difficulty with the debt sustainability objective is that it can only be achieved, and verified, over time, in fact over a very long period that extends over several years. Brazil cannot afford to wait for years until the FRL proves its mettle, if it ever does. The FRL needs to be completed to provide the fickle marketplace with assurance that Brazil's fiscal policy is firmly anchored to debt sustainability. In this section I explore the principles that can deliver such a guarantee and argue that they call for an adequate institutional arrangement. I outline some necessary, but not sufficient conditions. The institution must be backed by strong legislation. It must be unambiguously committed to the objective of debt sustainability. At the same time it must be able to cope with unexpected shocks in a way that preserves the political support without which any institution is fragile and therefore unlikely to establish immediate credibility.

6.4.1 Defining Debt Sustainability

Theory unambiguously establishes that the government budget constraint, and therefore debt sustainability, is an intertemporal condition that ties present and future budget balances to inherited debt. In this long-term perspective, annual budget balances are largely irrelevant provided that the whole path is anchored to the sustainability objective. This is why the LDO, which focuses on annual primary budget objectives, is not helpful. The LDO puts considerable emphasis on a particular realization of the budget that, in the true sense of debt sustainability, has a minor effect. The rule makes the setting and achievement of an annual target a litmus test of the ability and willingness of the authorities to abide by the budget constraint. In doing so, it artificially faults temporary deviations from the target, thereby detracting from equally important considerations, in particular, the countercyclical behavior of fiscal policy.

A better approach is to fully apply the logic of the intertemporal budget constraint, which treats debt sustainability as a long-term debt-to-GDP objective.[3] The operational solution is to define sustainability as a long-term debt-to-GDP target, and to be clear about the long term.

There is no optimal debt level. Leaving aside theoretical niceties,[4] a simple rule for the debt is: The lower, the better. However, initial conditions matter. They call for judgment as to whether the current debt level is acceptable and, if it is not, what is the desirable objective. This then requires an additional judgment on how quickly to bring down the debt level to its target level. Many considerations enter these judgments: the likely long-term growth performance, the demographic evolution, the usual length of business cycles, borrowing costs, the need to provide public goods and infrastructure, and so on. An important factor is that fast convergence to low target can be costly in terms of growth and the achievement of economic and social objectives. The trade-off is thus between the speed at which the vulnerability to vicious circles is reduced and the ability to smooth business cycles. There is no clear optimal response; the final decision has to be political as it will affect the general economy and concern transfers between generations. What is critical that the trade-off must be made explicit when the decision is taken.

The length of the target horizon must encompass a completed business cycle. Shorter horizons run the risk of missing the target because of temporary adverse conditions around the terminal date. The difficulty is that business cycles are of variable lengths and yet the target horizon must be set ex ante, long before conditions at the terminal point can be foreseen. So this is a conundrum with no perfect solution. One possibility is to set the terminal year after the current cycle is completed. This would be when the economy returns to a position—measured by the output gap, for instance—similar to that prevailing as the target was being set. Because it imparts quite a lot of ex ante uncertainty, this solution cannot deliver the quick benefits that Brazil needs. Another possibility is to aim at a horizon that exceeds the typical business cycle frequency and define the debt target as an average over the corresponding period. A third solution is to set rolling targets and horizons with margin errors. For example a debt target set for 2005 could be achieved in 2007, say, 40 to 45 percent of GDP, and periodically updated in 2006 for 2008, and so on. This is what inflation-targeting central banks do in using inflation targets. They occasionally do miss their targets but are able to explain why, as the Central Bank of Brazil did in 2003. Frequently missed debt targets are likely to be tolerated as long as a large portion of the debt is indexed. Thus lengthening the horizon can alleviate this problem.

6.4.2   Budget Structure, the Intertemporal Constraint, and Political Control

The budget structure—detailing public expenditures and taxes—is largely irrelevant for sustainability and macroeconomic stabilization. The structure is crucial for the achievement of general policy objectives, including equity, poverty alleviation, the provision of public goods, and so on, but what matters for debt sustainability and macroeconomic stabilization is the primary budget balance, the net of total spending and revenues.[5] Put differently, what is needed for fiscal discipline and debt sustainability is a credible promise to abide by the budget constraint, independently of the sources of revenue and of the way spending is utilized to achieve general economic and social objectives.

This distinction is crucial to understand the political aspects of debt sustainability restraints. The view that the budget is a prerogative shared by the government and the parliament or congress is deeply rooted in the design of democratic regimes, as it should be. Yet, regardless of this fundamental sovereignty, any budget remains subject to one limit, the intertemporal constraint. Debts become unsustainable when the policy makers reject this constraint. Put differently, debt sustainability is not something that sovereign governments can dispense with. Several have tried, and many will try, only to discover that they cannot once they face a crisis situation. What this means is that imposing a debt sustainability constraint is not an infringement on national sovereignty. This observation applies to arrangements that provide for debt sustainability because they must somehow limit the freedom to design fiscal policy. The executive and legislative authorities must give up something, simply the consequence of the unavoidable necessity to respect the intertemporal budget constraint.

The choice of a particular arrangement, however, is a matter of debate. Balanced budget laws and the FRL are examples of attempts at imposing the debt sustainability constraint. The FRL establishes limits on the size and structure of budgets, given revenues. Modifying the FRL, so that it applies to the budget balance, does not erode any the control of executive and legislative authorities over fiscal policy, it only changes the way the intertemporal constraint is applied. The first necessary condition therefore is the acknowledgment that sovereignty and the proper exercise of democracy are not hampered by the adoption of an institutional arrangement that removes the budget balance from the realm of the political and legislative process that delivers fiscal policy decisions.

Taking the decision on the budget balance out of the hands of policy makers is nevertheless a drastic step. Many countries have found ways to meet their budget constraints without such a step. All that is needed is that policy makers exercise adequate self-restraint. This is often the result of traditions and public awareness that frowns upon fiscal indiscipline. When historically policy makers have not felt the incentive to abide by this tradition, it has become necessary to formally impose the intertemporal constraint. The FRL has taken important steps in the direction of establishing transparency and honesty in the budgetary process, but as was previously noted, it does not deal effectively with the constraint. This is probably one reason why the markets continue to view with suspicion Brazil's commitment to fiscal discipline. The annual primary budget target further aims at filling the gap, and certainly serves a useful purpose. Two characteristics explain its limitations: it is a discretionary decision not embedded in a formally established institution, and it is too rigid to be upheld in front of unexpected adverse shocks, the next issue taken up.

6.4.3 Short- versus Long-run Objectives

Because the budget constraint is intertemporal, overall deficits are acceptable as long as they are clearly temporary. They are justified in the face of an economic slowdown or when a country needs to carry out substantial public investments. The key difficulty is to ensure that justified deficits will be reversed in the not too distant future, and durably so. The ability to put temporary fiscal deficits to good use requires combining rigid adherence to the long-run debt sustainability objective with shorter run flexibility.

The first objective calls for the adoption of rules, the second is best served with a dose of discretion. This is familiar dilemma, with no perfect answer. Strict rules are bound to be counterproductive in presence of unanticipated shocks. The costs involved are often seen as the price to pay for establishing and upholding credibility. This is certainly true, but the costs can become so high that they become politically unacceptable, thus threatening the viability of the rule.[6] Discretion is dangerous because the motivations for temporarily deviating from debt sustainability often cannot be ascertained. One solution is to limit discretion. For example, the FRL sets up severe restrictions in election years. Much as with rules, the list of desirable restrictions is too wide and unpredictable to be of much practical use. What is needed is good, reliable judgment.

6.5   A Taylor Rule for Fiscal Policy

6.5.1   Principles

From the considerations developed in the previous sections, a desirable approach would satisfy the following four conditions:

• Long-term debt sustainability requires setting a long-term target for the debt to GDP ratio.

• For the actual debt to converge to its target, ceteris paribus, the primary budget surplus should increase as the public debt b rises, which is due to past deficits or to the effect of indexation.

• Short-run flexibility allows the primary surplus to increase when the output gap g improves. Conversely, the primary surplus ought to decline—or the primary deficit should be allowed to increase—when the output gap decreases.

• When the interest rate i rises and raises the debt service ib, the primary surplus ought to increase in order to contain the overall deficit.

These four conditions suggest a rule of the following type:

$$s^* = \alpha + \beta(b - b^*) + \gamma ib + \theta g, \tag{1}$$

where s^* is the annual target primary budget surplus, b^* is the long-term target for the debt to GDP ratio, g is the output gap, and all variables are written as a ratio to GDP.[7] A positive β implies that the budget aims at closing the gap between the actual debt and its target, a positive γ corresponds to the need to tighten up the budget when the debt service rises, and a positive θ allows for the countercyclical use of fiscal policy. This is reminiscent of the Taylor rule used in the case of monetary policy, where the relative sizes of the policy parameters α, β, γ, and θ reflect the policy maker's preferences.

Much as central banks smooth the interest rate instrument, governments may wish to avoid large year to year swings in the budget balance. Thus the actual primary balance s can be written as

$$s = (1 - \rho)s_{-1} + \rho s^*. \tag{2}$$

This rule does not guarantee debt sustainability, however. To examine this issue, consider the evolution of the debt ratio (ignoring seigniorage):

$$\Delta b = -s + (i - n)b, \tag{3}$$

where n is the growth rate of nominal GDP.

Substituting (1) and (2) into (3) gives

$$\Delta b = -\rho\alpha + \rho\beta b^* - \rho\theta g + (1 - \rho)s_{-1} - [\rho\beta + n - (1 - \rho\gamma)i]b. \tag{4}$$

For the debt to eventually stabilize at the target level b^*, two conditions must be satisfied. First, the constant α must be compatible with the steady-state condition implied by (3), that the primary surplus is equal to $(i - n)b$:

$$\alpha = [(1 - \gamma)\bar{i} - \bar{n}]b^*, \tag{5}$$

where $\bar{i}$ and $\bar{n}$ are the long-term nominal interest and growth rates. Put differently, the choice of α is implicitly a choice of b^*.

The crucial question is whether the debt is sustainable, that is, whether the process (4) is dynamically stable. A necessary condition is that the coefficient of b be negative:

$$\rho\beta > (1 - \rho\gamma)\bar{i} - \bar{n}. \tag{6}$$

As expected, β must be large enough to deal with the "spontaneous" debt dynamics when the interest rate exceeds the growth rate.[8] Similarly smoothing $1 - \rho$ should be moderate enough to allow for prompt adjustment of the actual deficit to its target. Together, conditions (5) and (6) are sufficient to ensure that the public debt-to-GDP ratio b eventually converges to its target level b^*. It is possible to combine long-term debt sustainability and the temporary use of fiscal policy to deal with cyclical fluctuations.

6.5.2 Do Governments Actually Follow a Fiscal Rule?

Central banks usually reject the Taylor rule interpretation of monetary policy. While they may well admit that, on average, they behave that way, they consider the rule to be unrealistic as a guide to policy. Their claim is that they take into account a vastly wider set of considerations that cannot be subsumed by a simplistic rule. Yet there is now a large body of evidence that a Taylor rule provides a fairly good representation of central bank behavior. Could the same apply to fiscal policy? To do so, we explore whether actual primary budget surpluses behave according to (1) and (2) and, if so, whether the parameters reflecting policy makers' preferences satisfy the debt sustainability condition (6).

Ideally we would like to estimate the following equation derived from (1) and (2):

$$s = \rho[(\alpha - \beta b^*) + \beta b + \gamma ib + \theta g] + (1 - \rho)s_{-1}. \tag{7}$$

A complication arises because the debt target b^* is unobservable. It could be inferred from the data using (5).[9] Note that condition (5) implies the following restriction in (7):

$$\alpha - \beta b^* = [(1 - \gamma)\bar{i} - \bar{n} - \beta]b^*. \tag{8}$$

Table 6.3
Fiscal policy reaction function in Brazil

	Annual (1986–2002)	Monthly (1998–2003)
ρ (relative weight on rule s^*)	0.86	1.00
	4.05	8.40
γ (interest payments)	0.08	−0.18
	1.53	−0.46
θ (output gap)	0.35	0.01
	2.51	0.02
β (net debt lagged)	−0.05	0.21
	2.00	3.64
Adj R^2	0.47	0.09
DW	1.43	1.92
Sample period	86–02	98:02–03:02

Source: World Bank.
Notes: The dependent variable is the primary budget balance (% of GDP); constants are not reported. White heteroskedasticity-consistent t-statistics. The instruments are lagged output gap and interest payments, lagged US output and inflation.

This restriction can be used to estimate b^*, but it requires making further assumptions about the steady-state values of the interest and growth rates. More important, however, there is no reason to presume that the implicit debt target remains constant over the sample period. So one could impose restriction (8) and assume, alternatively, that b^* is a constant or follows a quadratic trend. However, if one takes the average sample value of the interest and growth rates to represent their steady-state values, this procedure fails to provide reasonable estimates for nearly all countries considered in tables 6.3 and 6.4. Under the maintained assumption that governments follow fiscal rules, these results can be seen as an indication that they do not actually adopt a debt target. Thus, if the debt consistency condition (5) is dropped, the fiscal policy rule is assumed to be

$$s^* = \alpha + \beta b + \gamma ib + \theta g, \tag{9}$$

and the estimated equation is

$$s = \rho[\alpha + \beta b + \gamma ib + \theta g] + (1 - \rho)s_{-1}. \tag{9'}$$

The estimate for Brazil is shown in table 6.3. For comparison, table 6.4 presents estimates for the OECD countries whose debts may be seen as approximately sustainable, though these are not entirely examplary

C. Wyplosz

Table 6.4
Fiscal policy reaction functions in the OECD

	Australia	Austria	Belgium	Canada	Germany	Denmark	Spain	Finland	France
ρ (relative weight on rule s^*)	0.50 5.96	0.58 3.54	0.88 4.40	0.44 4.53	0.68 5.01	0.59 2.30	0.28 2.18	0.65 7.93	0.54 2.79
γ (interest payments)	0.02 0.06	−1.10 −2.68	−1.48 −7.14	−2.55 −4.62	0.39 0.74	0.10 0.09	0.15 0.18	5.26 5.59	−1.48 −1.52
θ (output gap)	1.19 5.00	0.55 1.69	0.65 3.91	0.52 2.88	0.23 1.12	0.90 2.88	0.09 0.29	0.72 4.78	0.14 0.74
β (gross debt lagged)	0.07 1.12	0.10 3.81	0.22 12.08	0.25 7.31	0.06 1.13	−0.05 −0.78	0.13 2.27	−0.29 −4.64	0.13 2.41
Adj R^2	0.93	0.45	0.87	0.89	0.51	0.81	0.84	0.87	0.60
DW	2.70	1.62	1.70	1.66	1.74	2.53	1.84	2.00	2.42
Sample period	89–02	73–02	72–02	72–02	67–02	89–02	79–02	76–02	78–02

Source: *Economic Outlook*, OECD, CD-ROM December 2002.
Notes: The dependent variable is the primary budget balance (% of GDP); constant not reported. White heteroskedasticity-consistent *t*-statistics. The instruments are lagged out-

cases of fiscal rectitude. For Brazil, the data cover the period 1985 to 2002 and the debt concept is the gross debt. For the OECD countries, the database covers as many countries as possible over the period 1962 to 2001, with data coming from the OECD's *Economic Outlook* CD-ROM of December 2002. The output gap—estimated with an HP filter for Brazil and taken from OECD for the other countries—and net interest payments are instrumented to account for possible endogeneity. The unbalanced panel data estimation combines all OECD countries.[10]

The results in tables 6.3 and 6.4 provide limited evidence that Brazil and the OECD countries systematically operate a fiscal policy reaction function. For most countries the simple rule postulated here explains 80 percent or more of the primary balance fluctuations, much less in Brazil. In 9 of the 17 OECD cases under consideration, the debt stabilization coefficient β is significant and positive, and in one case,[11] it is significantly negative. This is also the case of Brazil, which may suggest that the debt process was unsustainable (more on this in section 5.3 below). In Brazil and in 10 OECD countries, fiscal policy is shown to be systematically countercyclical, with no case where θ is significantly negative.[12] The interest payment effect, on the one hand, does not appear to be relevant as γ is only positive and significant for 3

Table 6.4
(continued)

Greece	Ireland	Italy	Nether-lands	Portugal	Sweden	UK	USA	Panel
0.66	0.18	0.32	0.24	0.94	0.36	0.14	0.42	1
3.68	1.24	2.99	1.71	2.71	3.43	3.14	4.91	—
−1.03	−1.99	−0.42	6.55	0.20	4.69	5.92	−1.35	0.27
−3.52	−1.01	−1.27	0.87	0.59	1.98	1.78	−1.38	2.11
0.32	−1.25	0.26	2.49	0.37	2.13	1.25	0.79	0.24
2.05	−0.94	0.49	1.42	1.77	4.87	2.81	2.20	5.12
0.19	0.19	0.18	−0.43	0.08	−0.15	1.27	0.15	0.04
11.16	0.98	5.33	−0.75	1.46	−0.76	2.63	2.52	3.54
0.81	0.86	0.87	0.68	0.13	0.81	0.93	0.79	0.60
2.00	1.65	2.18	2.13	2.04	1.37	1.88	1.76	0.56
76–02	80–02	65–02	73–02	71–02	71–02	79–02	71–02	64–02

put gap and interest payments, with US output and inflation lagged for the non-US countries and EU12 output and interest payments lagged for the US. The cross section is GLS, unbalanced panel, with country and year dummies not reported.

Table 6.5
Comparison of estimates: Brazil and the OECD countries

	Brazil		OECD		
	Monthly	Annual	Average	Minimum	Maximum
ρ (smoothing)	1.00	0.86	0.49	0.14	0.94
γ (interest payments)	−0.18	0.08	0.70	−2.55	6.55
θ (output gap)	0.01	0.35	0.67	−1.25	2.49
β (debt level)	0.21	−0.05	0.12	−0.43	1.27

OECD countries, with 4 cases where it is significantly negative. On the other hand, all three policy parameters are found to be positive and statistically significant in the panel estimation. For Brazil, γ is positive but only significant at the 15 percent confidence level.

Table 6.5 shows comparisons of the estimates for Brazil in terms of the range (minimum, maximum, and average) found in the OECD countries. From the annual data, it is implicit that the Brazilian fiscal policy rule involves considerably less smoothing and less activism than that of the average OECD country. Yet the Brazilian estimate falls within the range of OECD estimates.

6.5.3 Debt Sustainability

The crucial question is whether, implicitly at least, the debt sustainability condition (6) is satisfied. Even if there is no debt target and the debt consistency condition (5) is not satisfied, the debt sustainability condition (6) implies that the authorities must ensure that the debt-to-GDP ratio is stationary. In this section we proceed to examine whether the debt sustainability condition (6) has been met. Since the interest and growth rates fluctuate from year to year, for the OECD countries we use the means over the period 1980 to 2002 to compute a floor β^* for parameter β:

$$\beta > \beta^* = \frac{(1 - \gamma\rho)\bar{\imath} - \bar{n}}{\rho}. \tag{6'}$$

In the case of Brazil, the fluctuations in both $\bar{\imath}$ (computed as the implicit rate on the debt, the ratio of net interest payments to net debt) and $\bar{n}$ are so wide that averages make little sense, so we can use the actual interest and GDP growth rates to compute an annual β^*. Until 1996, β^* was massively negative, meaning the debt was contained only because real interest rates were strongly negative. The situation changed afterward. The left-hand panel in figure 6.1 shows the evolution of the annual β^* obtained using the corresponding interest and GDP growth rates. From the figure we can infer that the fiscal rule over the period 1986 to 2002 was not geared toward debt sustainability.

However, the fiscal policy regime changed in 1998. In 2001, agreements between the federal and sub-federal authorities followed the debt consolidation agreements and the adoption of the FRL. To examine the impact of the regime change on the implicit fiscal policy rule, we need to estimate (9') using monthly data on the 1998 to 2003 sample. The results, which are displayed in table 6.3, are very different from those obtained with annual data. However, they must be treated with some caution because the shorter periods (1999–2003 and 2000–2003) reveal considerable parameter instability, such as might imply that Brazil followed no fiscal policy rule. Table 6.5 shows that the budget process since 1998 has not been smooth ($\rho = 1$) either. There is no indication of countercyclical action ($\theta = 0$) nor reaction to the debt service burden ($\gamma < 0$, nonsignificant), although attention was given to overall debt stabilization ($\beta > 0$, significant). The right hand-side panel of figure 6.1 shows that the debt stability condition was met occasionally but not systematically.

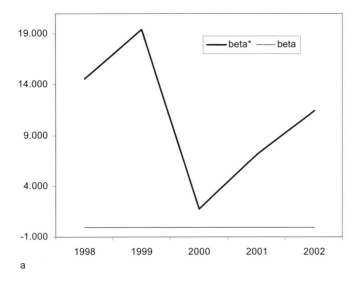

a

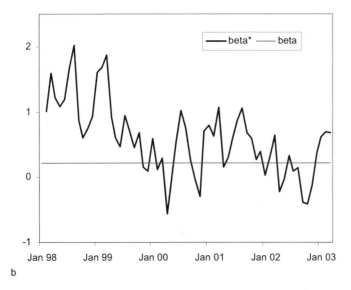

b

Figure 6.1
Debt stability condition $\beta > \beta^*$ in Brazil: (a) Annual estimates, 1998 to 2002; (b) monthly estimates, 1998 to 2003

Table 6.6
The stability condition $\beta > \beta^*$ in the OECD countries

	Aus-tralia	Austria	Bel-gium	Canada	Ger-many	Den-mark	Spain	Finland	France
β	0.07	0.10	0.22	0.25	0.06	−0.05	0.13	−0.29	0.13
β^*	0.04	0.08	0.11	0.21	0.01	0.06	0.05	−0.20	0.13

	Greece	Ireland	Italy	Nether-lands	Portu-gal	Sweden	United King-dom	United States	Panel
β	0.19	0.19	0.18	−0.43	0.08	−0.15	1.27	0.15	0.04
β^*	−0.33	−0.27	0.08	−0.21	0.01	−0.14	−0.12	0.11	−0.01

Note: The calculations are based on table 6.4.

Table 6.6 presents the estimates for the OECD countries. β and β^* are implied by the estimates shown in table 6.4. The table shows that with few exceptions, condition (6′) was satisfied.

6.5.4 The Fiscal Policy Rule Applied to Brazil

We now examine how fiscal policy rules would have worked in Brazil. We start by looking at a few counterfactual simulations of the primary surplus. The benchmark rule combines the coefficients presented in table 6.3 ($\rho = 1$, $\theta = 0.35$, $\beta = 0.21$) with the exception of γ, which is set at the minimum level (0.32) required to meet the sustainability condition (6′).

Figure 6.2 shows the corresponding baseline simulation of (9′) where α is chosen to correspond to a steady-state debt-to-GDP ratio of 35 percent, as in early 1998, and the steady-state interest rate is equal to the sample average. Interestingly the baseline counterfactual closely matches the actual evolution of the primary surplus. The actual policy was not different from the one that would have been adopted had the authorities tried to stabilize the debt while allowing for some counter-cyclical action and responding to interest rate-induced changes in the debt service. Of interest is the tightening that occurred in the wake of the two crises in 1998 and 2002.

The coefficient β estimated from annual data is not significantly different from zero. The first panel in figure 6.3 shows the simulation where $\beta = 0$. In this case the sustainability condition is not satisfied and the debt is sizable. As noted earlier, the choice of condition (6′) involves the setting of a debt target. The baseline simulation suggests

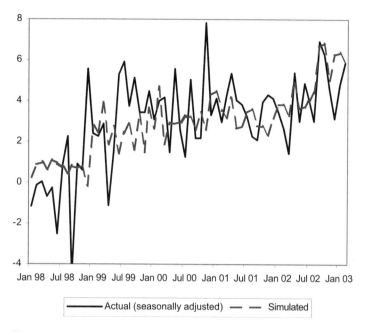

Figure 6.2
Baseline simulation of primary surplus; simulation of equation (6') with $\rho = 1$, $\gamma = 0.32$, $\theta = 0.35$, $\beta = 0.21$, $\bar{b} = 0.35$, and $\bar{i} = 15.9$

that the authorities could be trying to keep the debt-to-GDP ratio at its early 1998 level, or that they were only trying to stabilize the ratio at a level reached in the previous year when $\bar{b}_t = b_{t-1}$. The corresponding counterfactual is almost identical to the case where $\beta = 0$.

The interesting issue this result raises is how to deal with sharp changes in servicing debt. These are changes due to valuation effects through indexation to exchange and interest rates, and to expectation-driven changes in the interest rate. The first effect is captured by the debt-to-GDP ratio b, the second by the interest payment variable ib. We have already seen that in both Brazil and the OECD countries, the evidence that the budget is tightened when interest payments rise is at best limited. Among the OECD countries, few have issued indexed debts and are therefore less vulnerable to exchange and interest changes, so setting $\gamma = 0$ is understandable. In Brazil, on the other hand, where fluctuations in ib are frequent and often sharp, setting $\gamma = 0$ may seriously affect expectations.[13] The second panel in figure 6.3 shows that not reacting to changes in debt service actually does not

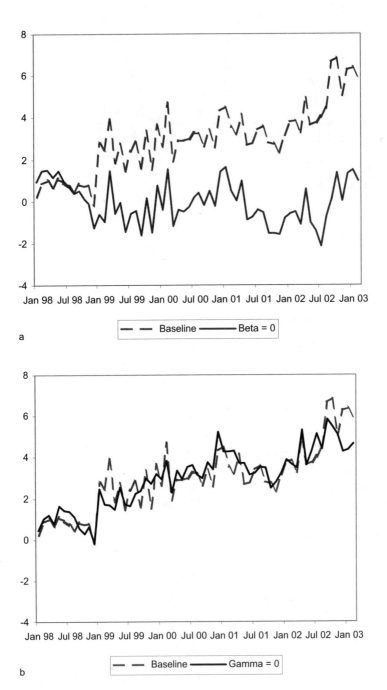

Figure 6.3
Other counterfactual simulations of primary surplus: (a) Case $\beta = 0$; (b) case $\gamma = 0$

seriously affect the path of the primary budget as long as the debt sus-tainability condition (6') is not satisfied.

6.5.5 Assessment

There is therefore evidence that several OECD countries have implic-itly followed fiscal rules that satisfy the debt sustainability condition but that the case of Brazil is muddled. Estimates of a policy rule are weak at best and not consistent. However, the simulated debt-stabilizing data in figure 6.2 do not show a trend markedly different from the actual evolution of the primary surplus over the recent period 1998 to 2003. Does this mean that governments should adopt fiscal rules of the type suggested here?

Just as central banks are inclined to implicitly follow a Taylor rule but are unwilling to commit to what they see as far too mechanical, governments are not likely to adopt fiscal policy rules, and rightly so. This conclusion clearly applies to Brazil. Because financial markets are apt to regard Brazil's commitment to debt sustainability as shaky, any adopted rule would have to be strictly followed over a significant period of time—measured in years and not in quarters. A rule feeding on highly volatile market sentiments might be too strict in periods of relatively benign market sentiment, and not strict enough during periods of alarming volatility. The rule might be good, on average, but generally misguided at times of impending crisis.

Put simply, a fiscal rule is not the quick fix that Brazil needs. Is there another logical approach? In the next section I show how reputation is established and debt sustainability delivered through institutions.

6.6 Scope for the Institutional Approach in Brazil

In Wyplosz (2002), borrowing from recent successes of inflation-targeting strategies,[14] I developed a number of economic principles that can be imported to fiscal policy, as I mentioned in section 6.3. Strong institutions backed by good legislation can provide the means to reassure jittery financial markets. In this section we will see how such principles can be used in Brazil.

6.6.1 Objectives, Targets, Instruments, and Indicators

In monetary policy the fiscal strategy depends on the specification of an objective. The specification includes the horizon at which the target is to be reached and some controllable instrument with an indicator that sends a clear signal regarding its use. Brazil has already taken important steps in this direction.

- The objective is debt sustainability. At the minimum it means that the debt is not allowed to grow faster than GDP. A more ambitious objective can be to stabilize or to reduce the debt-to-GDP ratio.
- The target is the debt-to-GDP ratio. Because of the partial endogeneity of debt to cyclical conditions, the horizon must be extended to business cycle length, and some margin must be allowed for unexpected events.
- The instrument is the primary budget. It is preferable to plan the overall budget, though it is affected by cyclical conditions. In theory, this calls for a cyclically corrected primary budget, but in practice, the approach suffers from high imprecision. Therefore the budget must be open to cyclical adjustments by authorities as needed.[15]
- The indicator is the expected debt, as predicted by the path of primary budget deficits. It requires making assumptions about the future course of the instrument and about the uncertainty associated with the interest rate and debt valuation.

In Brazil the FRL has set at all three government levels the targets concerning debt. All that is needed is to redefine these targets as percentages of GDP instead of revenues, and to break the current 15-year horizon down to shorter periods such as 5 years. The LDO effectively uses the primary balance as the policy instrument. Its triennial objective for the primary budget balance is well-adapted to the task. The 3-year objective for the debt-to-GDP ratio, currently treated as a commitment, should be replaced by a forecast, including a specification of the margin of the error (fan charts).

   Much as inflation targeting is not an automatic rule, a debt sustainability strategy is not meant to be a rigid commitment to pre-launched primary budget balances. The authorities must be willing to adjust the setting of the instrument, both to deliver an ex ante smooth convergence of the debt to its target and to deal with unexpected contingencies. The size and timing of debt adjustment remains a matter of broad judgment, to be carefully explained.

6.6.2   Institutional Arrangements
The main objective is to establish credibility. Of course, it takes years to demonstrate that a certain procedure delivers on its promises. Credibil-

ity can be achieved faster if proven failures are backed by sanctions by robust institutions. To this notion we now turn.

Sanctions   Sanctions seem to be a natural way of enforcing commitments. Yet sanctions are notoriously difficult to impose on legitimate governments. It is not clear how a federal government can be sanctioned other than by the electorate, when it is found to disregard its commitment to the rule of law. Lower levels of government can be financially sanctioned through the withdrawal of vertical transfers by the higher levels of government, but such a procedure is bound to trigger political difficulties.[16]

An Independent Budget Authority   A very different approach consists in delegating the instrument, the annual primary budget balance, to a politically independent authority. In such an arrangement all other aspects of the fiscal law—how much is to be spent on what and how revenues are to be collected—remain in the domain of normal political processes. The independent authority is given a target debt level by the relevant (target-dependent) level of government and has the exclusive right to mandate the primary (instrument-independent) budget balance. The government cannot legally submit a budget that does not meet the set target, nor can the parliament or congress approve a budget that gives a different primary balance. The budget authority is also entrusted with the responsibility of monitoring the execution of the budget law during the fiscal year. Equipped with an adequate staff, it has the right to mandate an adjustment in case of slippage, but the details (cutting spending or raising tax revenues) remain in the hands of the government.

The budget authority is composed of a group of recognized experts, much like the policy-setting committee in central banks. They are appointed by the highest political authorities for a long mandate that is compatible with the target horizon. Once appointed, they cannot be removed unless they violate the law. The authority must report on fully on the details of analysis that led to their decisions.

There remains the question of the participation of various levels of the government in budgetary decisions. Three possibilities are envisaged:

• *Delegate decisions on all budget balances to one budgetary authority.* Since targets will differ, so will the authority's choice of annual budget balances. The main advantage of this system is that it ensures overall consistency and equal treatment. A serious disadvantage is that lower levels of governments might not feel that they have a voice with the authority, so they could foster dissent among their electorates against dictates from Brasilia.

• *Each federal and sub-federal government level sets up its own authority.* This would require that the delegation of authority be similar enough horizontally and vertically to safeguard a clear federal framework. Targets would have to be agreed upon between the federal and municipal governments and between each municipal government and its local governments. The main advantage is greater political acceptability. The disadvantages include increased complexity, larger costs as possible returns to scale (experience, procedures) are lost and perhaps unequal levels of competence.

• *Intermediate solutions.* One federal authority could deal with the federal budget and provincial authorities could deal with all sub-levels with a province. Alternatively, a single authority could operate branches in each province.

A Watchdog Committee The political acceptability of an independent fiscal authority would be limited if it is perceived to be technocratic.[17] A scaled-down version can be envisioned in the form of a committee of "wise men" who would issue advice on the desirable primary budget target ahead of the government's budgetary exercise. This committee would also monitor the execution of the budget law and issue warnings and make recommendations if necessary.

The influence of the "wise men" would then depend on the willingness of the government to respond to their recommendations. Their credibility would thus depend on their clout with public opinion, the media, and the polity. This would argue in favor of choosing the "wise men" among well-known public figures at the expense of expertise, and possibly politicizing the process.[18]

Fiscal Rules: Existing Experiments Among governments there exist various forms of fiscal rules. Some rules are backed by explicit legislation, as in Brazil. Others are purely voluntary; they represent a public commitment by the government. The government can walk away from its commitments without any other cost than public disgrace. Nor can any government bind its successors to a budgetary commitment. It cannot be overemphasized that any law can be undone.

The problem with rules, as noted in section 6.3.2, is that they are bound to be occasionally counterproductive because of contingencies. This is why the rules in place usually either allow for escape clauses or are couched in vague terms.

The European Union's Stability and Growth Pact is legally backed and semi-hard. It mandates a ceiling to annual budget deficits (3 percent of GDP) and includes escape clauses. But these clauses are for exceptional cases (a recession of 2 percent automatically suspends the procedure; a recession of 0.75 percent allows for suspension). Recent experience has shown that the legal backing is not as firm as its proponents had thought.

Switzerland adopted in 2002 a law that obliges the federal government to run every year a structurally adjusted budget that is balanced. Unspecified exceptional circumstances allow for a suspension of the law. This rule eliminates the discretionary powers of fiscal policy makers and encourages them to use automatic stabilizers.

The rule adopted in 2000 by the Chilean government is voluntary and hard. The government committed itself to run every year a structurally adjusted budget surplus of 1 percent of GDP. There is no escape clause, only an adjustment for fluctuations in the price of copper.

The United Kingdom adopted in 1998 a Code for Fiscal Stability, approved by Parliament. This code does not include any quantitative target, although the Chancellor of the Exchequer has stated that "net debt will be maintained below 40% of GDP over the economic cycle." It mainly lays out principles for the good management of fiscal policy, which includes a vaguely defined golden rule. In 2003 the Chancellor announced plans to strengthen the procedure, including the adoption of an "open letter system" and the publication of a regular fiscal stability report to Parliament published on a pre-announced timetable.[19]

6.7   Conclusions

Brazil has taken in recent years a number of measures that should improve its highly vulnerable investment situation. Yet, vulnerabilities remain, as noted by the IMF, in the size and structure of Brazilian debt, its external borrowing requirement, and its slow economic growth.[20] The vulnerabilities, along with general uncertainty and a history of recurrent crises, currently weigh on Brazil's spreads and keep the economy on the brink at great economic and social crises. More recent improvements underline the benefits of the steps taken so far and should be seen as an encouragement to go further.

During 2003 the response to the market jitters has been to tighten both monetary and fiscal policies. This demonstrates that the new authorities are committed to correcting macroeconomic policy. The initially adverse conditions, inherited along with a skepticism regarding the new administration's intentions, has led to a policy stance that is more restrictive than strictly necessary. While there are signs that the message is being heard, the results are bound to be fragile, especially if the economy tips into a slowdown that is politically costly.

Is there a less costly and faster way of building up credibility? In this chapter, I argued that institution building has a useful role to play. If fiscal discipline can be enhanced by adequate institutions, then the macroeconomic policy mix can be somehow relaxed. This should not only help with growth and employment and provide the authorities with some leeway to attend to urgent social needs but also, crucially, reduce the risk of a political backlash.

A number of countries have recently adopted fiscal rules of various degrees of severity and legal backing. Fiscal rules can create impossible trade-offs: if they are hard and precise, they may prove to be too rigid in the presence of adverse shocks, or if they are flexible and self-imposed, they may lack credibility. It is interesting that most countries that had previously displayed a high degree of fiscal rectitude use the rules to enshrine or codify long-held practices. So they strengthen the control of the finance minister while dealing with spending ministers and various pressure groups that attach less importance to debt sustainability.

With its FRL and LDO, Brazil is a rare example of a country with a history of debt difficulties that has adopted a fiscal rule. Only twenty years ago, back in 1985, Brazil's the average budget balance was a surplus of close to 2 percent of GDP. So Brazil's debt problems are not entirely due to the original sin problem; its debt is either in foreign currency or indexed. All the episodes of debt explosion are the consequence of currency crises. This suggests that fiscal rules are useful for countries that are not exposed to the original sin.

Many countries, Brazil among them, can benefit from adopting budgetary institutions. If the establishment of an independent budget authority represents a departure from established practice, it is far less drastic than it seems. It does not affect the politically sensitive aspects of budgetary policy concerning the size and structure of the budget.

Depoliticizing the primary budget balance—already nearly done with the adoption of a target ahead of the budgetary procedure—does not differ in essence from the granting of instrument independence to the central bank. The intertemporal distributive effects of monetary policy and of the budget balance are limited.[21] Going one step beyond may be small sacrifice in view of the potential gain in credibility.

Notes

1. This is the point of chapter 2 by Blanchard in this volume.

2. In the shorter-run, Giavazzi and Missale (2003) make a convincing case for indexing a large portion of the debt to inflation instead of the interest and exchange rates.

3. This can be seen as practical implementation of the transversality, or no-Ponzi game, condition.

4. There are good reasons for some positive debt level: the fact that governments borrow on behalf on citizens on better terms, the need for a deep market for "riskless" financial instruments, the intergenerational equity view whereby future generations contribute to the purchase of public goods that deliver benefits over very long horizons.

5. It can be noted, however, that the structure matters because it can affect the ability of adjusting the balance. This happens, for instance, when spending items are mostly committed to mandated programs or to salaries. This may call for an explicit reserve that can be spent during times of downturns and for spending items that can be earmarked for possible deferral in case of booms.

6. This is what happened to the Argentinean Convertibility Law. It became so costly that it *had* to be removed.

7. It would perhaps be more intuitive to write the rule as $s^* = \alpha + \beta(1 + \gamma i)(b - b^*) + \theta g$, meaning the debt stabilization motive is strengthened when the interest rate rises.

8. As is well known, if $i < n$, the debt tend to stable for reasonable budget paths. Here the stability condition is less strict as we allow for the budget to react to fluctuations in the debt service. Obviously the stronger is the reaction, meaning the larger is γ, the less stringent is the condition on β.

9. This is the strategy followed by Favero and Giavazzi, chapter 3 in this volume.

10. The lagged endogenous variable is omitted, since it would result in inconsistent estimates, so we implicitly set $\rho = 1$. There no known reliable procedure to deal with this problem; see Kiviet (1995).

11. Finland underwent a major shock following the collapse of the Soviet Union.

12. In a recent similar exercise, Gali and Perotti (2003) examine subperiods and find some evidence of countercyclical policies in earlier periods.

13. Setting $\gamma = 0$ is not a sign of fiscal indiscipline and debt nonsustainability, however. As the debt sustainability condition (6') shows, β must be higher when γ is lower, and even higher is the (steady-state) interest rate relative to (steady-state) GDP growth.

Interestingly, to some extent, a low γ can be compensated by a small amount of budget smoothing (a high β), which is a characteristic of the Brazilian budgetary process.

14. See, for example, Mishkin and Schmidt-Hebbel (2001) and Svensson (1999).

15. A similar concern applies to monetary policy, which should favor the real interest rate rather the nominal rate. All inflation-targeting central banks retain the unambiguous nominal rate. Note that two inflation-targeting central banks, in Mexico and Peru, use monetary aggregates.

16. The recent experience in Europe with the Stability and Growth Pact well illustrates this point.

17. Much the same used to apply in many countries, to the concept of an independent central bank and the delegation of power to technocratic monetary policy committees. Some early examples are the experiments in Germany and the United States.

18. Since 1969 Belgium has established a High Council of Finance whose tasks include ensuring the sustainability of the public debt. The Council's influence is limited, as Belgium's high public debt, which is currently worth 100 percent of GDP, would suggest. This is largely due to the oversight being introduced ex post.

19. The fiscal stability report is prepared by the Treasury, not by an independent budgetary authority. Quoting the Treasury: "Some authors have argued, drawing explicit parallels with monetary policy, for the delegation of fiscal stabilization policy to an independent committee (an independent Fiscal Policy Committee). However, the establishment of such a body would be inconsistent with parliamentary tradition in the UK, and would challenge parliamentary sovereignty" ("Fiscal Stabilization and EMU", HM Treasury, June 2003, p. 5).

20. IMF (2003, p. 5).

21. Because the budget balance has strong intertemporal effects, the budget authority is charged with protecting the future generations.

References

Gali, J., and R. Perotti. 2003. Fiscal Policy and Monetary Integration in Europe. Unpublished paper. University Pompeu Fabra.

Goldfajn, I. 2002. Are there reasons to doubt fiscal sustainability in Brazil? Technical Note 25. Banco Central do Brasil.

Goldfajn, I., and E. R. Guardia. 2003. Fiscal rules and debt sustainability in Brazil. Unpublished paper. Banco Central do Brasil.

Goldstein, M. 2003. Debts sustainability, Brazil, and the IMF. Unpublished paper. Institute for International Economics.

International Monetary Fund. 2003. IMF concludes Article IV consultation with Brazil. Public Information Notice 03/38. IMF.

Kiviet, J. 1995. On bias, inconsistency and efficiency of various estimators in dynamic panel data models. *Journal of Econometrics* 68: 53–78.

Mishkin, F., and K. Schmidt-Hebbel. 2001. One decade of inflation targeting in the world: What do we know and what do we need to know. Working Paper 8397. NBER.

Missale, A., and F. Giavazzi. 2003. Public debt management in Brazil. Unpublished paper. Universita Bocconi.

Svensson, L. E. O. 1999. Inflation targeting as a monetary policy rule. *Journal of Monetary Economics* 43: 607–54.

Wyplosz, C. 2002. Fiscal discipline in EMU: Rules or institutions? Paper prepared for the Group of Economic Analysis of the European Commission. Graduate Institute of International Economics, Geneva.

Comment on Chapter 6

Rogério L. F. Werneck

Wyplosz's main proposal is the creation of an independent watchdog for fiscal policy in Brazil. I will concentrate my comments on that proposal.

I am unconvinced that the creation of an independent fiscal authority is the best solution to the problem of guaranteeing that the public sector debt in Brazil will remain under control in the medium to long run. I also have serious doubts about the political feasibility of this idea in Brazil. My general impression is that Wyplosz goes too far in trying to apply to the problem a solution borrowed from recent successful arrangements in monetary policy making.

Of course, it is tempting to see successes in inflation targeting as showing the way to what can be done at the fiscal policy front. But the differences between the problems faced at the two fronts are too important not to be taken into account. In decisions involving debt sustainability, the relevant time span is much longer and there is more scope for differences in time preferences and the right timing to react. One could also argue that the degree of complexity of proper considerations of cost and benefits is widely different. This makes it difficult therefore to simply "delegate the task of setting the annual primary balance to an independent authority."

The prescription then of leaving unavoidably complex decision making in economic policy to a group of "wise men" can only be used sparingly. It is no panacea. In Brazil recent experience with supposedly independent regulatory agencies in electricity supply and telecomm areas has proved to be somewhat problematic. In the end the quality of the staffing of the agencies reflected the quality of the policy that was effected by the government in the first place. There is a sharp divide between what happened in these areas and in the administration of monetary policy, about which the Lula government has proved to have much more sensible ideas. The idea of putting an independent watchdog at the fiscal front can lead to serious political fights and be extremely damaging to the positive steps already taken in enhancing fiscal policy credibility.

At the end of the chapter, almost as an afterthought, Wyplosz concedes that an independent fiscal authority may be too far-fetched. He proposes, instead, that the committee of "wise men" could advise on the desirable primary surplus, and possibly issue warnings and produce a debt sustainability report. That may be more sensible. More generally, it seems wiser to find ways to reduce the perceived risk of the debt going out of control, instead of looking for a device that could guarantee that would not happen.

There is much to be done in this direction. With increased transparency some of the shortcomings of the Fiscal Responsibility Law could be reduced and perhaps eliminated. Although periodic publication of the estimated cyclically corrected primary balance could be manipulated, a legal requirement of publication could be an important course of action. In addition a requirement of periodic publication of detailed stress-tests, though rough, could increase the political costs of persisting on unsustainable paths, at least on the more obvious ones. There is a lot that can be done before reaching the point of delegating decision making to an independent group of experts. The challenge is to design institutions capable of handling complex economic policy problems. This is of course, much more complicated than prescribing the creation of a committee of so-called wise men every time there is a problem of intricate complexity to be faced.

IV

Country Risk and Domestic
Political Risk in Brazil

7 Learning to Trust Lula: Contagion and Political Risk in Brazil

Marcus Miller, Kannika
Thampanishvong, and Lei
Zhang

7.1 Introduction

To the dismay of those who believed that emerging market lenders could "quarantine" individual countries in crisis, the collapse of the Argentine currency board in late 2001 was followed by a rise in Latin American sovereign spreads as capital flows to the region came to a "Sudden Stop" (Calvo et al. 2002a). Brazil—the dominant economy of the region, operating with a floating exchange rate, inflation targets, and an internationally respected central bank governor—suffered more than the average.

As figure 7.1 shows, in 2002 sovereign spreads in Brazil rose to more than twice the EMBI + (without Brazil). Although Brazil's public debt appeared to be sustainable, following a substantial reduction in its external debt during the preceding four years, the country was nevertheless exposed to the risk of self-fulfilling crisis.[1] In the view of Fraga and Goldfajn (2002), while the debt-to-GDP ratio would decline if real interest rates moved toward single figures,[2] debt could become an unsustainable burden with persistently high interest rates—and/or low growth.

Global factors were not propitious. Following the collapse of Enron in the United States, US junk bond rates rose well over 500 basis points for a year, from mid-2002 to mid-2003 (see figure 7.1). Returns on US high yield bonds provided an effective floor to emerging market sovereign spreads, and as fears of lack of accountability undermined trust in emerging markets, EMBI + spreads (without Brazil) were pushed to a peak of about 1,000 basis points in the second half of 2002. Although Calvo and Talvi (2002b) have put primary emphasis on the "Enron effect" in explaining Brazilian sovereign spreads, figure 7.1 suggests that other factors were in play as Brazilian country risk rose to a peak

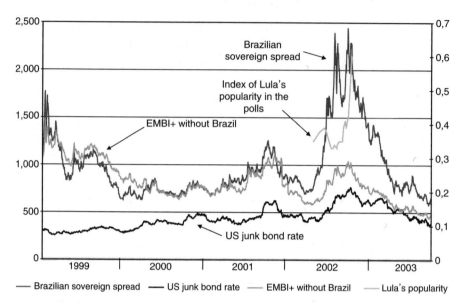

Figure 7.1
Sovereign spreads, US Junk bond rates and opinion polls. Source: Supplied by Marcio
Garcia, PUC-Rio

of over 2,000 basis points in late 2002, far higher than the average of
other emerging market countries.

In the light of East Asian experience, regional contagion is surely
an issue to be considered. Argentina had defaulted in December 2001 to
January 2002, leading to the largest bond restructuring in history—and
some direct empirical tests for contagion as reported below. But what
appeared to "spook" financial markets in summer of 2002 was domestic politics, in particular, the upcoming October election. With Lula da
Silva, the charismatic leader of the left-wing Workers' Party (PT), as
the front-running candidate, markets feared unilateral debt restructuring. It is hardly surprising that, as the polls swung in his favor, sovereign spreads increased sharply, since foreign banks had substantial
exposure to Brazil. The sovereign spread widened from around 700
bps in March to around 2,000 bps in September, as Lula moved from
less than 30 percent to over 40 percent in the public opinion polls.
Figure 7.2 gives the opinion poll results for the four presidential candidates for almost a year preceding the election; the index of Lula's popularity (rescaled) is also shown in figure 7.1 for the six months right
before the election.

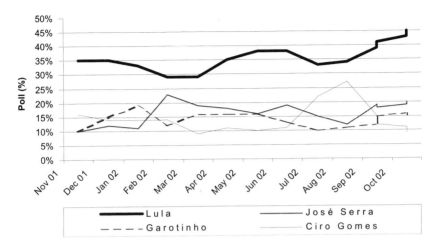

Figure 7.2
Opinion polls prior to the presidential election. Source: Opinion Polls taken by IBOPE (OPP169–OPP422)

In the months following Lula's victory, however, Brazil's sovereign spread declined from a peak of 23 percent to around 13 percent in January 2003. The spread fell below 6 percent in October 2003, due, we believe, to markets recovering from the initial panic over the prospect of a left-wing administration.

In this chapter we analyze sovereign spreads in an environment where an untested left-wing candidate is expected to win an election. Williamson (2002) suggests that international investors were afraid that the Lula government would imitate the Argentine default: "If Argentina could ultimately be forced into doing what it tried so hard to avoid ... can [international investors] be certain that Brazil run by a president with a past record of sympathizing with default will not take the easy way out?" Williamson (2002, p. 14). We agree that if the experience of neighboring countries is indeed used as a guide to the behavior of an incoming government, domestic politics can provide a powerful channel for contagion.

What if Lula did *not* intend to renege on Brazil's debts but had decided to adopt market-friendly policies due, say, to the persuasive efforts of the Ministry of Finance and the central bank? As debts are honored and repudiation resisted, sovereign spreads should decline, with expectations of future radical repudiation being revised downward.

Our key contributions in this chapter are twofold. First, we show that contagion and political risk are not mutually exclusive—that political risk can be a channel for contagion. Second, we show that in the circumstances prevailing in Brazil, a successful transition from Left to Right involved both the adoption of market-friendly policies by the incoming government and the restoration of market confidence. We further contribute an analysis of the IMF's role in providing policy pre-commitment and liquidity support, which extended the time period for the market to learn to trust the Lula government.

The discussion proceeds as follows. In section 7.2, we report empirical evidence from econometric studies of contagion and of multiple equilibria, and we review some of the relevant theoretical literature, including that on Global Games that generate unique equilibrium.

In section 7.3, we introduce a Sudden Stop model. This allows us to see how a drying-up of capital flows leads to high sovereign spreads in a political climate driven by fears of debt default and restructuring. A similar interpretation of the 1994–95 Mexican crisis was given in Sachs, Tornell, and Velasco (1996), but our model differs in that the choice for the government is the rate of default on debt rather than how fast debt is inflated away.

The macroeconomic implications of domestic politics in the run-up to an election are analyzed in section 7.4. Along the lines of Alesina (1987), we distinguish between the political preferences of Right and Left (where the latter are more prone to default on debt), and then we calculate sovereign spreads endogenously, using election probabilities. To understand events after the election, it is essential to consider different varieties of left-wing behavior, which we characterize as Far-left and Moderate-left. In the appendix we describe an extended two-sided process in scenarios where Lula gradually shifts his policy toward being market-friendly and where the markets use Bayesian updating steadily to reduce their expected default probability if he does not default. In section 7.5, however, we postulate that Lula promptly shifts his policy preferences to Moderate-left, and the market, which initially expects default with a high probability, follows by revising the default probability down to zero so long as no default takes place when Lula assumes office. This is a special case of Bayesian learning. The IMF's role in dealing with the confidence crisis is discussed in terms of providing liquidity support in exchange for policy pre-commitments endorsed by all candidates for election. In section 7.6, we offer some concluding remarks.

7.2   Literature Survey: Empirical Evidence and Theory

7.2.1   Empirical Evidence: Contagion, Multiple Equilibria, and Politics

The evidence from currency crises in emerging markets during the 1990s suggests an important role for contagion across countries— as well as weak fundamentals and exogenous shifts in expectations (Agénor et al. 1999; Claessens and Forbes 2001). Contagion is the core explanation in an empirical study of Markov-switching regimes by Marcel Fratzscher (2000, 2002), for example. In another time-series study, by Jung Yeon Kim (2001), a latent variable measuring contagion was found to have an important role in causing a series of crises in East Asian emerging markets.

Figure 7.3 focuses on Latin American sovereign spreads, showing separately the rates for Brazil, Argentina, and the rest of Latin America. Two factors support a role for contagion in the Brazilian crisis. First is that an event such as the Argentine default is the type of public signal that can coordinate private agents' expectations on a bad equilibrium[3] (Masson 1999); second is the analogy from East Asia, where a fundamentals-driven crisis in Thailand in mid-1997 led to a full-blown liquidity crisis in Korea the following Christmas. Is Argentina to Brazil, what Thailand was to Korea?

Using a VAR approach, Boschi (2003) detects a small but noticeable reaction of Brazilian spreads to the Argentine turmoil, but the analysis of correlation coefficients (corrected for heteroscedasticity) shows no evidence of contagion. These results suggest that Argentina is an isolated case.

Based on forward rates in the bond market, Favero and Giavazzi (2002) offer evidence for the role of political factors in explaining Brazilian interest rates. They note that the upward shift in the term structure of forward rates that occurred between February 2002 and May 2002 could be linked to electoral uncertainty, and that forward-looking data as of mid-2002 indicated another upward shift in spring 2003, when the new government was to take office after the election. They argue that Brazilian term premia reveal market concern about the sustainability of the debt—before the IMF target for fiscal surplus was adopted (and later increased).

Fitting a nonlinear Markov-switching model to daily data for Brazilian sovereign spreads from November 2001 to October 2002, Goretti and Taylor (2004) and Goretti (2004) provide evidence in favor of

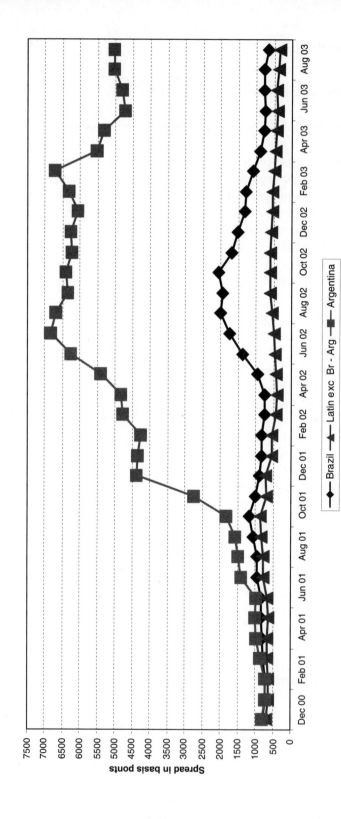

Figure 7.3
Sovereign spreads for Brazil, Argentina, and the rest of Latin America. Sources: JP Morgan and EMTA

financial contagion from the Argentine crisis as well as of political uncertainty during the pre-election period in Brazil. In the latter study, political developments, together with US high-yield spreads and news of IMF actions, are included as factors that can trigger a regime shift from "tranquillity" to "turmoil."[4] In the equation determining Brazilian spreads, Goretti (2004) finds that the state variable for this regime shift adds some 600 basis points to Brazilian country risk: so political factors have a distinctly nonlinear impact on Brazilian spreads. The direct effect of regional financial contagion on the latter is captured by a size-dependent coefficient on Argentine spreads, 0.125 for spreads above 60 percent, but only 0.031 for spreads below this threshold.

Goretti's econometric findings indicate that Brazilian spreads of about 20 percent could be explained in large part by direct contagion from Argentina in default (7 or 8 percentage points) augmented by financial "turmoil" triggered by political and other factors indicated above (adding 6 more percentage points); the remainder is given by a constant term. The substantial direct influence attributed to regional contagion and the relatively limited effect of domestic politics are in contrast with the account developed below, where we examine how and why the Argentine default may have had its impact *through political channels*.

7.2.2   Theoretical Literature

Self-fulfilling Crises and Coordination Failure   In their interpretation of the Mexican crises of 1994–95, Sachs, Tornell, and Velasco (1996), hereafter STV, use a political-economy model to show that a government with a sufficiently high debt-income ratio can face a self-fulfilling crisis if creditors charge high interest rates, anticipating that the government is about to inflate the debt away and devalue its currency. In the STV model, multiple equilibria can occur at some levels of the relevant state variable (i.e., the ratio of debt to income) but not at other levels. In situations of indeterminacy, rumors are important, and events—such as the Chiapas uprisings and the assassination of presidential candidate Luis Donaldo Colosio—can become focal points for drastic shifts in creditor expectations. Their opinion is that the Tequila crisis of 1994–95 was a consequence of shifting to a panic equilibrium.

While STV go on to develop a game-theoretic model of events, Cole and Kehoe (1996), in their account of the same crisis, focus on general equilibrium considerations. In this interpretation, investors, fearing that Mexico would not be able to honor its commitments, were not willing to buy new Mexican government bonds. The investor panic that ensued made the financing problem facing the government— sustainable with normal rollover—suddenly become impossible. They found that this sort of self-fulfilling prophecy was possible for government debt in an interval they called the crisis zone. The size of the crisis zone depends crucially on the average length of maturity of government debt (a low level of debt to GDP can still lead to crisis if the maturity of debt is very short). The selection of equilibrium is attributed to "sunspots," meaning due to random variables not connected with fundamentals of the model. In their numerical calibration, Cole and Kehoe concluded that Mexico was in the crisis zone, and they characterized the Tequila crisis as a self-fulfilling crisis. In a subsequent analysis of alternative monetary regimes for Latin America, Araujo and Leon (2003) adopt a similar multiple-equilibria approach and find that Brazil is in the crisis zone as well and thus exposed to the risk of self-fulfilling crisis.

Global Games and the Uniqueness of Equilibrium The literature discussed above effectively assumes that there is a representative creditor, so the issue of coordination among creditors is not explicitly addressed. It may, however, be the lack of coordination among creditors that leads to the Sudden Stop[5] and forces the country to default on its debt (Radelet and Sachs 1998; Ghosal and Miller 2003). In marked contrast to the multiple-equlibria approach is a newly emerging paradigm, where agents act with individual rationality and with private information. The result is a unique equilibrium, as crises only occur when fundamentals fall to a critical threshold. This so-called rational model of crises was developed by Morris and Shin (1998), who appeal to the Global Games paradigm of Carlsson and van Damme (1993). In Morris and Shin's classic account of a speculative attack, agents obtain private but correlated signals on economic fundamentals. They use the signals to coordinate their actions by calculating a critical common-knowledge threshold for attacking the currency.

The Morris-Shin model has recently been extended to include the role of the IMF by Corsetti, Guimares, and Roubini (2003), hereafter CGR. The CGR model assumes there are a large number (a continuum) of fund managers who have lent on a short-term basis to a small open economy and who face the decision of whether or not to roll over lending, with payoffs depending on taking the "right decision". To determine when to withdraw, creditors use a trigger strategy based on their private signals of the rate of return achieved by the borrower; the Global Games approach ensures a unique level of fundamentals when all creditors exit. They go on to show that when the IMF is willing to provide liquidity support and faces similar economic incentives as the fund managers, the threshold level of returns triggering creditors' exit remains unique—and is lower the larger the size of IMF intervention.

To get this interesting result, it is assumed that the IMF moves simultaneously with other creditors. This leaves open the question of what would happen if there were a large player who moves first. Can "herding" emerge? CGR do briefly consider the case where the IMF moves before the withdrawal decision by fund managers, and they observe that "one can build examples in which fund managers will disregard their private signal, and just conform to the IMF move: they will roll over debt if the IMF opens contingent credit lines to the country, and withdraw otherwise." But note also that with sequential moves the action of IMF becomes a public signal, so it can play the role of a "sunspot" in coordinating the decisions of fund managers. (In a recent paper Angeletos et al. 2003 show that multiple equilibria may also arise because the reaction of the central bank to the crisis generates *endogenous* public signals.)

Another interesting feature of CGR analysis is the possible strategic complementarity between the provision of liquidity by the IMF and the reform efforts of the domestic government. Our interpretation of role of the IMF also stresses strategic complementarity, but this is secured by the explicit use of the IMF's "conditionality."

Domestic Politics   In a contemporary IIE policy brief Williamson (2002) examined the pessimism about Brazil's economic prospects that gripped financial markets in the summer of 2002. Appealing to the theory of self-fulfilling crisis discussed above, he judged that Brazil's fundamentals, both in regard to domestic and external debt, were in what he calls an "intermediate situation," meaning the zone where things are ripe for self-fulfilling crisis. He went on to argue that the market's choice of equilibrium was strongly influenced by the political situation in Brazil and that sovereign spreads before the election reflected political developments. He noted, however, that there was a prospect, after the election, for Brazilian sovereign spreads "to drop furthest under a left-wing government that shows itself to be responsible, because the market's ever-present fear of a left-wing government renouncing Brazil's debts would be once and for all laid to rest" (Williamson 2002, p. 15).

Most of the existing self-fulfilling crisis models assume a single sovereign decision maker, but the ideas can be carried over to a two-party case, Left and Right, as in Alesina (1987). Assume, for concreteness, that rollovers lead to satisfactory debt service by whichever party is responsible, while panic leads to default by Left but not Right. Then the appointment of a left-wing government will lead to multiple equilibria, but a right-wing government will be associated with a unique, no-default equilibrium. (If there is an election pending so that the nature of the party responsible is not determined, the uncertain prospect of the left-wing gaining power may be enough to generate multiple equilibria.)

Chang (2002) analyses the way in which electoral uncertainty and capital flows interact in a small open economy. Two candidates run for office, one "pro-business" and the other "pro-labor," with objectives biased toward entrepreneurs or workers, respectively. The electoral outcome matters for the investment decision because of its implication for the choice of tax policy. A pro-business victory promises low capital income taxes, so capital inflows continue, but a pro-labor electoral victory results in a Sudden Stop in investment and capital flows. This is because the pro-labor government is known to favor a capital levy and, given its social preferences, cannot commit not to impose excessively high taxes on investment returns. In the "politicoeconomic" equilibrium before the election, self-fulfilling crises are possible, and it is shown that pre-electoral policy agreements, where the pro-labor party ties its hands, can contribute not only to financial stability but also to the chances of a pro-labor victory in the elections.[6]

7.3   Determining of Sovereign Spreads

7.3.1   Chronology of Events and Time Line

The chronology of events is as follows. First, the public opinion polls are revealed, indicating the ex ante probability of each party being elected. Second, the creditors determine whether or not to roll over their short-term lending, that is, set A, where $A \in \{0, b\}$ is the amount that is rolled over of b, the amount of existing short-term debt. When $A = 0$, creditors panic and refuse to roll over.[7] The possibility of a crisis triggered by rollover failure is discussed in more detail in Alesina et al.

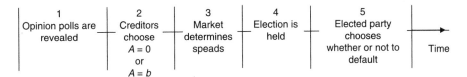

Figure 7.4
Chronology of events

(1990), where the confidence crisis reflects a coordination problem among investors making investment decisions at different dates.[8] When $A = b$, however, creditors roll over all their lending. Third, the market forms (rational) expectations of the government's default rate, δ^e, which determines the sovereign spreads on the debt that is rolled over, A; specifically, creditors use the ex ante probability of each party being elected to form the expected rate of default and the sovereign spread. Next, the election is held. Finally, the elected party chooses whether to default or not by minimizing its losses subject to given default expectations. The sequence of events is presented in figure 7.4.

7.3.2 The Model

Consider a small open economy with substantial government debt held in private hands, where inflation has been held in check by inflation targets operated by an independent central bank. To service the debt, the government can choose either to tax or to default—using involuntary debt restructuring to lengthen the term of the debt for example, or possibly to write it down. Where τ is the tax rate (i.e., tax yield divided by GDP), and δ the default rate—a measure of how costly the debt restructuring will be to creditors[9]—the government minimizes the following loss function:

$$\min_{\delta}\{\lambda_i y^2 + \tau^2 + I_\delta C_i(\delta)\}, \tag{1}$$

where y is a percentage deviation from full employment (natural rate), λ indicates the relative importance to the government of welfare losses associated with output. (Here we index the parameters λ and C by i, indicating different political parties.) In addition to welfare losses associated with output and taxes, we assume that there are extra costs related to debt default, $I_\delta C(\delta)$, where I_δ is an indicator function that is equal to 1 if there is a default and zero otherwise. The extra costs of default reflect direct sanctions imposed by creditor countries, temporary suspension of the borrowing country from world capital markets, and other transaction costs associated with restructuring and repudiation. Specifically, we assume that the cost of default is quadratic in δ:

$$C_i(\delta) = Z_i + \alpha_i \delta^2, \tag{2}$$

where both Z_i and α_i are positive because the costs imposed reflect "punishment" for the act of default itself (breaking the terms of the debt contract) and for the degree of debt restructuring (value loss to creditors).

Let all debts be short-term (one period) so that the government faces the following budget constraint:

$$\tau + \delta b + A = (1 + \delta^e)b, \tag{3}$$

where b is the quantity of debt as a fraction of GDP, A is the amount of debt that is rolled over, and δ^e is the expected default rate. In the derivations that follow, we first characterize equilibrium for given A in the absence of a fixed cost Z, and then we look at how introducing the fixed cost changes the selection of equilibrium.

We begin with the case where $A = b$, so the government is unlikely to avail itself of the option to default. But what if creditors panic and refuse to roll over? To analyze this case later—a Sudden Stop to use Calvo's phrase[10]—we set $A = 0$ and find that default and restructuring are real possibilities.

We assume that creditors move first to determine whether to roll over the existing debts, then the interest rate for debt contracts is determined by rational expectations before the government chooses its policy. Actual default is beneficial to the government since it reduces taxes: but a government that retains the option of defaulting may face a higher expected default rate in the equilibrium.

Given the foreign interest rate r^*, we assume that interest parity holds for this small open economy, and that there will be no expected depreciation or appreciation of the domestic currency. So sovereign spreads reflect the expected default rate:

$$r = r^* + \delta^e, \tag{4}$$

where r is the domestic interest rate.

Aggregate demand is simply given by

$$y = -r,$$

where y measures the percentage deviation from full employment output; for simplicity we ignore the effect of taxes on output. Normalizing the foreign interest rate to zero, we arrive at

$$y = -\delta^e. \tag{5}$$

The government's decision is specified as a one-period problem with the following chronology: (1) creditors determine whether or not to roll over their short-term lending,[11] namely set A; (2) given A, creditors form expectations of the government's default rate, δ^e (which determines the sovereign spread on its borrowing, b); (3) conditional on these expectations, the government decides whether or not to default. As it moves last, the government clearly faces a time-consistency problem, which may lead to multiple equilibria, as in Sachs et al. (1996) and Obstfeld (1996).

Minimizing the loss function in (1), subject to the given expected default rate of δ^e, gives rise to the following best response for the government:

$$\delta = \frac{(1+\delta^e)b^2 - Ab}{(\alpha_i + b^2)}. \tag{6}$$

Substituting (2), (5), and (6) into (1) yields minimum losses with a given expected default rate

$$L^D = Z_i + \lambda_i(-\delta^e)^2 + (1+\delta^e)^2 b^2 - 2bA(1+\delta^e)$$
$$+ A^2 - \frac{[(1+\delta^e)b^2 - Ab]^2}{(\alpha_i + b^2)}. \tag{7}$$

Rational expectations on the part of creditors imply that

$$\delta^e = \delta. \tag{8}$$

In the absence of the fixed cost Z, we obtain the *time-consistent equilibrium* as

$$\begin{cases} \delta_D^e = \delta_D = \frac{b^2 - Ab}{\alpha_i}, \\ \tau_D = b - A. \end{cases} \tag{9}$$

If the creditors decide to roll over all their lending, setting $A = b$, then $\delta_D^e = \delta_D = 0$ and $\tau_D = 0$. Now consider what Calvo describes as a Sudden Stop, which we represent as complete rollover failure so that creditors set $A = 0$. In that case, $\delta_D^e = \delta_D = b^2/\alpha_i$ and $\tau_D = b$. This may

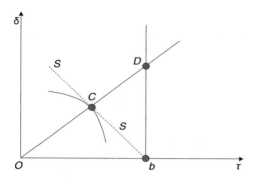

Figure 7.5
Time-consistent and pre-commitment equilibria

appear to be an extreme assumption as typically not all debt is short term, falling due for repayment at the same time. It is, however, common in the analysis of crisis (e.g., see Sachs et al. 1996) and may reflect the fact that failure to service longer term debt can trigger "acceleration clauses," calling for immediate repayment: that is, even long-term debt becomes payable on demand in the crises.

The Sudden Stop equilibrium is illustrated in figure 7.5, where the horizontal and vertical axes indicate the tax rate and the actual default rate, respectively. As can be seen from equation (1) the absolute minimum of the loss function (given δ^e) is at the origin. The ellipse sketched in figure 7.5 indicates an iso-loss function. Assuming $\delta^e = 0$, the budget constraint is given by the downward-sloping line SS going through point b. Subject to this budget constraint, the government's optimal default rate is at point C, where there is a strictly positive default rate. This shows that *in the absence of lump sum costs of default*, government promises of no default are not credible. Varying δ^e traces out the line OD showing all the "short-run" optimal choices of the government; this is government's best response function described by (6), setting $A = 0$. Substituting the rational expectations requirement (8) into (3), with $A = 0$, gives the best response function of the creditors (indicated by vertical line Db in the figure). The intersection between OD and bD gives the time-consistent (Nash) equilibrium at D. However, under the complete rollover, $A = b$, there also exists another time-consistent (Nash) equilibrium at O.

It is clear from the figure that with rational expectations on the part of creditors, equilibrium must satisfy the restriction that $\tau = b$ after a Sudden Stop. In normal times the budget constraint would be far closer to the origin: technically, with r^* set to zero, it would be at the origin if $A = b$. So one may interpret τ as the extra taxes needed to finance the Sudden Stop.

If there is a complete rollover—meaning creditors have chosen $A = b$—the unique time-consistent equilibrium is $\delta = 0$ and $\tau = 0$ (regardless of α_i). However, if creditors have decided not to roll over the debt, namely $A = 0$, whether the government would default or not depends on the fixed cost Z. If $Z < b^4/(\alpha_i + b^2)$, default will be the unique time-consistent equilibrium, but if $Z > b^4(\alpha_i + b^2)/\alpha_i^2$, no default will be the only time-consistent equilibrium. In what follows we assume that the former case represents the left-wing party and the latter case the right-wing party.

7.4   Sovereign Spread and Political Risk

In the presidential election, Lula da Silva, a charismatic former trade union leader, was the candidate of the left-wing Workers' Party (PT). Despite the verbal commitments by the PT regarding the maintenance of economic stabilization policies (inflation control, honoring contractual obligations, and a primary budget surplus needed to service debt obligations of 3.75 percent of GDP in 2003), it appears that uncertainty as to his economic proposals nevertheless triggered panic in financial markets fearing the use of unilateral repudiation to deal with the debt problems facing Brazil.

7.4.1   A Simple Political Economy Model with No Default by the Right-Wing

To see how political factors can impact on sovereign spreads, we modify the model along the lines of Alesina (1987) by introducing two political parties with different preferences: left-wing (L) and right-wing (R), see Thampanishvong (2002). We denote by π the ex ante probability of the left-wing party being elected, as indicated by the pre-election polls—for example.[12] To simplify the analysis, moreover, we follow Rodrik and Velasco (1999) by assuming that the *right-wing party always repays debt in the face of a Sudden Stop: while the left-wing party always chooses to default and restructure*. Conditional on the Sudden Stop,[13] the sequence of events is as follows: (1) creditors use the ex ante probability for each party to be elected to form the expected rate of default δ^e, (2) the election is held, and (3) the elected party chooses whether to default by minimizing its losses subject to given default expectations.

With political uncertainty, rational expectations on the part of creditors imply

$$\delta^e = E(\delta) = \pi\delta(L) + (1 - \pi)\delta(R),$$ (10)

where E denotes the mathematical expectation, and $\delta(L)$ and $\delta(R)$ are the ex post default rates for the left- and right-wing parties respectively.[14] These results may be summarized in the following proposition:

Proposition 1 *Sovereign spreads and political uncertainty.* Assume that creditors fail to roll over debt before an election in which both parties have the same preference parameter (α) but the left-wing has a significantly lower fixed cost parameter (Z), so default by an incoming government will depend on the fixed cost. Assume further that the left-wing government prefers to default while the right-wing government prefers to honor its debts. Pre-election sovereign spreads will then be increasing in π, the perceived probability of a left-wing victory.

Formally, let $\alpha_L = \alpha_R = \alpha$, $Z_L \le b^4/(\alpha + b^2)$ and $Z_R \ge b^4(\alpha + b^2)/\alpha^2$, then the expected default rate is given by $\delta^e = \pi b^2/[\alpha + (1 - \pi)b^2]$ which is increasing in π. If the left-wing party is elected, the post-election outcomes are $\delta_L = b^2/[\alpha + (1 - \pi)b^2] > 0$ and $\tau_L = \alpha b/[\alpha + (1 - \pi)b^2] < b$. If the right-wing party is elected, the outcomes are $\delta_R = 0$ and $\tau_R = (\alpha + b^2)b/[\alpha + (1 - \pi)b^2] > b$.

Figure 7.6 illustrates. (The axes are as defined in figure 7.5, but here we also use the vertical axis to represent the mathematical expectation of the default rate.) As the left-wing government always defaults

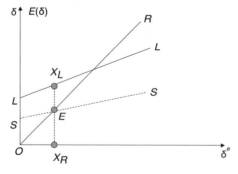

Figure 7.6
Sovereign spreads and political uncertainty

and the right-wing always honors its debts, the corresponding reaction functions (conditional on gaining office) are LL and the horizontal axis, respectively. Before the election the mathematical expectation of the default rate, $E(\delta)$, is a weighted average of these two reaction functions, as shown by SS in the figure. This mathematical expectation matches the expected rate of default δ^e at E, where SS crosses the 45-degree line labeled OR, and the rational expectation constraint is satisfied. Immediately after the election, the left-wing is expected to default at the rate X_L, with no default by the right-wing (see X_R). The predicted ex post jump in sovereign spreads after a left-wing victory, EX_L, will shrink as the pre-election polls swing to left, shifting SS closer to LL.

Consider the situation when the right-wing party holds power, but an election looms, as in Brazil in 2002. Clearly the prospect of the left-wing being elected will increase sovereign spreads even though the current government has no intention of defaulting. This is consistent with surges in Brazilian spreads as and when Mr. da Silva's popularity soared: but note that if Lula is almost sure to win, there will be little ex post jump in the spread.

7.5   Policy Adaptation, Market Learning, and IMF Intervention

The Alesina-style model outlined above assumes that the policy preferences of both parties are well known. But there was in fact considerable uncertainty as to what Lula's economic policies might be, Williamson (2002). In terms of market indicators, the interest rate term structure, using the pre-election forward rate data, was expected to rise in early 2003—the date on which Lula was expected to take office—and to go on rising for some time thereafter, Favero and Giavazzi (2002). This seems to be consistent with expectations of a left-wing government that will probably default. As noted above, however, sovereign spreads have declined steadily since the election, as shown in figures 7.1 and 7.3. An important determinant was that Lula learned to become market friendly and shifted his announcements during the campaign accordingly. But the default premium also depended on how the market perceived the change in policy stance of Lula. In this section we provide a stylized account of Lula's policy adaptation, together with instant Bayesian learning by the market as default is avoided, to explain a prompt decline in sovereign spreads.[15] (In an appendix to this chapter we give a more realistic, two-sided process, where Lula gradually shifts his policy toward being market friendly, and the markets use Bayesian updating steadily to reduce their expected default probability if he does not default.)

Note that the political-economy approach with market-learning allows a channel for contagion. Where should the market get its ideas of what a new government in Brazil might do? Why not look at what happened in its southern neighbor less than a year before the Brazilian election, where the departure of Argentine President de la Rua led to debt repudiation? *The Economist* (2003, p. 39) took such a view: "Over the past year, fears of default, stoked by Argentina's insolvency and the past radicalism of Lula and his Workers' Party (PT), helped push up interest rates and the value of the dollar."

7.5.1   Sovereign Spreads: Going Up or Going Down?

In figure 7.7 we summarize the state of expectations before Lula's adoption of Moderate-left policy and the market's learning about this. Thus the pre-election "political equilibrium" shown as E is as described in the previous figure. If we assume that debt contracts signed before the election last for some time after the election, the forecast rate of default conditional on Lula's victory will increase as indicated by the jump from "political equilibrium" to the point labeled "conditional forecast of postelection spreads" (D_0) as the electoral uncertainty is resolved. After Lula has taken office, and it is time to revise short-term debt contracts signed before the election, the equilibrium would then shift to the "time-consistent" outcome shown as D_1, characterized by the perceived response function for the left-wing party labeled "Mar-

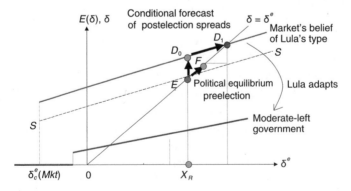

Figure 7.7
Forecasts of postelection default rates

ket's belief of Lula's type." We can assume that D_1 is a weighted average of the response functions of the Far-left and Moderate-left with considerable weight (possibly 1) on the former (see appendix).

Thus, while the conditional forecast of interest rates given a right-wing victory is that they will fall to zero and stay there, the *conditional* forecast of interest rates given a left-wing victory is that they rise first to D_0 and then to D_1. This is, of course, qualitatively consistent with the *unconditional* market expectations of rising interest rates noted by Favero and Giavazzi, indicated by the arrow from E to F (where E is an unconditional forecast of the spreads immediately before the election, and F is the weighted average of the two time-consistent equilibria 0 and D_1).

These forecasts reflect the fear that the incoming administration would stick to the radical-left policies described in the Workers' Party program of December 2001 (PT, 2001) which "spoke of denouncing the existing agreement with the IMF and auditing and renegotiating the external debt ... [and of] a complete revision of the policy of giving priority to the payment of debt service" (Williamson 2002, p. 12). As Williamson goes on to point out: "it is hardly surprising that foreign investors should have taken fright at the prospect of a party with such a policy agenda coming to power." But, there were, in fact, determined efforts made by Ministry of Finance and the central bank to warn Lula that such policies would lead to a state of financial crisis and to persuade him that adapting his policies to avoid crisis would be in his own political interest. Although the incoming president had made a commitment to replace the head of the central bank and the Minister of Finance, he nevertheless decided to retain in their posts other key policy makers in both institutions. Furthermore the prospect of a successful transition was boosted by raising the target for primary budget surpluses above that promised to the IMF by the outgoing administration (see below). We postulate that Lula (who had said of himself, "Sou uma espécie de metamorfose ambulante"; Época 2001) shifted his policy preferences. However, the market, which initially expected default with high probability, only revised the default probability down to zero[16] when no default was observed after Lula took office in January 2003.

Even if Lula was planning to pursue the policies of a Moderate-left government, would this be sufficient, in and of itself, to avoid default when he took office? To answer this question, we include in figure 7.7 the response function of a Moderate-left government (where we simply use a higher value for α to illustrate the adaptation of policy). The policy shift shown in the figure has the property that despite the increase in the critical value δ_c^e, a Moderate-left government is still forced into default. This is because the political equilibrium based on the market's fears generates default expectations above the critical level for a Moderate-left administration, $\delta^e(E) > \delta_c^e(\textit{Moderate-left})$. To avoid default in such circumstances, it is essential not only that Lula adopts market-friendly Moderate-left policies but also that the market knows and believes that he has done so. To buy the time needed for such a process of "learning to trust Lula," other policy actions are called for.

In fact the IMF approved Brazil's request for a 15-month standby credit of US$30 billion (7.5 times Brazil's IMF quota of $4 billion) to support the country's economic and financial program, of which $10 billion was made available under the Supplemental Reserve Facility "adding that much extra to the funds potentially available to defend the real before the election" (Williamson 2002). To ensure policy compliance, the IMF agreed to disburse $24 billion of the promised funds in 2003 only after the new government took office and accepted the conditions, including the target for a public sector primary surplus of 3.75 percent of GDP in 2003 (and no less than this for 2004–2005).[17] Although the candidates were not formally required to endorse the program, as proposed by Truman (2002) following the model of Korea 1997, in its Letter of Intent (IMF, August 2002a) the incumbent government assured that Fund that "the core elements of the programme have been explained to the leading candidates, and they have committed to support them," an assurance that the IMF publicly accepted (IMF, September 2002b).

In understanding the declining path of interest rates, "the biggest event when Lula came to office in 2003 is that nothing happened."[18] This idea can be captured in a model of Bayesian learning where not defaulting is enough to persuade the market that Far-left policies have been dropped. Formally, we postulate that the market's belief of Lula's type is a weighted average of a Far- and Moderate-left, where the former has a far higher propensity to default than the latter. That is to say, we assume the Far-left will default for sure, but the Moderate-left will only do so when interest rates are very high.[19]

Since Lula had shown his willingness to adopt the market-friendly policies of the Moderate-left, we indicate in figure 7.8 how IMF support can help implement a successful transition. (To focus on the process of learning, we assume in figure 7.8 that Lula's election was seen as a sure thing, i.e., $\pi = 1$, which rules out the postelection jump in

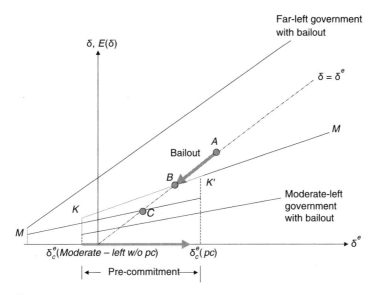

Figure 7.8
Bailouts and policy pre-commitment

spreads and implies that unconditional market expectations of post-election spreads depend only on the response function of the left-wing. So point A corresponds to point D_1 in figure 7.7.) Where A represents the political equilibrium after a Sudden Stop, a partial bailout will lower country risk, as shown by the arrow from A to B in the figure (and a complete bailout will cut sovereign spreads to zero). Incorporating a bailout in the response functions for Moderate- and Far-left governments and taking a weighted average gives the stepped schedule MKM shown in the figure, passing through B on the 45-degree line $(\delta = \delta^e)$ with a step down at K, where $\delta^e = \delta_c^e$ (*Moderate-left without pre-commitment*). Formally, in the absence of pre-commitment, the response function for the left-wing government is obtained as

$$\delta = (1 - P_0)\frac{(1+\delta^e)b^2 - Ab}{(\alpha_F + b^2)} + P_0\frac{(1+\delta^e)b^2 - Ab}{(\alpha_M + b^2)}, \tag{11}$$

or alternatively,

$$\delta = \frac{(b^2 - Ab)(1 - P_0)}{(\alpha_F + b^2)} + \frac{P_0(b^2 - Ab)}{(\alpha_M + b^2)} + \left(\frac{(1 - P_0)b^2}{(\alpha_F + b^2)} + \frac{P_0b^2}{(\alpha_M + b^2)}\right)\delta^e, \tag{12}$$

where P_0 is the prior probability attached to the prospect of the Left-wing being moderate. Note in the figure that without any increase in policy pre-commitment, market expectations will force the Moderate-left government to default even with the provision of liquidity support as the point labeled B far exceeds the default trigger for Moderate-left government without pre-commitment.

If, however, policy pre-commitment succeeds in shifting the default trigger to the right of B, as shown by the arrow on the horizontal axis, there need be no default by the Moderate-left government. From the fiscal conditionality attached to the loan, it is clear that the IMF was concerned to check the moral hazard effects of providing a bailout many times the Brazilian quota. As fiscal policies are not formally incorporated in the model, we represent the commitment to the IMF fiscal targets by increasing the lump-sum cost of default Z_M, which increases δ_c^e, the expectation trigger, defined as

$$\delta_c^e = \frac{\sqrt{Z_M(\alpha_M + b^2)}}{b^2} + \frac{A}{b} - 1.$$

Increasing the default trigger for the Moderate-left government as shown in the figure has the effect of shifting the "step" in the market response function to the right. As a result market interest rates fall to point C, where lower portion of the schedule $MK'M$ now intersects the 45-degree line.[20] Note that the line segment of $MCK'M$ to the left of $\delta_c^e(pc)$ is the weighted average of the schedule "Far-left government with bailout" and the horizontal axis where the weights are P_0 and $1 - P_0$ respectively.

Clearly, for default to be avoided, the trigger value achieved by the pre-commitment has to lie above the level of sovereign spreads achieved by the bailout alone, meaning the two arrows in the figure must overlap. (The fact that the pre-commitment itself brings down market rates of interest raises the possibility of multiple equilibria. This occurs when the default trigger for Moderate-left government lies between point B and C in the diagram: so market expectation will trigger the default, point B, or no default, point C.) In the Brazilian case it appears that the effect of the partial bailout together with policy conditionality was sufficient for Lula to avoid strategic default.

7.5.2 Contagion

While it may appear that the financial crisis was "home-grown," our account includes a powerful channel for contagion, namely the source of the response functions we characterize as Far-left and Moderate-left and the weights attached to them. Brazil may differ from Argentina in many respects, but both had a sufficiently high level of external debts to make them vulnerable to a crisis of confidence in the international capital market (Williamson 2002). Possibly the model of Moderate-left behavior is that of Social Democratic parties in Chile and elsewhere as Williamson suggests. But could the image of the certain-to-default Far-left not be based on events in Argentina that took place less than a year before the Brazilian election? Contagion could thus raise country risk by shifting prior beliefs about the nature of an incoming left-wing government. It could also raise country risk by changing the weight attached to the prospect of a Far-left government. The potential link between politics and contagion implied by equation (11) can be summarized as follows:

Proposition 2 (*Contagion and Politics*)   Default expectations depend on parameters α_F and $1 - P_0$, which are subject to contagious infection: a decline in α_F and/or P_0 increases the likelihood of default.

As learning is immediate, in section 7.5.1 we gave merely a simplified account. We ignored, for example, efforts made by the incoming administration to "manage expectations." In fact, as *The Economist* (p. 39, January 4, 2003) noted, "Since the final weeks of the election campaign, Lula has worked hard to turn investor panic into mere wariness. He has stressed that Brazil means to pay its debt and has chosen ministers who seem ready to carry that promise through." Moreover the target for the primary fiscal surplus was increased to 4.25 percent of GDP, half a percent above what was promised to the IMF (*Financial Times* 2003). So, instead of simple Bayesian updating, beliefs could be subject to manipulation by the new government.[21]

7.6   Conclusion

In this chapter, we interpret the high Brazilian country risk in 2002 and the Sudden Stop in capital flows as reflecting "political equilibrium" in a context where, for the first time, a charismatic left-wing leader had a strong run for office. We show how, for reasons suggested by Alesina, sovereign spreads will move in line with opinion polls, rising with the popularity of the left-wing candidate. It is argued that as the behavior of the potential left-wing president was uncertain, the situation was ripe for contagion from neighboring Argentina, where default followed the end of a right-wing administration.

The finding of a regime shift in mid-2001 reported by Goretti and Taylor (2004) and Goretti (2004) provides some econometric support for what we describe as a Sudden Stop—and the latter gives evidence of political and other factors that may have triggered it. Goretti's (2004) estimates also indicate substantial regional contagion—but only when Argentine spreads pass a threshold of 60 percent. By contrast, our account makes the transmission of contagion depend on Brazilian political developments: this "interaction effect" helps us account for what has happened outside Goretti's sample period, namely the rapid decline in sovereign spreads as Lula took office and pursued prudent policies.

We conclude that the evidence clearly supports the existence of a panic equilibrium (with no rollover and high sovereign spreads) associated with the anticipation of the left-wing victory. Avoiding default was, in our view, achieved by process of transition in which Lula was first persuaded to adjust his policies and then the market learned to trust Lula. If over time Lula becomes more market-friendly, prior probabilities of radical repudiation will be revised as debts are honored and repudiation resisted, bringing down real interest rates and allowing for continued growth without default. IMF support, both financially and in the formation of credible policy, appears to have played a key supporting role in buying time for this transition process.

Appendix: Modeling the Adjustment of Policy and of Perception

A crucial feature of the Brazilian experience was that Lula learned to become market-friendly and shifted his announcements during the campaign accordingly: together with market learning of his revised policies, this led to a fall in sovereign spreads. In this appendix we model the former as a random choice of preferences between those of the Far-left and those of Moderate-left, where the probability of Lula selecting Moderate-left policies increases monotonically over time (e.g., due to the good offices of both the central bank and the Ministry of Finance). Market learning is described by a process of Bayesian updating, where the prior attached to Lula being Moderate-left steadily increases in the absence of default.

Let ρ denote the probability per unit of time of drawing a low-valued preference parameter α_L (which leads to default), and let $1 - \rho$

be the complementary probability of drawing a high-valued pre-ference parameter α_H (which leads to no default). We define two (con-stant) extreme types of left-wing government: the Far-left, which defaults for sure ($\rho_F = 1$), and the Moderate-left, which never defaults ($\rho_M = 0$).

To capture the fact that Lula shifted his policy stance substantially toward Moderate-left during and after the election, we use a model of learning. As described in the next paragraph, this requires an upper bound of the market belief of Lula's type, which declines over time. Let this be given by $\rho_{\text{lula}}(t) = \omega(t)\rho_M + [1 - \omega(t)]\rho_F$, where $\omega(t)$ lies be-tween 0 and 1, $0 \leq \omega(t) \leq 1$, and increases to 1 over time. Obviously $0 \leq \rho_M \leq \rho_{\text{lula}}(t) < 1$, and $\rho_{\text{lula}}(t)$ declines toward ρ_M.

To incorporate Bayesian learning in an analytically tractable way, we first assume that markets believe that Lula can be one of two different types, either defaulting with a high probability $\rho_{\text{lula}}(t)$, or with a low probability ρ_M. Just after the election, the financial markets attach a prior probability P_0 to the belief of the prospect that Lula is Moderate-left of type ρ_M (and the complementary probability $1 - P_0$ to the pros-pect that it is $\rho_{\text{lula}}(t)$).

How will these priors evolve over time? Let P_t be the market's prior belief at time t that Lula is Moderate-left, conditional on observing that he has not defaulted in the previous t periods. If there is no default at period t, the prior belief of a Moderate-left government at period $t + 1$ can be obtained using the Bayesian updating rule:

$$P_{t+1} = \frac{P_t(1 - \rho_M)}{P_t(1 - \rho_M) + (1 - P_t)(1 - \rho_{\text{lula}}(t))}. \tag{13}$$

The complementary probability is thus

$$1 - P_{t+1} = \frac{(1 - P_t)(1 - \rho_{\text{lula}}(t))}{P_t(1 - \rho_M) + (1 - P_t)(1 - \rho_{\text{lula}}(t))}.$$

Dividing the two equations above yields

$$\frac{P_{t+1}}{1 - P_{t+1}} = \frac{1 - \rho_M}{1 - \rho_{\text{lula}}(t)} \frac{P_t}{1 - P_t}. \tag{14}$$

Let $V_t = P_t/(1 - P_t)$. Then (14) becomes a first-order difference equation

$$V_{t+1} = \frac{1 - \rho_M}{1 - \rho_{\text{lula}}(t)} V_t$$

with the solution

$$V_t = f(t)V_0, \tag{15}$$

where

$$f(t) = \frac{(1 - \rho_M)^t}{[1 - \rho_{lula}(t-1)][1 - \rho_{lula}(t-2)] \cdot \ldots \cdot [1 - \rho_{lula}(0)]}.$$

Solving for P_t yields

$$P_t = \frac{f(t)[P_0/(1 - P_0)]}{1 + f(t)[P_0/(1 - P_0)]}. \tag{16}$$

Consider a simple case where $\rho_M = 0$, meaning the Moderate-left government never defaults. As long as Lula has not defaulted, the process of Lula's adoption of Moderate-left policies will imply that $\rho_{lula}(t) \to \rho_M$ or the default probability of Lula will decline asymptotically over time.

Since $\rho_M \leq \rho_{lula}(i) < \rho_{lula}(i-1)$, it is obvious that

$$\frac{1 - \rho_M}{1 - \rho_{lula}(i-1)} > \frac{1 - \rho_M}{1 - \rho_{lula}(i)} \to 1.$$

This implies that both $f(t)$ and P_t are increasing over time. So, as Lula adapts his policies, markets will believe that Lula is less likely to default.

How would learning affect the ex ante default rates? If the market believes Lula is of the type of Moderate-left, the resulting default rate must be

$$\delta_M = 0.$$

If, however, the market believes that Lula is of the type of $\rho_{lula}(t)$, the default rate will be

$$\delta_F = \frac{b^2}{\alpha_L + b^2}(1 + \delta_t^e).$$

Given the market's priors, the ex ante spreads for Lula in the presence of learning and policy adaptation can be expressed as

$$\delta_t^e = E_t(\delta_t) = P_t[\rho_M\delta_F + (1 - \rho_M)\delta_M]$$
$$+ (1 - P_t)[\rho_{lula}(t)\delta_F + (1 - \rho_{lula}(t))\delta_M]$$

$$= (1 - P_t)\rho_{\text{lula}}(t)\delta_F$$

$$= (1 - P_t)\rho_{\text{lula}}(t)\frac{b^2}{\alpha_L + b^2}(1 + \delta_t^e)$$

assuming that $\rho_M = 0$.

This implies the expected default rate

$$\delta_t^e = \frac{(1 - P_t)\rho_{\text{lula}}(t)[b^2/(\alpha_L + b^2)]}{1 - (1 - P_t)\rho_{\text{lula}}(t)[b^2/(\alpha_L + b^2)]}. \tag{17}$$

Since both $1 - P_t$ and $\rho_{\text{lula}}(t)$ are decreasing over time, δ_t^e declines monotonically. This gradual downward adjustment in sovereign spreads is more realistic than the simple step-change used in the text, and it corresponds broadly to the time-profile of Brazilian spreads depicted in figure 7.3.

Notes

For their helpful comments, we thank Renato Flores, Emanuel Kohlschen, and participants in the PUC-Rio seminar, particularly Olivier Blanchard, Arminio Fraga, Marcio Garcia, Francesco Giavazzi, Pedro Malan, and our formal discussant Dionísio Días Carneiro. We are also grateful to Chuck Blackorby, Martin Ellison, Adrian Penalver, Neil Rankin, Peter Sinclair, Michael Spagat, and John Williamson for their observations and to Elba Roo for research assistance. This research has been supported by ESRC grant R000239216 "Moral Hazard and Financial Institutions" and by the CSGR at Warwick.

1. According to Sebastian Edwards, Brazil's debt ratio was expected to decline as long as the primary surplus was maintained, "Brazil's only hope of avoiding collapse," *The Financial Times* (August 5, 2002). See also Williamson (2002) and Goldstein (2003) for discussions of debt sustainability.

2. "The current primary surplus of 3.75 percent of gross domestic product guarantees a declining debt to GDP ratio as long as the inflation-adjusted interest rate paid by the government on its publicly traded debt does not exceed GDP growth by more than 7 percentage points," Fraga and Goldfajn (2002).

3. Atkeson (2001), Boonprakaikawe and Ghosal (2003), and Hellwig (2002) show how the existence of public signals can generate multiple equilibria even in models with private signals.

4. In the equation determining the probability of transition to turmoil, the variable measuring Lula's popularity is statistically significant and positive, but high yield spreads in developed markets have a stronger impact on the transition probability, though statistically less significant. In addition there is a positive effect of a dummy variable for bad news from IMF.

5. This resembles the bank-run equilibrium of Diamond and Dybvig (1983) in that it can take place when fundamentals are in good shape.

6. Chang stresses, as we do, that recent market volatility in Brazil cannot be fully understood without reference to the electoral outlook, but his account omits the evolution of left-wing policies and the role of the IMF in helping to avoid default while learning takes place.

7. As Mexico experienced in 1994 when despite the signal of impending crisis the government failed to place its debt in the auction.

8. Employing an infinite-horizon model, they showed that there exist more than one possible equilibria: one in which the investors roll over and the government honors its obligations, and the other in which investors refuse to buy any public debt, anticipating that future investors will do likewise. So the government is forced to repudiate.

9. A low value of δ could involve debt rollover, while a high level could indicate outright default.

10. See Calvo et al. (2002a).

11. In the absence of creditor coordination, this could be the outcome of panic.

12. Ideally one would explain how these probabilities are determined.

13. Note that in the case where creditors voluntarily roll over, $A = b$, the result is trivial no matter which party wins the election. The sovereign spread would be zero.

14. In a more complete model of the political process, this probability would be endogenous as the candidates select programs to gain votes.

15. See Driffill and Miller (1992) and Altug et al. (2000) for other applications of Bayesian learning that might arise after changes of political and economic regimes.

16. This is a special case of Bayesian learning. It is qualitatively similar to the more general two-sided process, described in the appendix, where Lula shifts his policy preferences increasingly to be more market-friendly and the markets reduce their expected default probability accordingly.

17. The Lula government raised the target to 4.25 percent, further reassuring overseas investors, *The Financial Times* (2003, p. 22, March 31).

18. Arminio Fraga's comments at the PUC-Rio meeting.

19. Hence, if only the Moderate-left can avoid default for one period, market interest rates will fall sharply as the market learns its true type.

20. Obtained by setting to zero the second term on the right-hand side of equation (11).

21. Models of strategic learning that may be useful in this context include Cripps (1991), Ellison and Valla (2001), and Rosal and Spagat (2003).

References

Agénor, P., M. Miller, D. Vines, and A. Weber, eds. 1999. *The Asian Financial Crisis: Causes, Contagion and Consequences*. Cambridge: Cambridge University Press.

Alesina, A. 1987. Macroeconomic Policy in a Two-Party System as a Repeated Game. *Quarterly Journal of Economics* 102(3): 651–78.

Alesina, A., A. Prati, and G. Tabellini. 1990. Public confidence and debt management: A model and a case study of Italy. In R. Dornbusch et al., eds., *Public Debt Management: Theory and History.* Cambridge University Press, pp. 94–124.

Altug, S., F. Demers, and M. Demers. 2000. Political risk and irreversible investment: Theory and an application to quebec. Discussion Paper 2405. CEPR.

Angeletos, G.-M., C. Hellwig, and A. Pavan. 2003. Coordination and policy traps. Presented at the European Summer Symposium in Macroeconomics (ESSIM), Athens (May). CEPR.

Araujo, A., and M. Leon. 2003. Speculative attacks on debts and optimum currency Area: A welfare analysis.

Atkeson, A. 2001. Comment on Morris and Shin. *NBER Macroeconomics Annual.* 15: 162–71.

Boschi, M. 2003. International financial contagion: Evidence from the Argentine crisis of 2001–2002. Mimeo. University of Essex.

Boonprakaikawe, J., and S. Ghosal. 2003. Public signals and multiple equilibria. Presented at Warwick Summer Research Workshop on Financial Crises: Theory and Policy. University of Warwick.

Calvo, G. A., A. Izquierdo, and E. Talvi. 2002a. Sudden Stops, the real exchange rate and fiscal sustainability: Argentina's lessons. Mimeo. Inter-American Development Bank.

Calvo, G. A., and E. Talvi. 2002b. Lula effect? Look again! Mimeo. Washington, DC.

Carlsson, H., and E. V. Damme. 1993. Global games and equilibrium selection. *Econometrica* 61(5): 989–1018.

Chang, R. 2002. Electoral uncertainty and volatility of international capital flows. Available at *http://econweb.rutgers.edu/chang/brazil1.pdf.*

Claessens, S., and K. Forbes, eds. 2001. *International Financial Contagion.* Boston: Kluwer Academic Publishers.

Cole, H., and T. Kehoe. 1996. A self-fulfilling model of Mexico's 1994–1995 debt crisis. *Journal of International Economics* 41: 309–30.

Corsetti, G., B. Guimares, and N. Roubini. 2003. The tradeoff between an international lender of last resort to deal with liquidity crisis and moral hazard distortions: A model of the IMF's catalytic finance approach. Presented at the European Summer Symposium in Macroeconomics (ESSIM) in Athens. CEPR.

Cripps, M. 1991. Learning rational expectations in a policy game. *Journal of Economic Dynamic and Control* 15: 297–315.

Diamond, D., and P. Dybvig. 1983. Bank runs, deposit insurance, and liquidity. *Journal of Political Economy* 91: 401–19.

Driffill, J., and M. Miller. 1992. Learning and inflation convergence in the ERM. *Economic Journal* 103(417): 369–78.

The Economist. 2003. Lula's burden of hope. January 4, pp. 39–40.

Edwards, S. 2002. Brazil's only hope of avoiding collapse. *Financial Times*, August 5, p. 17 (London edition).

Ellison, M., and N. Valla. 2001. Learning, uncertainty and central bank activism in an economy with strategic factors. *Journal of Monetary Economics* 48: 153–71.

Época. 2001. Frases de Lula. Available at *http://revistaepoca.globo.com/Epoca/0,6993,EPT426959-2011,00.html*.

Favero, C., and F. Giavazzi. 2002. Why are Brazil's interest rates so high? Università Bocconi, Milanno. IGIER.

Financial Times. 2003. Lula's 100 days. March 31, p. 22.

Fraga, A., and I. Goldfajn. 2002. Trust Brazil: Investors' concerns about the country's debt levels are unfounded. *Financial Times*, September 18, p. 19 (London edition).

Fratzscher, M. 2000. What causes currency crises: Sunspots, contagion or fundamentals? Mimeo. EUI. Available at *www.csgr.org*.

Fratzscher, M. 2002. On currency crises and contagion. Working Paper 139. ECB.

Ghosal, S., and M. Miller. 2003. Co-ordination failure, moral hazard and sovereign bankruptcy procedures. *Economic Journal* 113(487): 276–304.

Goldstein, M. 2003. Debt sustainability, Brazil and the IMF. Working Paper 03-1. Institute for International Economics.

Goretti, M. 2004. Understanding the Brazilian currency turmoil in 2002: An empirical analysis. Mimeo. University of Warwick.

Goretti, M., and M. P. Taylor. 2004. Brazil and the 2002 Currency Turmoil: A story of financial contagion and political mistrust? Mimeo. University of Warwick.

Hellwig, C. 2002. Public information, private information, and the multiplicity of equilibria in coordination games. *Journal of Economic Theory* 107(2): 191–222.

IMF. 2002a. Brazil—Letter of intent, memorandum of economic policies, and technical memorandum of understanding. International Monetary Fund, Washington, DC.

IMF. 2002b. IMF approves US$30.4 billion stand-by credit for Brazil. Press Release 02/40. International Monetary Fund, Washington, DC.

Kim, J. Y. 2001. Currency crisis contagion, capital flows, and sovereign ratings: Empirical studies on (Asian) emerging markets. PhD dissertation. University of Warwick.

Masson, P. 1999. Contagion: Monsoonal effects, spillovers and jumps between multiple equilibria. In P. Agénor et al., eds., *The Asian Financial Crisis: Causes, Contagion and Consequences*. Cambridge: Cambridge University Press, pp. 265–80.

Morris, S., and H. S. Shin. 1998. Unique equilibrium in a model of self-fulfilling currency attacks. *American Economic Review* 88(3): 587–97.

Obstfeld, M. 1996. Models of currency crises with self-fulfilling features. *European Economic Review* 40(3–5): 1037–47.

PT (Partido dos Trabalhadores). 2001. Concepção e diretrizes do programa de governo do PT para o Brasil. Available at *http://www.pt.org.br* (see under Diretrizes).

Radelet, S., and J. Sachs. 1998. The East Asian financial crisis: Diagnosis, remedies and prospects. *Brookings Papers on Economic Activity* 1: 1–90.

Rodrik, D., and A. Velasco. 1999. Short-term capital flows. Working Paper 7364. NBER. Available at *http://www.nber.org/papers/w7364*.

Rosal, J. M., and M. Spagat. 2003. Structural uncertainty and central bank conservatism: the ignorant should shut their eyes. Mimeo. Royal Holloway College, University of London.

Sachs, J., A. Tornell, and A. Velasco. 1996. The Mexican peso crisis: Sudden death or death foretold? *Journal of International Economics* 41: 265–83.

Thampanishvong, K. 2002. Incorporation of electoral uncertainty into the crisis model with self-fulfilling feature. MSc dissertation. University of Warwick.

Truman, E. M. 2002. Brazil needs help. *Financial Times*, June 25, p. 19 (London edition).

Williamson, J. 2002. Is Brazil next? *International Economics Policy Briefs*. PB02-7. Institute for International Economics, Washington, DC.

Comment on Chapter 7

Dionísio Carneiro

Miller, Thampanishvong, and Zhang explore a combination of self-fulfilling elements present in the rise of the spreads, and they single out the positive effect of learning about the true Lula in the subsequent fall of the spreads. By making use of contrasts between multiple-equilibria and single-equilibria results, they add political contagion as a trigger to in an optimal default setting, *and* take the position that the recent market volatility cannot be fully understood without reference to electoral outlook. They take markets' prior estimates of the "probability" of default using the perception of Lula's chance of winning and the likelihood that Brazil would imitate Argentina. These estimates of default risk are ultimately updated by the fact that the true Lula, as representative of the Brazilian Left, turned out to be much more moderate than market agents were led to believe when they considered the case of Argentina.

My comments focus on (1) the models used by the authors, (2) the authors' characterizations of left-wing and right-wing, (3) the idea that the threat of contagion from Argentina was a source of market panic, (4) the role of exchange rate flexibility and IMF, and (5) the importance, underlined by the authors, of trusting Lula's ability to perceive the political advantage of adopting sensible policies as opposed to the authors' analysis of the markets learning to trust Lula.

Comments on Models

The rational default model in section 7.3 has two features: First, it assumes fixed rates as external debt b depends only on δ and not on devaluation. In my view, this is not a fair description of the Brazilian situation in 2002, as the fixed exchange rate regime had been abandoned in 1999. Since then, exchange rate depreciation has played an important corrective role in external accounts. Second, in the sequence of events described by the model, creditors first decide the level of rollover and estimate δ^e; then government decides whether or not to default. This setup implies that rollover rate is the "cause" of default, and this is unrelated to the government's actual behavior. The trigger value for default would combine Rudi Dornbusch's "Sudden Stop" and "politically motivated default." However, the latter is not related, in the model, to the politicians' rhetoric, contrary to the evidence of PT promises and discourse up to the second half of 2002.

Left and Right

From Miller, Thampanishvong, and Zhang's cost function of the default rate $C(\delta) = Z + \alpha\delta^2$ and b, which is defined as the size of debt subject to default, we find that right-wing is characterized by its "good behavior" when debt b is low and α is high, whereas left-wing is characterized by high b and low α. By this reasoning, former president Cardoso would be left in 2002 because of high b and of the size of dollar-linked debt, especially because of the effect of floating *real* on the share of dollar-linked debt, b, which increases in the adverse scenario. If anything in this context, left should mean high b and low α even when $R > 0$. Before August 2002 Palocci and (Venezuela's president) Hugo Chávez had more in common than the authors acknowledge, as both considered "debt repayment ... [as] part of neoliberal strategy." The characterization of left and right results appears to be convenient in the authors' willingness to identify right with low probability of default, and because of the observed link between spreads and results of surveys on voters' intentions.

Argentina as a Trigger Factor

At the end of section 7.3.2, the problem posed is where the market should get its ideas of what a new government might do. The discussion considers what has happened in neighboring Argentina. However, this is not satisfactory. In their attempt to introduce the importance of contagion to the episode, the authors set up a correlation between JPM EMBI + spreads—an information value that may be exaggerated. When one calculates volatility by way of corrected (Lyons and Schmuckler 2000 used by Forbes and Rigobon 2001) correlations for this period, the figures are consistent with another view: the correlation actually

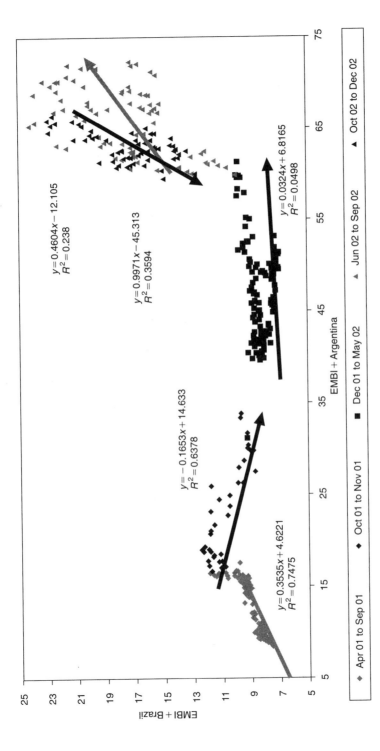

Figure 7.9
Contagion between EMBI + Brazil and Argentina (tripped % p.a.). Sources: JP Morgan and Galanto Pesquisas

Table 7.1
Measures of correlation EMBI + Brazil versus EMBI + Argentina (%)

	EMBI + Argentina variance	Correlation R^2	Coefficient R^2 adj
Pre-crisis			
January 2002–March 2001	0.06	69	69
Postcrisis			
April 2001–September 2001	0.24	89	69
October 2001–November 2001	0.24	−80	−56
December 2001–May 2002	0.17	22	14
June 2002–September 2002	0.05	51	54
October 2002–December 2002	0.03	60	74

Sources: JP. Morgan and *Galanto Pesquisas Econômicas*.
Note: *Variances were calculated on daily basis.*

declines after the Argentine default (at the time, market analysts referred to this phenomenon as decoupling). The correlations were subsequently aggravated because of the general sell-off of Brazilian debt.
This was due to the simple fact that the debt was liquid, as large
holders of high-risk debt adjusted their portfolios in response to the
Argentine default. This episode had little to do with where markets
were "getting their ideas," however. In 2002 correlations were smaller.
In contrast to what had happened in early 2001, as the Argentine crises
loomed, periods of higher volatility did not lead to higher correlation.
From 2001 onward higher volatility was accompanied by lower correlations (see figure 7.9 and table 7.1).

Lumping of Different Behavior in Different Episodes

Some post-2003:2 lessons suggest some alternative explanations to
the authors' approach here. First, Argentina's importance for Brazilian
2002 problems is somewhat overstated. The direct impact in 2002 was
dominated by decoupling and the opening channel for contagion. For
example, Kirchner's declaration on default was made after the terms
of the agreement had been settled between Argentina and the IMF.
Second, the importance to the IMF in improving Brazil's chances of
success after Argentina's default is ignored by the authors. Third, the
building of confidence had little to do with the ability of markets learning to trust Lula, but more with Lula's learning to trust market-friendly

policies and taking serious steps to consolidate minimally sensible macropolicies. Clearly, he saw the political benefits to be reaped from this change in intentions. Indeed, as inflation was reduced as a consequence of the restrictive monetary policies, public support for the new government was sustained.

Evaluation of the IMF's Role and Flexible Exchange Rate

The IMF agreement was not a dividing issue in the presidential campaign after July as the authors claim. Before the IMF agreement was pre-announced, no candidate defended IMF policies. Liquidity from the IMF was important to preventing default in 2002, but this was the same way it had been in the 1998 elections when the IMF did not prevent the collapse of the system. This suggests that exchange rate regime rather then politics and perception played a more important role than the political economy models used by the authors.

The decision to increase the supply of dollar-linked assets and float the *real* contributed more to the Sudden Stop than any political opinion surveys. On these issues one can't ignore the fact that two different viewpoints exist. The first may be called the macro-free view of expected default and actual default, which is essentially political and not economic in focus. The second concerns the effect of the macrodetermined interest rate, size of debt, exchange rate, and politicians' ability to learn from inflation results, the disorganizing effects on the economy, and the voters' evaluation of the candidates' commitment to stabilization. Pragmatism and sound macropolicies, rather than ideology and market tolerance, appear to have been a stronger force in the Brazilian 2002 to 2003 episode than it is represented in the view expressed in the chapter.

References

Forbes, K., and R. Rigobon. 2000. Contagion in Latin America: Definitions, measurement and policy implication. NBER Working Paper 7885.

Lyons, R., and S. Schmukler. 2000. Fragility, liquidity and risk: The behavior of mutual funds in crises. Paper prepared for the project on Financial Contagion and How it Spreads.

8 Credit, Interest, and Jurisdictional Uncertainty: Conjectures on the Case of Brazil

Persio Arida, Edmar Lisboa Bacha, and André Lara-Resende

8.1 Introduction

Real interest rates have been extraordinarily high since the *Real* Plan stabilized inflation in 1994. Until 1999, one might argue, the macroeconomic policy was not in order. There was no primary budget surplus, the exchange rate was pegged and overvalued, and interest rates were primarily oriented to sustain the level of international reserves. The adoption of a floating exchange rate at the beginning of 1999 marked the start of a new phase. The public sector accounts showed a primary surplus on a systematic and sustained basis, and the real exchange rate depreciated to the point where the country started to produce record high trade balance surpluses, and significantly reduced the current account deficit. Real interest rates have been, on average, lower than before, although they are still exceptionally high when compared with those of other emerging market countries. However, why is it that the interest rate remains so high?

The explanations offered for this phenomenon can be labeled as "bad equilibrium," "insufficient fiscal adjustment," and "sequence of negative shocks" hypotheses. Section 8.2 briefly reviews these hypotheses. Whatever their relative merits in explaining why interest rates have been so high since the adoption of a floating exchange rate, we argue that there is something more fundamental linking the inexistence of local long-term domestic credit to the persistence of high short-term interest rates.

Section 8.3 introduces the concept of "jurisdictional uncertainty" and argues that it is the reason for the nonexistence of a long-term domestic credit market. The concept of jurisdictional uncertainty is distinguished from related risk concepts in section 8.4. The negative consequences of jurisdictional uncertainty for private savings and investment are spelled out in section 8.5. Section 8.6 argues that the adverse consequences of jurisdictional uncertainty have been misinterpreted as market failures that require state intervention. These interventions have varied over time but can be gathered into four categories: restrictions to currency convertibility, artificial term lengthening of public debt, compulsory saving funds, and forced savings through inflation—with the latter now replaced by "incomeless" taxes. Section 8.7 reviews each of these interventions and argues that they aggravate the effects of jurisdictional uncertainty. A very simple two-equation reduced-form open economy macro model is presented in section 8.8 to show the impact of each intervention on the short-term interest rate and on the exchange rate, under the assumption of a credible inflation-targeting monetary policy. A discussion of policy implications closes the chapter in section 8.9.

8.2   Current Interpretations of High Interest Rates

Three general lines of argument can be identified in the debate about the reason why real interest rates are so high in Brazil.

The first is that monetary policy after inflation stabilization has been too conservative. In the period of pegged and overvalued exchange rates (1994–1998), high interest rates were required to compensate for the risk of devaluation. After the adoption of a floating exchange rate (1999–to date), monetary policy was caught in a "bad equilibrium." The argument is that very high real interest rates raise the risk on public debt. It should thus be possible to obtain the same rate of inflation, everything else remaining constant, with a lower real interest rate and a lower risk on public debt. This is what we call the "good equilibrium."

The double equilibrium hypothesis then presupposes fiscal dominance in an open economy. Inflation is sensitive to the exchange rate, but the exchange rate responds to the risk on public debt. When the domestic public debt is high, the attempt to control inflation primarily through monetary policy may result in a perverse outcome: high real interest rates worsen the fiscal disequilibria, and increase the default risk and the risk premium demanded by creditors.

The double equilibrium model is internally consistent. Its empirical relevance, however, has not yet been established. Moreover interest rate smoothing considerations may render it unattractive in practice. A central bank concerned with the credibility and the coherence of policies through time would hardly dare to make the abrupt interest rate cut required to reach the good equilibrium.

A second hypothesis is that the fiscal adjustment is still insufficient. Despite a large primary surplus, the burden of public debt is very high and puts pressure on the interest rate. The public sector high financing requirements compete for the scarce available savings, raising the market-clearing interest rate. Government spending crowds out private investment and prevents the economy from growing.

The third hypothesis is that there was an unusual series of adverse shocks, external and internal, in the last couple of years: the burst of the Nasdaq bubble, the rationing of domestic energy supply, September 11, the collapse of Argentina, and finally, in 2002, the fear of an electoral victory of the Workers' Party and the so-called Lula risk. In the wake of these shocks, the macroeconomic policy, although adequate, has not yet had sufficient time to produce results for economic recovery and lower the interest rates. An inflation-targeting monetary policy should attempt to smooth interest rate volatility in the trajectory toward long-run equilibrium. Thus, in the absence of additional adverse shocks, it should be only a question of time before the Brazilian real interest rate converges to the levels of other stable economies. In addition the central bank is not independent and has therefore to establish its reputation. Interest rates are high ex post but not necessarily ex ante because the public has doubts that political interference will prevent the central bank from complying with the inflation target.

These alternative interpretations are not mutually exclusive. A sustainable improvement in the fiscal regime, preferably in the form of a contraction of public expenditure, will certainly reduce the equilibrium rate of interest. It is also clear that Brazil has not been able yet to extract the full potential of the macroeconomic policies put in place in 1999. The explanation above, however, misses an important point behind the persistently high interest rates in Brazil. We believe that a policy-related distortion, of a resilient nature, is impeding the convergence to real equilibrium interest rates compatible with those observed internationally.

Before we elaborate on this conjecture, we need to call attention to a relatively forgotten point in the debate on high interest rates: the absence of local long-term bond and credit markets. In the literature this fact is used to explain why, unlike in other countries, monetary policy is less effective in Brazil (smaller wealth effect), or private financing for long-term investment is so small. The connection between the lack of a

local long-term interest rate structure and the high short-term real interest rate has, however, gone unnoticed. The reason seems to be that
the threads establishing such connection go beyond the usual macroeconomic channels covered in the literature.

8.3 Jurisdictional Uncertainty

We start by noting that there are some local instruments used for long-
term credit tied to government development banks with compulsory
funding, but no market as such exists. Experience shows that it is
possible to lengthen maturities through tax incentives (e.g., income tax
deferment in private pension plans) or through decisions of fund managers required to hedge long-term liabilities (e.g., the case of pension
funds willing to buy long-term price-indexed assets). Although there
are some other specific exceptions, such as the financing of durable
goods, the local long-term bond market is small and, symptomatically,
restricted to Treasury bonds with a captive institutional demand, and
with an inflation adjustment factor ("IGP-M") calculated by an independent, nongovernmental institution. There is, however, a large long-
term credit market open to Brazilian debtors where the jurisdiction
is foreign. Access to this market is restricted to the government, large
companies—firms whose size justifies the cost of verification of credit
quality—and large banks. The credit risk is thus Brazilian, but these
same firms that obtain long-term credit outside the country are by and
large unable to obtain financing with equivalent maturity in the domestic market.

The existence of a long-term credit offshore but not on-shore is
not explained by the location of the creditors' decision-making center.
There are resident creditors with decision centers offshore and nonresi-
dent creditors with decision centers in the country. The same creditors
act on both markets, but they are only willing to lend long-term offshore. The inexistence of a local long-term credit market is also not
explained by the currency of denomination of contracts. Despite the
legal restrictions for the local issuance of dollar-indexed private debt,
not even Brazil's Treasury finances itself locally with long-term dollar-
linked bonds. There is no long-term credit market on-shore, not in *reais*
nor in foreign currency.

Regardless of the residence of the creditor or of the currency of
denomination of the contract, long-term credit is only available if the
jurisdiction is foreign. It is the jurisdiction—the uncertainties associ-

ated to the settlement of contracts in the Brazilian jurisdiction—that is at the root of the inexistence of a large long-term domestic credit market.

The absence of long-term offshore credit denominated in *reais* should also be noticed. The execution of offshore contracts in *reais* would in the event of litigation necessarily refer to the Brazilian jurisdiction, because Brazil is the issuer of the reference currency. Although signed offshore, credit contracts are thus subject to the uncertainties of the Brazilian jurisdiction. The credit contracts in *reais* that exist offshore are synthetic assets denominated in *reais* but settled in dollars. They mirror domestic credit instruments, exclusively of a short-term nature, that exist in Brazil. The contracts that underlie such synthetic assets make it explicit that the risks of execution and settlement are exactly equivalent to those of the assets in *reais*, to which they are referred. They are mirror images of Brazilian credit contracts, and really just vehicles launched by financial institutions that make a profit by bearing the responsibility of complying with the legal requirements for converting dollars into *reais*. Such contracts would disappear if the *real* were fully convertible.

Credit is thus restricted to the short term in Brazil or the long term in dollars offshore, since only the later escapes the risk of the Brazilian jurisdiction. Table 8.1 illustrates the situation. The left-hand side of the table refers to short-term financial contracts and the right-hand side to long-term contracts. The lines describe the currency denomination of the contracts (in *reais* or in dollars); the columns describe the jurisdiction (Brazil or offshore). Short-term contracts are available in both denominations and locations while long-term contracts are available only in dollar terms and under offshore jurisdiction.

Table 8.1 shows that long-term credit exists only when the jurisdiction is not Brazilian. The critical divide is the jurisdiction, not the denomination currency. There are legal restrictions on the private

Table 8.1
Credit contracts in Brazil

	Short term		Long term	
	Brazil	Offshore	Brazil	Offshore
Reais	Yes	Yes	No	No
Dollars	Yes[a]	Yes	No[a]	Yes

a. Restrictions apply to private debtors.

issuance of domestic debt with dollar indexation clauses but these restrictions do not apply to the Treasury. There are short-term contracts denominated in *reais* in both jurisdictions but not long-term contracts. Because the legal foundation of the domestic currency is of necessity Brazilian, offshore contracts in *reais* are "contaminated" by the Brazilian jurisdiction. Short-term external finance in *reais* mirrors short-term internal finance. Long-term credit is therefore only available offshore and denominated in foreign currencies, which is the only way to avoid the reference to events defined in the Brazilian jurisdiction.

The refusal to extend long-term credit in the domestic jurisdiction signals the presence of an important uncertainty factor. This affects, to use Keynes's (1963) terminology, "the stability and safety of the money contract" by which savings are made available to the government and other debtors. It is an uncertainty of a diffuse character that permeates the decisions of the executive, legislative, and judiciary and manifests itself predominantly as an anti-saver and anti-creditor bias. The bias is not against the act of saving but against the financial deployment of savings, the attempt to an intertemporal transfer of resources through financial instruments that are, in the last analysis, credit instruments.

The bias is transparent in the negative social connotation of figures associated to the moneylender—"financial capital" by opposition to "productive capital,""banker" as opposed to "entrepreneur." The debtor is viewed on a socially positive form, as an entity that generates jobs and wealth or appeals to the bank to cope with adverse life conditions. This bias may be observed more or less everywhere, but it is particularly acute in Brazil, probably because of the deep social differences and the high levels of income concentration in the country. Cultural and historical factors could also have facilitated the dissemination of this anti-creditor bias.

The depth of this bias in Brazil may be inferred from the answers to a recent elite opinion survey conducted by two Brazilian political scientists (Lamounier and Souza 2002), and summarized in table 8.2. Confronted with the dilemma between the enforcement of contracts and the practice of social justice, only 48 percent of the 500-plus respondents considered that contracts have always to prevail over social considerations. Surprisingly enough, only 7 percent of the members of the judiciary said that they were prepared to judge contracts independently of social considerations, and a full 61 percent answered that the achievement of social justice justifies decisions in breach of contracts.

Table 8.2
Contract enforcement according to the Brazilian elite

	Executive	Legislative	Judiciary	Total[a]
Contracts must be enforced independently of their social effects	77	44	7	48
Judge has to perform a social function, and the quest for social justice justifies decisions in breach of contracts	15	39	61	36
Other answers	08	17	32	16
Total	100	100	100	100

Source: Lamounier and De Souza (2002).
a. Includes businesspeople, union members, journalists, members of religious orders, NGO-members, and intellectuals.

The concept of jurisdictional uncertainty conforms to the growing consensus among economists and political scientists that the social, economic, legal, and political organizations of a society, meaning its institutions, are a primary determinant of its economic performance (North 1981). In the Brazilian case, jurisdictional uncertainty may thus be decomposed, in its anti-creditor bias, as the risk of acts of the Prince changing the value of contracts before or at the moment of their execution and as the risk of an unfavorable interpretation of the contract in case of a court ruling. Overcoming jurisdictional uncertainty involves recasting both what Acemoglu and Johnson (2003) call "private rights institutions," which protect citizens against expropriation by the Prince, and "contractual institutions," which enable private contracts among citizens.

A long-term domestic market does not exist because there are no long-term financial savings available under Brazilian jurisdiction. The "preferred habitat" (Modigliani and Sutch 1982) of savers is the very short term. It is a distortion resulting not from an intertemporal consumption allocation decision but rather from the reluctance of individuals and firms to make their savings available for the long term under domestic jurisdiction. Banks and financial intermediaries share the same reluctance and only hold medium-term securities under the particular circumstances that we discuss below.

This reluctance has roots in our recent history, punctuated by the loss of value of long-term financial contracts, as a result of the manipulation of indexation, changes of monetary standard, freezing of financial assets, judicial annulment of clauses of readjustment in foreign currency, normative acts of the Brazilian internal revenue service affecting the taxation of ongoing contracts, and so on. The long tradition of delays in the payment of credits against the government, as exemplified by the difficulty of cashing in on indemnity or judicial orders of payment, reinforced the reluctance to invest in long-term debt instruments. Jurisdictional uncertainty worsened after the 1988 Constitution introduced the possibility of changes in the interpretative emphasis between conflicting constitutional principles, particularly the subordination of private property to its social function.

The longest maturity for which there is a financial domestic market varies with circumstances and the perception, more or less acute, of the jurisdictional uncertainty. In Brazil this maturity was seldom over one year, and in times of stress the duration of savings instruments contracted to levels close to one day by massive concentration on overnight banking deposits. It is only through artifices, such as the indexing of public debt to the daily overnight interest rate and the regulation of captive markets (pension funds' compulsory investments and banks' reserve requirements), that the average tenor of domestic public debt is today around two and half years. In contrast, under foreign jurisdiction, the external public debt has an average maturity of 12 years, and Brazil 40 is a liquid bond.

Let T be the maximum term for which there exists a domestic debt market, as determined by the jurisdictional uncertainty. For terms above T, this uncertainty makes the domestic market disappear, although there is still an interest rate term structure for external debt. This means that, for maturities longer than T, the jurisdictional uncertainty cannot be evaluated quantitatively; that is, it cannot be expressed as an add-on to the interest rate prevailing in the long-term external markets, and the domestic market ceases to exist. But up to T there is a near perfect arbitrage between dollar-denominated interest rates in the domestic and international markets. Thus, for short-term debt maturities, the jurisdictional uncertainty is embedded in the spread over the riskless US Treasury rate that has to be paid to investors to hold short-term Brazilian government debt on-shore.

8.4 Jurisdictional Uncertainty and Other Risk Concepts

To clarify our concept of jurisdictional uncertainty, it is useful to spell out its characteristics to distinguish these from related concepts in the literature. Although associated with lack of confidence in the monetary standard, jurisdictional uncertainty is not restricted to mere apprehension about the purchasing power of the currency being maintained in the long run. If it were so, there would be many long-term credit instruments, both domestic and offshore, indexed to the domestic price level. Even in the absence of possible inflationary and devaluation losses, few investors are willing to buy long-term financial instruments in the domestic jurisdiction. Jurisdictional uncertainty cannot thus be solely connected to the risk factors involved in price level and exchange rate volatility.

Jurisdictional uncertainty is also not to be confused with frontier or transfer risk. The market knows how to price frontier risks for different maturities, as demonstrated by the spread differences between CDs issued by Brazilian banks offshore with and without the "dollar constraint" clause. Frontier risk alone cannot inhibit the development of a long-term domestic credit market.

Jurisdictional uncertainty is also not be confused with credit risk. Like the frontier risk, credit risk can be priced for different maturities, as demonstrated by the existence of long-term offshore credit for the Brazilian Treasury as well as for large firms and financial institutions. The spread paid by Brazil's Treasury long bonds over US Treasury paper of similar duration, which has conventionally been denominated country risk, is the market estimate of the country's long-term credit risk offshore.

Jurisdictional uncertainty affects all types of long-term mercantile activities in the country. But it should not be confused with the risk of doing business in Brazil, where the difficulties faced by firms include logistic problems of transport and ports, complex legal and labor legislation, and high crime rate. Jurisdictional uncertainty results from an anti-creditor bias, and not an anti-business bias. This is evident in the willingness of foreign firms to make long-term private direct investment in the country but not to extend local long-term credit even to associated firms. It is also shown by the fact that business firms are often benefited as debtors by the materialization of the jurisdictional uncertainty in its anti-creditor bias.

Jurisdictional uncertainty is, in our view, what gives substance to the so-called original sin of international finance, as identified by Eichengreen and Hausmann (1999), namely the incapacity of issuance of long-term external debt denominated in the national currency. Jeanne (2002) argues that the original sin is the result of lack of credibility of domestic monetary policy in a context of fixed exchange rates. We consider this interpretation to unduly restrict the problem to risks posed by the volatility of foreign exchange and interest rates. If this were the only problem, a local dollar-indexed long-term market for financial contracts would exist. It is true that there are legal restrictions to local long-term contracts in foreign currency, but even Brazil's Treasury, which is not subject to such restrictions, finds it difficult to finance itself with dollar-indexed long-term bonds in the local market.

Eichengreen, Hausmann, and Paniza (2003) mention countries such as Chile, Israel, and India that are able to issue long-term debt denominated in national currency on-shore but not offshore. For us, this impediment is not an ingrained, original sin. Rather, it is a problem of small size (as international financial markets need bulky issues to give them liquidity), or else the consequence of these countries having inconvertible currencies. Local pension funds and other long-term institutional investors with long-term obligations in local currency are not affected by such inconvertibility but foreign investors are. Thus what the three-country experience seems to indicate is that there are three requirements for a country to be able to issue long-term debt offshore in domestic currency: a good local jurisdiction, large debt size, and currency convertibility.

8.5   Impact on Private Savings and Investment

Jurisdictional uncertainty is therefore the reason behind the inexistence of long-term credit and long-term financial instruments. The diffuse and nonquantifiable way by which it affects the real value of long-dated financial contracts precludes the development of a large long-term financial market. Savers cannot be expected to be receptive to holding long-term financial contracts if it is impossible to price in the uncertainty affecting their purchasing value.

Jurisdictional uncertainty reduces the overall availability of credit. Secured debt contracts are not sufficient to stimulate credit supply because the judicial system renders the right of creditors to repossess the collateral difficult to exercise. The quality of enforcement of guarantees is poor because both the law and the jurisprudence are biased toward the debtor. Even if the creditor has sufficient knowledge of the debtor and feels comfortable to lend to him for a long period, jurisdictional uncertainty will make his credit illiquid. If the original creditor needs the resources and has to sell its credit instrument, no one will be willing to buy it at a fair price. The credit cannot be fairly priced by someone who does not share the same knowledge of the debtor as the original creditor. Long-term credit instruments are therefore illiquid. Bilateral relationships might work, but jurisdictional uncertainty precludes the possibility of multilateral impersonal transactions that involve credit over long time periods. The consequence is the almost complete collapse of a long-term financial market. In the nomenclature of Kiyotaki and Moore (2001), jurisdiction uncertainty negatively affects both the borrowing constraint and the resalability constraint. Viewed from another angle, the term structure of local interest rates is truncated. Among other consequences this precludes markets from revealing long-term inflationary expectations.

Jurisdictional uncertainty not only precludes the existence of a long-term financial market but distorts savers' behavior in at least five ways:

• In the absence of currency convertibility, it increases the short-term interest rate required by savers to deploy their financial wealth in the local debt market.

• It reduces overall savings because it is a risk pertaining to the postponement of consumption.

• It makes savers attach a high value to the reprogramming of their financial wealth, thus keeping it short term and in the most liquid form possible.

• It induces savers to transfer their long-term financial wealth offshore.

• It increases savers' preference for forms of wealth allocation that do not depend on financial intermediation, searching for direct forms of real investment.

Consequently jurisdictional uncertainty distorts capital formation in three different ways:

• Small and medium size firms, for which the cost of credit verification is high, do not have access to long-term finance. Consequently their investments are restricted by their profits.

• Large firms, with access to the external credit market, have to deal with the risky consequences of currency mismatch.

• Cash-rich firms, small or large, tend to overinvest in their own businesses.

8.6   Distorting Policy Reactions in Brazil

In a comparison with emerging market economies, the strong impact
of jurisdictional uncertainty on short-term interest rates stands out
in the Brazilian case. The reason seems to be that among emerging
market economies with weak jurisdiction, Brazil appears to be unique
in its developing a large "de-dollarized" captive short-term domestic
market for its public debt. Other Latin America countries have a dollarized market for local short-term financial assets. Besides Brazil, the
only two Latin countries without financial dollarization are Chile and
Colombia. Chile, as is indicated by its investment-grade credit rating,
does not suffer from jurisdictional uncertainly. Colombia only recently
lost its investment-grade status because of high drug-related risks, but
it has traditionally followed very responsible financial policies. What
makes Brazil special is its large public debt market in domestic currency under substantial jurisdictional uncertainty. This explains both
the lack of a long-term credit market and an unusually high short-term
interest rate. Table 8.3 summarizes our point of view. Short-term interest rates and local long-term credit markets depend on the quality of
the jurisdiction and the degree of currency convertibility. (A third determinant, the long-term stability of the local monetary standard is
ignored for simplicity, as this is frequently subsumed under a good
jurisdiction.) If the jurisdiction is strong and the currency convertible,
short-term interest rates are low and there exists a long-term credit
market in domestic currency, certainly domestically, and also abroad

Table 8.3
Jurisdiction and currency convertibility

	Jurisdiction	
Currency convertibility	Strong	Weak
Yes	Low short-term interest rates	Dollarization with moderate short-term interest rates
	Long-term credit in domestic currency locally and abroad (if the country has scale)	No long-term domestic credit
No	Low short-term interest rates	High short-term interest rates
	Long-term credit locally but not abroad in domestic currency	No long-term domestic credit market

if the country's securities market is big. Mexico after NAFTA would illustrate this situation. If the jurisdiction is strong but the currency is not convertible, short-term interest rates are low and the domestic currency long-term credit market flourishes locally but not abroad. India falls into this category. If jurisdiction is weak but currency is convertible, the local short-term financial market is dollarized with moderate interest rates. This is the case of Peru. Finally, if the jurisdiction is weak and the currency is not convertible, domestic short-term interest rates are high and no long-term domestic credit market can exist. This, in our view, is the case of Brazil.

The persistence of very high short-term interest rates has caused agents other than the Brazilian Treasury to resort to bank credit only occasionally to avoid bankruptcy. Alternatively, they might exercise their lobbying power to transfer to the Treasury the responsibility for paying their debts. In the 1990s this is precisely what happened. Local states and municipalities transferred their public liabilities to the Union under favorable conditions. Rural debtors and banks were bailed out by the Union through programs such as Proes and Proer. The Brazilian Treasury is the only agent that ends up systematically paying high interest rates over time.

Policy decisions that disregard holders of financial instruments are directly responsible for Brazil's jurisdictional uncertainty. These decisions were particularly detrimental in the early 1980s, leading to triple-digit inflation. This began with monetary correction (government debt inflation-adjustment factor) being pre-fixed at artificially low levels in late 1979. A purge of monetary correction indexes took place at the beginning of all inflation stabilization attempts in the 1980s, and a financial assets freeze occurred in the Collor Plan of 1990. Simonsen (1995) documents these interventions in his analysis of the rise and fall of inflation indexation in Brazil.

Independently of the various measures directly hurting the holders of financial instruments, most economic policy decisions that aggravated jurisdictional uncertainty were probably a consequence of mistaken attempts to correct its effects. Policy makers noted the limits to economic growth imposed by the unavailability of long-term domestic savings. They, however, did not interpret this unavailability to be due to jurisdictional uncertainty but to a market failure that required policy intervention. The general purpose of the policies was therefore to create mechanisms of capital formation under the command of the government, on both the mobilization of long-term domestic savings and the financing of fixed investment. They were organized along five dimensions:

• Limited currency convertibility. Capital controls, administered in a discretionary form, imposed severe restrictions on foreign investment of residents. The purpose was to create "captive" savings that could thus be directed by the government to finance domestic real investment.

• Mechanisms of compulsory long-term savings (FGTS, PIS/PASEP) administered by government agencies and banks (CEF and BNDES).

• Artificial lengthening of the maturity of financial investments, both for public debt and private sector credits. This term lengthening has traditionally been made through (1) tax measures that strongly penalize financial investments of very short maturities (IOFs), (2) regulations that make compulsory for certain classes of agents (pension funds, insurance companies) the acquisition of long-term government bonds, and (3) incentives for the retention of long-term government debt by financial intermediaries, even in the absence of resources of final investors for such maturities.

• Practices at the level of public enterprises to increase savings and investment. Examples are (1) payment of benefits to employees through transfers to pension funds instead of direct salary increases, (2) use of monopoly power over tariffs and public sector prices with the objective of extracting society's resources for the financing of public investment (such resources as a rule were not transferred to the Treasury as dividends but rather reinvested in the expansion of the public enterprises themselves), and (3) use of public enterprises as vehicles for the absorption of long-term foreign savings through external debt.

• Seignorage as a mechanism to generate and channel forced savings to the public sector, a mechanism further explored by the creation of public sector commercial banks.

The importance of interventions through public enterprises has lately diminished, due to privatization, creation of independent regulatory agencies, establishment of limits for sponsoring firms' transfers to their employees' pension funds, and the progressive subcontracting of the management of such funds. The use of inflation to promote forced savings has also had its form of expression substantially altered since the stabilization of inflation with the *Real* Plan. Forced savings through inflation were replaced by distorting taxation, which we will denominate "incomeless" taxes in section 8.7 below.

There are two common threads to this collection of economic policy responses. The first is the subordination of microeconomic efficiency to macroeconomic considerations. The welfare cost of the constraints imposed on the freedom to allocate wealth and savings was deemed smaller than the aggregate welfare gains to be obtained from the availability of long-term domestic credit. Overcoming what government perceived as a serious market failure was considered to be welfare improving despite the obvious misallocation of resources. The second thread is the form of the policy response. In all cases the decision power of the bureaucracy was increased. Three examples are of interest. First, the convertibility restriction empowered the bureaucracy to decide who, and under what conditions, is authorized to transfer wealth abroad. Second, the artificial lengthening of public debt maturity increased the dependence of financial intermediaries to the lender of last resort. Third, the power to decide the deployment of compulsorily-held savings has always been maintained in the hands of the bureaucracy. Wealth holders were never allowed to choose the manager of their savings. "Portability" of long-term compulsory savings never came into existence.

The increase in the bureaucracy's power resulted from the confluence of passions, interests, and tradition. Passions as private agents were perceived to be myopic to their own long-run interests and passive in their reactions to the interventions of an omniscient government able to implement optimum control of economic activity. Interests are expressed through the political articulation of private groups supporting the control of the bureaucracy over the deployment of compulsory savings into alternative investments, in view of their privileged access to the state and their capacity to mold its policies for private profit. Tradition derives from the historical cultural experience of state control over mercantile activities, and state control was particularly strong in Brazil until very recently. These forces seem to be at the root of the interventionist bias that worsened the impact of jurisdictional uncertainty on the short-term interest rate, as we show in the following section.

8.7   Effects of Policy Interventions

This section considers successively the allocation and growth-distorting consequences of convertibility restrictions, artificial lengthening of public debt maturities, compulsory saving funds, and "incomeless" taxes.

8.7.1 Convertibility Restrictions

In the pegged exchange rate system that prevailed in Brazil from the period of World War II to the beginning of 1999, restrictions to convertibility gave the government the power of ordering priorities on the use of scarce international reserves. This monopoly power was used to allocate reserves primarily to the importing of capital goods and essential raw materials. Until the 1990s the restrictions on convertibility, for all practical purposes, were strict; some exceptions were admitted but only in special cases and administered in discretionary form. The result was the emergence of an enormous parallel exchange rate market, without legality but tolerated, through which there passed a good share of foreign exchange operations. A gradual loosening of the restrictions to convertibility only occurred after the *Real* Plan, with the consequent reduction in the parallel exchange rate market.

The loosening of restrictions that occurred with the so-called CC-5 mechanism was nonetheless partial. In the first place, not all agents can transfer resources abroad. Big institutional savers (pension funds and the technical reserves of insurance companies) do not have permission to invest abroad. Second, the transaction costs are high because of complex compliance requirements. Third, there are limits on the remittances. Large values need previous authorization from the central bank. Moreover a mere administrative decision can reverse this situation of relative liberalization. The CC-5 mechanism maintained intact the legal and administrative instruments of convertibility control, since it was just a normative expedient to create a fissure for international currency transfers without altering the restrictive foreign exchange laws. The power of the bureaucracy was not reduced. Examples are (1) the double exchange rate system that is still in place, the "commercial" and the "floating," and arbitrage between the two markets can be suspended at any time by central bank decision, (2) the normative power of the central bank to impede, at any moment, the remittances of foreign exchange abroad, and (3) the stigmatization of the CC-5 by allegations of anti-patriotism and even criminality.

With the floating of the exchange rate in 1999, the pursuance of active monetary policy (in the sense of the ability to drive local interest rates away from the external rate) became compatible with free capital mobility. The very idea of a quantitative scarcity of foreign exchange ceased to apply. Nonetheless, there has been no substantive progress in the mechanisms of convertibility. The central bank continues to retain the power to suspend convertibility by administrative fiat.

The rationale for controls changed with floating exchange rates. The fear nowadays of adopting full convertibility is that the capital migration toward a better jurisdiction might be of such magnitude that no stable equilibrium will exist in the foreign exchange market; severe depreciation and an erosion of the tax base will necessarily follow from the liberalization of the capital account. This attitude may be viewed as another example of the fear to float. More fundamentally, however, capital controls signal to private agents how monetary authorities view the exchange rate system. In a context of fixed exchange rates, the maintenance of capital controls signals that the monetary authorities perceive the pegged rate as being overvalued. In a context of floating exchange rates, the maintenance of capital controls signals that the monetary authorities do not believe that there is an acceptable market premium to compensate for jurisdictional uncertainty. The underlying assumption is that capital flight will occur regardless of how depreciated the exchange rate is.

8.7.2 Artificial Debt Term Lengthening

Because of jurisdictional uncertainty, there is no long-term domestic financial market. The government, however, wishes to increase the maturity of public debt to make monetary policy more effective and reduce the roll-over risk, and thus the credit risk of public debt. Policy actions have been pursued on two different fronts. Policy makers have tried to force investors to extend the maturity of their portfolios through administrative and fiscal measures that penalize short-term financial investments. The results obtained were very limited. As a consequence attention was drawn to financial intermediaries. The lengthening of debt terms turned out to depend on the willingness of financial intermediaries to make the necessary term transformation, carrying long-term bonds with funding of a very short-term nature. Thus, as of January 2004, a full 46 percent of the domestic federal debt was held by local commercial banks—33 percent voluntarily and 13 percent compulsorily. Out of this total, 56 percent is estimated to have been held by government-owned banks and 44 percent by private banks. The domestic financing counterparts to these assets are mostly CDs with daily liquidity (after an initial 30-day holding period) and automatic drawing rights. An additional 44 percent of the domestic debt was in banks' clients' funds (FIFs), enjoying daily liquidity, if not automatic drawing rights, regardless of the maturity of the underlying debt instrument. Thus 90 percent of the federal domestic debt can be said to have its maturity artificially lengthened through the intervention of the commercial bank system.

The result of this intermediation under fixed rate debt instruments is a high interest rate mismatching risk, which for many years called for high premiums on the carrying of debt and also some implicit form of insurance by the central bank. Until the creation of the LFT (floating rate bonds based on the daily central bank reference rate) in 1986, this debt intermediation process with maturity mismatch increased significantly the public debt cost. The introduction of the LFT eliminated the mismatch risk between the interbank financing rate and the interest rate received by the financial intermediary when carrying government bonds. The LFT, however, has duration of one day and, as we have seen, virtually no final buyer outside the banking sector or the funds they manage.

Although since the creation of the LFT a substantial proportion of the public debt has had daily financial indexation, the central bank continues to try to lengthen maturities with fixed rate instruments. As of January 2004, 51.1 percent of the domestic federal debt was in LFTs, and 12.6 percent in fixed rate bills (as for the rest, 21.0 percent was dollar indexed, and 15.3 percent held in inflation protected instruments). Such lengthening increases the effectiveness of monetary policy but has high fiscal costs, because the government only manages to place fixed rate instruments when financial intermediaries expect falling rates, and thus high carryover profits. Experience shows that whenever the expectations become frustrated, the central bank is forced to buy back the fixed-rate debt at subsidized rates to avoid insurmountable losses and the risk of a systemic crisis. As there is no long-term funding—especially not at fixed rates—on the part of the nonbank public, the debt, as we have seen, is almost entirely carried by financial intermediaries. As these are, as a collective, maturity mismatched, the central bank has to offer an implicit bailout insurance that ends up forcing it to exchange the debt, at unfavorable prices, in critical moments. Jurisdiction uncertainty requires thus an implicit bilateral agreement between financial intermediaries and the central bank to create the impression of long-term duration for the public debt. The ensemble of measures of induced term lengthening and restrictions to very short-term placements create furthermore a negative signaling effect that makes the saver more unwilling to finance the public debt.

8.7.3 Compulsory Savings

The use of inflation by the government as a mechanism to extract forced savings gave signs of exhaustion at the beginning of the 1960s. The structural reforms of the second half of that decade aimed at replacing part of the forced savings due to inflation by institutional mechanisms of compulsory savings, notably FGTS, PIS-PASEP, and the unification of the social security funds.

The reforms that the military regime introduced in this period also included "monetary correction," an attempt at neutralizing the perverse effects of inflation on savings through price indexation. The indexation of financial assets was designed to preserve the real value of the recently created instruments of compulsory savings and to stimulate long-term voluntary savings. The fixed 6 percent interest rate inflation-adjusted passbook savings account was the first attempt to create a government guaranteed, indexed retail savings instrument. The resources of the savings accounts would be primarily directed for the financing of investment in housing.

The surcharges for social security, FGTS, and PIS-PASEP were initially designed as savings, that is, as a compulsory intertemporal income transfer, without impact on the permanent income of wage earners. Over the years, however, the monetary correction lagged behind inflation and at times was set at rates lower than expected inflation. Apart from the losses in purchasing power to wage earners, many barriers of access to their compulsory savings funds were erected. Besides, investment in projects without profitability, as well as the misuse of funds to finance current government spending, required successive increases in the tax rate of compulsory savings to keep the overall system able to finance new investment projects.

Because of bad management and departures from the original objectives of the instruments of compulsory savings, wage earners came to understand that the surcharges did not effectively represent deferred income but merely taxes without counterpart of future individual income. This perception transformed the compulsory surcharges into a tax wedge between the income paid by the employer and the income received by the employee.

The quantitative importance of such compulsory saving mechanisms can be visualized in Brazil's 2002 consolidated national accounts (IBGE 2004). Gross national savings this year were R$249 billion. Social security contributions added up to R$181 billion, whereas family contributions to pension funds, FGTS, and PIS/PASEP were R$22 billion.

The difference between the cost of labor for the firm and the net income received by the wage earner shifted employment from the formal to the informal sector of the economy where the tax wedge did not apply. If computed only as wage-related payments not directly received by the workers (e.g., social security, compulsory accident insurance, contribution to education, and contributions to the so-called S's training schemes), this wedge represents 49.7 percent of the monthly formal sector wage, according to Amadeo and Camargo (1996). If one includes the extra yearly 13th salary plus paid vacations and holidays, and other benefits such as family allowances, maternity leaves, and food and transport vouchers (neither of which is available in the informal sector), the difference adds up to 86.9 percent of the basic monthly formal sector wage. Since labor productivity is lower in the informal sector, there is a reduction in the average productivity of the economy as a result. Therefore the tax-induced labor displacement process diminished natural output, with adverse implications for the equilibrium rate of interest, as discussed in section 8.8.

8.7.4 "Incomeless" Taxes

The price stabilization achieved by the 1994 *Real* Plan revealed the magnitude of the public sector deficit, which had previously been masked by the inflation-related forced transfer of savings to the government. The adjustment of the public sector accounts became imperative. But the reduction of expenditures was harder to implement due to the increase of tax earmarking under the 1988 Constitution. The reduction of real spending through administrative delays in the release of nominal payments, an otherwise effective mechanism of budget control under high inflation, became much less effective after price stabilization. The second-best alternative was to raise the income tax or to institute a national value added tax. Fiscal federalism, however, supported by the 1988 Constitution, forced the federal government to transfer nearly 50 percent of income tax and federal value-added tax (IPI) revenues to the states and municipalities. The deadlock in the discussion over the redistribution of a new national value-added tax on consumption, to replace the existing state-level valued-added taxes on production, made any attempt at rational reform of the tax system unviable.

In face of the constitutional inflexibility on spending, the restriction on external financing, and the political difficulties in rationalizing the tax system, the only remaining alternative was to increase the so-called social contributions, namely the cumulative and distorting taxes that are levied on sale proceeds and financial transactions.

The tax burden reached very high levels even by standards of advanced economies: 35.9 percent of GDP in 2003, up from 25.8 percent in 1993 (BNDES 2001; Afonso and Araújo 2004). This increase in the tax burden permitted the generation of high primary surpluses (4.3 percent of GDP in 2003) and a relative stabilization of the debt-to-GDP ratio. The distorting burden caused by the increase in the tax burden, however, was enormously aggravated because it was heavily dependent on turnover taxes—on sale proceeds or financial transactions (COFINS, PIS/PASEP, CPMF, IOF, and ISS). A full 47 percent of the increased tax burden between 1993 and 2002 was in the form of such taxes, which came to represent 25 percent of the total tax burden in the latter year (income taxes stood for 20 percent, value-added taxes [IPI and ICMS] for 25 percent, wage bill taxes for 23 percent, and sundry taxes for the remaining 7 percent).

Such turnover taxes are levied regardless of the generation of income. The adverse effect on output is evident. Used on a vast scale, they tend to create a dichotomy in the industrial structure (Bodin 2003). On one side, there are small businesses that are only made viable through tax evasion. On the other side, there are large firms, with oligopolistic power of trademark-based product differentiation, enjoying sufficiently high profit margins over sales to be able to comply with taxation requirements. Average sized firms, however, which are unable to operate evading taxes in view of their visibility, are hard put to pay taxes on turnover.

Industrial dichotomy makes the domestic goods supply curve steeper. Informal sector firms cannot increase output in face of growing demand because of compliance risks. The reason is that with a larger output the risks of remaining informal increases, and the firm has to pay turnover taxes. Profitability disappears with the passage to the formal sector unless the firm has above average management. The formal sector, in turn, responds to the increase in demand by raising margins and prices because it is almost exclusively composed of large firms with oligopolistic pricing power, capable of attending the complex demands of fiscal compliance.

Apart from the industrial dichotomy, the widespread use of turn-over taxation was bolstered by its political attractiveness. Voters can hardly figure out the share of income absorbed by taxes levied on sale proceeds and financial transactions. In the process of equilibrating public sector finances, the traditional populism was replaced in Brazil by what might be called fiscal populism. Traditional populism is here defined as the attempt to influence voters by resorting to easy money or higher spending not backed by taxes. The stop and go process thus generated was aptly called the electoral business cycle. In contrast, under fiscal populism there is no tolerance for deviations of inflation relative to target or for fiscal deficits. Voters are to be seduced by higher expenditures, and little concern is given to whether taxation is detrimental to growth or extremely distorting in its allocation effects. The consequence of fiscal populism is an increase in overall taxation and government spending as a proportion of GDP. The macro picture given by the fiscal deficit and monetary policy seems sound, but natural output is reduced.

8.8   Jurisdictional Uncertainty and the Interest Rate

We are now at the point of our discussion where we can link jurisdictional uncertainty to the reasons for extraordinarily high interest rates in Brazil. Jurisdictional uncertainty as well as the distortions created by policy makers were already in place when the inflation-targeting regime was introduced in 1999. It would thus be misleading to interpret the workings of the distortions under inflation targeting as defects or inadequacies of the inflation-targeting regime alone or of its underlying macro model. Our task is to insert the distortions provoked by jurisdictional uncertainty and government interventions into the inflation-targeting framework. We can then examine how a sustained and encompassing program aimed directly at remedying the jurisdictional uncertainty might lower the interest rate. The model here is a simple version of the usual forward-looking short-term open macro model. Its purpose is to illustrate how the distortions associated with jurisdictional uncertainty affect the central bank rate of interest.

We assume a strict inflation-targeting framework. The short-term nominal interest rate i_t is set by central bank independently of other policy objectives such as minimizing output fluctuations or achieving interest smoothing. This is not realistic. Since the adoption of the inflation-targeting regime, interest rate smoothing was prevalent with the exception of discontinuities provoked by major shifts in expected inflation. We also have the evidence that in some circumstances central bank prefers to miss the target than facing a too severe contraction in output (e.g., the accommodative stance adopted after the 2001 shocks). The rationale for assuming strict inflation targeting is just simplicity.

We will also disregard central bank credibility issues. Under full credibility and no disturbances, actual and expected inflation coincide with the target and time-invariant inflation rate π^*. The assumption works as a rough approximation to reality. Despite not having formal independence, the central bank has enjoyed in practice substantial control over monetary policy instruments. Markets acknowledge the accountability and transparency of the central bank since the adoption of inflation targeting. Not having formal independence or fixed mandates for board members, however, is extremely costly in some circumstances, as exemplified by the surge in inflation expectations after the election of Lula in the last quarter of 2002.

Equations (1) and (2) summarize the model:

$$\pi^* = F\left[x_t, E_t x_{t+1}, \frac{e_t}{e_{t-1}}, (i_t - \pi^* - r_t)\right], \tag{1}$$

$$G\left[(1 - p)(1 + i_t)\left(\frac{e_t}{E_t e_{t+1}}\right) - (1 + r^*)\right] = N\left(\frac{e_t}{1 + \pi^*}\right). \tag{2}$$

Equation (1) is a reduced-form domestic goods market equilibrium condition under a fully credible inflation-targeting policy. We take x_t as the current output gap, $E_t x_{t+1}$ as the expected output gap, e_t/e_{t-1} as the ratio between the current nominal exchange rate and last period's exchange rate, and r_t as the equilibrium interest rate. Given the inflation target π^* and the equilibrium rate r_t, the central bank sets the nominal interest rate as a function of the actual and expected output gaps and the exchange rate depreciation.

In equation (1) we define the equilibrium rate of interest, r_t, as the real rate of interest required to keep aggregate demand equal to the natural rate of output; any factor changing the natural rate of output affects the equilibrium rate of interest as well. In particular, both a positive productivity shock and a cut in government spending reduce the equilibrium rate. The variables of $F(.)$ are mutually constrained: if both current and expected output gaps are zero and the real exchange rate is constant $(e_t/e_{t-1} = 1 + \pi^*)$, then the real rate of interest $i_t - \pi^*$ is equal to the equilibrium rate, r_t.

Equation (2) is the balance of payments equilibrium under the simplifying assumption that the level of international reserves is constant. The left-hand side captures capital flows as a function of the interest rate spread. The variable $(1 + i_t)(e_t/E_t e_{t+1})$ is the rate of return in dollars of an investment in reais, and r^* is the external risk-free interest rate in dollars. Variable p captures all of the risks involved in short-term arbitrage. There are credit risks (domestic debt repudiation), contractual risks (court rulings or acts of the Prince interfering with the compliance of contractual obligations), and frontier risks (capital controls blocking remittances). The risks are simplified here as all-or-nothing events. The right-hand side gives net exports as a function of the current real exchange rate.

The capital flows described in equation (2) differ from the formulation given by Blanchard (chapter 2 in this volume) in three ways. First, we do not differentiate between Treasury and central bank liabilities. Second, we take p as exogenously given. In Blanchard's formulation p is a function of the interest rate because a higher interest rate increases the default risk. (It may also be argued that p is a function of the exchange rate as well, in the sense that the more devalued the currency is, the bigger is the risk of the introduction of capital controls.) Third, we leave risk aversion considerations in the background. Sudden Stops are captured in the analysis by shifts in the $G(.)$ function.

The model determines simultaneously the domestic interest rate set by the central bank and the exchange rate as a function of the equilibrium interest rate, the external risk-free interest rate, the default probability, the current output gap, and expectations on the future output gap and the exchange rate.

It would seem sensible to adopt, under full central bank credibility, a rational expectations approach in which the one-period-ahead expected values of the output gap and the exchange rate coincide with the true conditional expectations. However, local financial markets are truncated at the long end, making the deployment of the full apparatus of conditional expectations artificial. Thus, to simplify matters, we have chosen to skirt the modeling of learning dynamics by which expectations evolve over time and assume that expectations are exogenously given.

Figure 8.1 illustrates the model, with the domestic interest rate in the vertical axis and the exchange rate in the horizontal axis. For simplicity, we assume $\pi^* = 0$. The domestic equilibrium (1) is upward sloped.

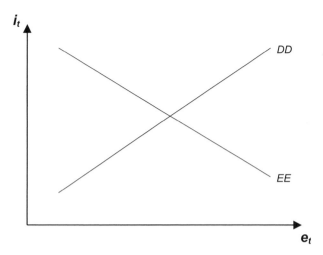

Figure 8.1
Simple model of interest and exchange rate equilibrium

An increase in the real exchange rate (a larger value of e_t) requires a higher interest rate for inflation to remain constant. The external balance equation (2) is downward sloped. An increase in the real exchange rate increases both net exports and capital inflows; external balance requires then a lower interest rate to reduce capital inflows. Note that if p is sensitive to the interest rate, as in Blanchard (chapter 2 in this volume), the external balance curve could be upward sloped.

The following exercises are straightforward:

• A productivity increase raises the natural rate of output, reduces the equilibrium rate of interest, and shifts the domestic balance curve *DD* to the right.

• A reduction in the risk factor p shifts the external balance curve *EE* to the left.

• An increase in the risk-free foreign interest rate shifts *EE* to the right. The same holds true for any adverse shocks to capital flows.

• A reduction in the expected output gap shifts *DD* to the right.

• A more depreciated expected exchange rate shifts *EE* to the right.

With the help of this simple model, it is possible to discuss the effects of a comprehensive program aimed at reducing the jurisdictional uncertainty in terms of an inflation-targeting regime.

Suppose that agents perceive such a program to be sustainable over time, with the unwinding of the distorting policy responses reinforcing their perception about the quality of the domestic monetary standard. Then:

Making the currency convertible reduces p. The reason is that the risk of blockage of capital remittances would disappear. As a consequence curve EE shifts to the left. This may explain why countries with bad jurisdiction but currency convertibility (including the legalization of local bank deposits in US dollars) show lower interest rates.

Abandonment of attempts to lengthen artificially the maturity of public debt reduces the bailout-related debt costs. A smaller p value captures this effect, shifting EE to the left.

Replacement of distorting "incomeless" taxation makes the DD curve flatter, as smaller increases in interest rates are needed to offset the expansionary effects of a depreciated exchange rate.

A balanced reduction of expenditure and taxes (reversing the "fiscal populism") works like a productivity shock (larger natural output), reducing the output gap and shifting DD to the right.

Elimination of mechanisms of forced savings increases the productivity of aggregate investment, increasing the natural rate of output and shifting DD to the right.

The signaling effect of attempts to extricate distortion from policy responses reduces the equilibrium interest rate, shifting DD to the right, since savers require lower rates to deploy their wealth in domestic debt instruments.

To sum up, unwinding the policy responses to the jurisdictional uncertainty reduces the short-term interest rate required to keep inflation on target while the net effect on the exchange rate cannot be predicted on a priori grounds. Removing "financial" distortions (convertibility restrictions and artificial debt term lengthening) appreciates the exchange rate, and removing "real" distortions (compulsory savings and "incomeless" taxes) depreciates the exchange rate.

8.9 Final Remarks

To our results above we need to add some words of caution. Critical to our results is the assumption that the issues posed by jurisdiction uncertainty are addressed in a coherent and sustainable mode. However, it is easy to think of scenarios in which the unwinding of policies can backfire. For example, convertibility might be perceived as a brief and unique window of opportunity to elude local jurisdiction. The expected exchange rate would increase as a result, shifting the curve *EE* to the right.

The reduction of public debt maturity might be perceived as increasing the vulnerability of the public sector to portfolio shifts by private investors. The fear of debt monetization would increase the expected exchange rate, shifting the curve *EE* to the right.

The dismantling of forced savings mechanisms might reduce the funding available for long-term investment if savers remain reluctant to buy long-term debt instruments. In this case the expected output gap would increase as the next period natural rate of output shrinks, and the *DD* curve shifts to the left.

The substitution of "easy to evade" income taxes for "easy to collect" "incomeless" might raise doubts about government revenue. If government spending is perceived as constant, the expected output gap increases, shifting *DD* to the left.

It is important then to ensure that the removal of distortions is perceived as an improvement of the domestic jurisdiction, but the removal alone may not be sufficient. The distortions created by the misguided policy reactions to jurisdictional uncertainty are only part of the problem. Jurisdictional uncertainty has deep institutional roots in the executive, the legislative, and the judiciary branches of the state. If property rights are violated in the process of dismantling these distortions, for instance, it will be very hard to convince agents that the problem of jurisdictional uncertainty is being tackled appropriately. In particular, a big bang approach can be dangerous. Because jurisdictional uncertainty is the result of history, restoring confidence in the jurisdiction is per force a long road. Increased tradability and economic integration with a good jurisdiction can signal an improvement of the domestic jurisdiction, as we have learned from the development of local capital markets in countries entering the European Union.

Although a discussion of policy guidelines to deal with local jurisdictional uncertainty is outside the scope of this chapter, a step-by-step announced program, with well-defined criteria for moving from one phase to the next, could well be the best way to go. The dismantling of forced savings, for instance, could be done at the margin and over a certain number of periods. The road to convertibility could be paved by strengthening the prudential framework, limiting the scope of capital controls in the transition phase, as well as setting proper international reserve requirements (see Arida 2003). A more stringent regulatory framework could reduce the bailout costs caused by excessive exposure of financial intermediaries to maturities mismatch. The reduction of distorting taxes could be achieved by adopting strict budget-balancing rules that are perceived as legally and politically viable.

Note

This work was presented in the seminar on Inflation Targeting and Debt: The Case of Brazil, jointly sponsored by the Instituto de Estudos de Política Econômica da Casa das Garças, Departamento de Economia da Pontifícia Universidade Católica do Rio de Janeiro, and the World Bank. Rio de Janeiro, December 12–13, 2003. We are indebted for comments to Arminio Fraga, Arthur Candal, Dionisio Carneiro, Eduardo Gianetti da Fonseca, Elena Landau, Fabio de Oliveira Barbosa, Fernando Sotelino, Luiz Orenstein, and Marcio Garcia, as well as participants in seminars at Instituto Rio Branco, MIT Club of Brazil, and Universidade de São Paulo.

References

Acemoglu, D., and S. Johnson. 2003. Unbundling institutions. NBER Working Paper 9934. August.

Afonso, J. R., and E. Araújo. 2004. Uma análise da carga tributária global estimada. Unpublished Technical Note. Available at *www.joserobertoafonso.ecn.br*.

Amadeo, E., and J. M. Camargo. 1996. Instituições e o mercado de trabalho no Brasil. In J. M. Camargo, ed., *Flexibilidade do Mercado de Trabalho no Brasil*. Rio de Janeiro: Fundação Getúlio Vargas, pp. 47–94.

Arida, P. 2003. Aspectos macroeconômicos da conversibilidade: O caso brasileiro. Available at *www.iepecdg.com*.

BNDES. 2001. Informe-SF, n. 29. Available at: *www.federativo.bndes.gov.br*.

Bodin de Moraes, P. 2003. Favelização da indústria: As conseqüências destruidoras da tributação ineficiente. *O Estado de São Paulo*, May 2.

Eichengreen, B., and R. Hausmann. 1999. Exchange rates and financial fragility. Proceedings of the Seminar on *New Challenges for Monetary Policy*. Kansas City: Federal Reserve Board of Kansas City, pp. 329–68.

Eichengreen, B., R. Hausmann, and U. Paniza. 2003. The pain of original sin. Available at: *http://emlab.berkeley.edu/users/eichengr/research/ospainaug21-03.pdf*.

IBGE. 2004. Instituto Brasileiro de Geografia e Estatística, Contas Nacionais/Contas Econômicas Integradas–2002. Available at *www.ibge.gov.br*.

Jeanne, O. 2002. Why do emerging economies borrow in foreign currency. Prepared for the Inter-American Development Bank Conference on Currency and Maturity Mismatching: Redeeming Debt from Original Sin. Washington, DC, November 21–22.

Keynes, J. M. 1963. Inflation and deflation. In *Essays in Persuasion*. New York: Norton.

Kiyotaki, N., and J. Moore. 2001. Evil is the root of all money. Claredon Lectures I, November 26. Discussion Paper 110. Edinburgh School of Economics.

Lamounier, B., and A. de Souza. 2002. As elites brasileiras e o desenvolvimento nacional: fatores de consenso e dissenso. São Paulo: Instituto de Estudos Econômicos, Sociais e Políticos de São Paulo. Available at: *www.augurium.com.br/termometro.php*.

Modigliani, F., and R. Sutch. 1982. Debt management and the term structure of interest rates. In A. Abel, ed., *The Collected Papers of Franco Modigliani*, vol. 1. Cambridge: MIT Press.

Simonsen, M. H. 1995. *30 Anos de Indexação*. Rio de Janeiro: Editora da Fundação Getúlio Vargas.

North, D. 1981. *Structure and Change in Economic History*. New York: Norton.

Comment on Chapter 8

Arminio Fraga

Interest rates have indeed been extraordinarily high in Brazil since the 1980s, in both real and nominal terms. Although hyperinflation was wiped out by the Real Plan of 1994—a plan largely designed and implemented by the co-authors of the chapter under discussion—real interest rates have remained particularly high. Arida, Bacha, and Lara-Resende argue that an understanding of this phenomenon requires the introduction of the concept of jurisdictional uncertainty. In this brief comment I will argue that the concept is useful, but mostly if one is trying to determine the root causes of the high cost of bank credit rather than the reasons for the high basic rate of the economy.

First a bit of terminology: the chapter focuses mainly on what I have called the basic rate of the economy, the Brazilian equivalent of the Fed funds rate, that is, the rate paid by the government for short-term borrowing and lending against Treasury collateral. Since 1995 the real basic rate in Brazil has averaged some 15 percent! One could also focus on the average real rate charged on a bank loan. The current weighted average of interest rates charged across all loans is close to 45 percent, a figure also worthy of attention.

The standard analyses of interest rate determination tend to focus on the fiscal and monetary regimes, and on trends of saving, investment, growth, and productivity. Concepts typically used include default, expropriation, exchange rate, and convertibility risks. For bank spreads, one must also look into the ability to post collateral and to enforce contracts, the efficiency of the legal system, tax and regulatory wedges, and so on.

An important point of chapter 8 seems to be that the view that the high rates are mainly driven by a historically weak fiscal regime is insufficient to explain the very high basic rates. Arida and colleagues argue that in large part, a number of second best responses to the absence of long-term credit are the main root cause of the problem. These policy errors include restrictions on exchange rate convertibility, forced or artificial debt maturity lengthening, mandatory saving schemes, and a number of tax distortions. While at the margin there is no doubt that they are right, a cursory look at China, India, and Korea over the last few decades uncovers many, if not all, of these policies but not the sky-high real interest rates found in Brazil.

On the other hand, the path of interest rates in Brazil over the last decade does seem to tell us quite a lot: the 1980s were a decade of fiscal irresponsibility, debt defaults and reschedulings, asset freezes, hyperinflation, and much more. Real interest rates were almost all the time in double digits during this period. Then in 1994 came the *Real* Plan, followed by four years of fiscal deficits, even at the primary level, and a fixed and overvalued exchange rate. The combination of fiscal and exchange rate risk was perhaps the key causal factor explaining the 20 percent average for real interest rates during these four years. After the 1998 and early 1999 crisis the primary budget of the Brazilian government moved to a surplus, which has ranged from 3 to 4.25 percent of GDP since then. The exchange rate was forced into floating and has stayed that way since then as Brazil moved to an inflation-targeting regime. During these five years real interest rates have averaged about 10 percent, despite the significant crises of 2001 (Argentina, Nasdaq, power blackout) and 2002–2003 (a confidence crisis driven by fear of populist policies by the then opposition). This significant drop seems to be fully explained by the strengthening of the fiscal regime and the move to a floating exchange rate.

Now the Workers Party government of President Lula da Silva, which took over in 2003, has demonstrated its commitment to macroeconomic stability and real rates have fallen further, regardless of the need to counter the massive exchange rate depreciation of 2002 with tight monetary policy. This is best seen through the decline in the yield of long-dated inflation-linked government bonds, which have dropped from 13 percent in early 2003 to 8.5 percent in early 2004, the lowest such yield in a long time. If sound macro policies are maintained, real interest rates are likely to continue to decline toward levels found in most countries. The process will take some time as credibility in the long-term soundness of the macroeconomic regime in Brazil is still tainted by a history of exotic behavior.

Summing up, I found the discussion in the chapter to have many relevant academic and policy points worth pursuing further. The focus on jurisdictional risk is warranted, especially if one is trying to explain the very high cost of bank credit, a point the Central Bank of Brazil and others such as Armando Castelar Pinheiro have been emphasizing in their research over the years. However, for understanding the high real basic rate, I remain convinced that the evidence still favors the more conventional explanations based on weak macro regimes (with emphasis on fiscal and exchange rate issues), low savings, and a long history of misbehavior.

Index